ART WORLDS

HOWARD S. BECKER

ART WORLDS

UNIVERSITY OF CALIFORNIA PRESS
Berkeley • Los Angeles • London

University of California Press
Berkeley and Los Angeles, California
University of California Press, Ltd.
London, England
© 1982 by
The Regents of the University of California
Printed in the United States of America

1 2 3 4 5 6 7 8 9

Library of Congress Cataloging in Publication Data

Becker, Howard Saul, 1928–
  Art worlds.

  Bibliography: p.
  Includes index.
  1. Arts and society. 2. Popular culture.
3. Arts—Psychology. I. Title.
NX180.S6B42   700'.1'03   81–2694
ISBN 0-520-04386-3   AACR2

Contents

Illustrations

Preface

Maybe the years I spent playing the piano in taverns in Chicago and elsewhere led me to believe that the people who did that mundane work were as important to an understanding of art as the better-known players who produced the recognized classics of jazz. Growing up in Chicago—where Louis Sullivan's democratic philosophy was embodied in the skyscrapers of the downtown I loved to prowl around and Moholy-Nagy's Institute of Design gave a Midwestern home to the refugee Bauhaus' concern for the craft in art—may have led me to think that the craftsmen who help make art works are as important as the people who conceive them. My rebellious temperament may be the cause of a congenital antielitism. Learning the "Chicago tradition" of sociology from Everett C. Hughes and Herbert Blumer surely led to a skepticism about conventional definitions of the objects of sociological study.

All those things had a part in forming the attitude of this book, quite different from the one with which sociologists usually approach the arts. I have treated art as the work some people do, and have been more concerned with patterns of cooperation among the people who make the works than with the works themselves or with those conventionally defined as their creators. In doing that, I have found it natural to use the style of analysis I and many others have used in analyzing other kinds of work and work settings. That has inevitably meant treating art as not so very different from other kinds of work, and treating people defined as artists as not so very different from other kinds of workers, especially the other workers who participate in the making of art works.

The idea of an art world forms the backbone of my analysis. "Art world" is commonly used by writers on the arts in a loose and metaphoric way, mostly to refer to the most fashionable people associated with those newsworthy objects and events that command astronomical prices. I have used the term in a more technical way, to denote the network of people whose cooperative activity, organized via their joint knowledge of conventional means of doing things, produces the kind of art works that art world is noted for. This tautological definition mirrors the analysis, which is less a logically organized sociological theory of art than an exploration of the potential of the idea of an art world for increasing our understanding of how people produce and consume art works. Each chapter approaches that idea from a slightly different vantage point, suggesting the important features of art worlds, outlining how they come into existence and persist, noting how their operations affect the form and content of art works, and reinterpreting standard questions in analyses of the arts in ways suggested by all the foregoing.

I think it generally true that sociology does not discover what no one ever knew before, in this differing from the natural sciences. Rather, good social science produces a deeper understanding of things that many people are already pretty much aware of. This is not the place to pursue that argument. But I should say that whatever virtue this analysis has does not come from the discovery of any hitherto unknown facts or relations. Instead, it comes from exploring systematically the implications of the art world concept. Though the basic idea seems commonplace, many of its implications are not. Thus, it seems obvious to say that if everyone whose work contributes to the finished art work does not do his part, the work will come out differently. But it is not obvious to pursue the implication that it then becomes a problem to decide which of all these people is *the* artist, while the others are only support personnel.

Because my focus has been on forms of social organization, I have frequently compared art forms and works which have quite different reputations as art. I have spoken of Titian and comic strips in the same breath and have discussed Hollywood film scores or rock-and-roll tunes as seriously as the work of Beethoven or Mozart. In fact, since the problem of reputation is central to the analysis, such comparisons occur frequently. I remind readers who find them offensive that the principle of analysis is social organizational, not aesthetic.

This approach seems to stand in direct contradiction to the dominant tradition in the sociology of art, which defines art as something more special, in which creativity comes to the surface and the essential character of the society expresses itself, especially in great works of genius. The dominant tradition takes the artist and art work, rather than the network of cooperation, as central to the analysis of art as a social phenomenon. In light of this difference, it might be reasonable to say that what I have done here is not the sociology of art at all, but rather the sociology of occupations applied to artistic work. I would not quarrel with that way of putting it.

I have not argued directly with the more traditional point of view, except in the final chapter, and deal with some of its most important preoccupations only glancingly. It is not that those concerns cannot be dealt with in the terms proposed here, but they are not central to the approach I have taken, and so have a subordinate place in my discussion. Furthermore, I have put those questions in a way that makes them relevant to what I want to talk about and thus does not deal with them adequately in their own terms. I am not sure that the two styles of analysis conflict or contradict one another. They may just be two different sets of questions asked of the same empirical materials.

I have, of course, not been the first to think about the arts in this way. There is a hearty tradition of relativistic, skeptical, "democratic" writing about the arts. The example of such ethnomusicologists as Charles Seeger and, especially, Klaus Wachsmann gave me much to think about and to imitate. William Ivins' *Prints and Visual Communication* started me thinking about many of the problems I take up later and provided some of the tools needed to work on them. Harrison and Cynthia White's analysis of the world of nineteenth-century French painting suggested the advantages of studying *all* the artists of a period rather than only the great names. These, and other sources I have used liberally in the text, indicate something of the tradition that lies behind what I have done. Like all traditions, its makers are not responsible for what latecomers do in its name.

Acknowledgments

Because this book focuses on the networks of cooperation and assistance through which work gets done, I am even more conscious than most authors of how what I have done depends on what a multitude of people and organizations have done for me. I cannot be detailed and specific in my thanks—it would take forever. So I have listed names alphabetically and let it go at that, which doesn't mean that I am not truly grateful.

I began the work on which the book is based in 1969–70, when I was a Fellow (supported in part by a fellowship from the National Institute of Mental Health) of the Center for Advanced Study in the Behavioral Sciences; there is no better place for the kind of aimless exploratory inquiry I was ready for that year. I completed the first draft of the complete manuscript in 1978–79, while I was a Fellow of the John Simon Guggenheim Memorial Foundation. I thank both organizations for their support. In addition, I have been a member of the Sociology Department of Northwestern University since 1965; it has been a wonderful and encouraging intellectual home.

Portions of this book first appeared in somewhat different form in the following journals and books, and are adapted here with the permission of the original publishers:

"Art as Collective Action," reprinted from *American Sociological Review* 39 (December 1974): 767–76, with the permission of the American Sociological Association.

xii

"Art Photography in America," reprinted from *Journal of Communication* 25 (Winter 1975): 74–78, with their permission.

"Art Worlds and Social Types," reprinted from *American Behavioral Scientist* 19 (July 1976): 703–18, with the permission of Sage Publications.

"Arts and Crafts," reprinted from *American Journal of Sociology* 83 (January 1978): 862–89, with the permission of the University of Chicago Press.

"Stereographs: Local, National and International Art Worlds," reprinted from Edward W. Earle, ed., *Points of View: The Stereograph in America—A Cultural History* (Rochester, N.Y.: Visual Studies Workshop Press, 1979), pp. 88–96, with their permission.

"Aesthetics, Aestheticians, and Critics," reprinted from *Studies in Visual Communication* 6 (Spring 1980): 56–68, with their permission.

Publishers have granted permission to quote from the following works:

Anthony Trollope, *An Autobiography*, University of California Press

William Culp Darrah, *World of Stereographs*, William C. Darrah

Patricia Cooper and Norma Bradley Buferd, *The Quilters: Women and Domestic Art*, Doubleday & Company, Inc.

Raymonde Moulin, *Le Marché de la peinture en France*, Les Editions de Minuit

Françoise Gilot and Carlton Lake, *Life with Picasso*, McGraw-Hill Book Company

Michael Baxandall, *Painting and Experience in Fifteenth Century Italy*, Oxford University Press

Barbara Herrnstein Smith, "Fixed Marks and Variable Constancies: A Parable of Literary Value," by permission of the author

Vivian Perlis, *Charles Ives Remembered: An Oral History*, Yale University Press

The following friends and colleagues helped in all sorts of ways: Bernard Beck, Nan Becker, H. Stith Bennett, Bennett Berger, William Blizek, Philip Brickman, Derral Cheatwood, Kenneth Donow, Edward Earle, Philip Ennis, Carolyn Evans, Robert Faulkner, Eliot Freidson, Jane Fulcher, Blanche Geer, Barry Glassner, Hans

Haacke, Karen Huffstodt, Irving Louis Horowitz, Everett C. Hughes, Bruce Jackson, Edward Kealy, Robert Leighninger, Leo Litwak, Eleanor Lyon, Arline Meyer, Leonard Meyer, Dan Morganstern, Chandra Mukerji, Charles Nanry, Susan Lee Nelson, Richard Peterson, Ellen Poole, Barbara Rosenblum, Clinton Sanders, Grace Seiberling, Barbara Herrnstein Smith, Carl Smith, Malcolm Spector, Anselm Strauss, Helen Tartar, Susan Vehlow, Gilberto Velho, Klaus Wachsman, Brenda Way, and Nancy Weiss.

1 • Art Worlds and Collective Activity

*IT WAS MY practice to be at my table every morning
at 5:30 A.M.; and it was also my practice to allow myself no mercy. An old groom, whose business it was to
call me, and to whom I paid £ 5 a year extra for the
duty, allowed himself no mercy. During all those years
at Waltham Cross he was never once late with the coffee
which it was his duty to bring me. I do not know that I
ought not to feel that I owe more to him than to any
one else for the success I have had. By beginning at that
hour I could complete my literary work before I dressed
for breakfast.*
ANTHONY TROLLOPE, 1947 [1883], p. 227

The English novelist may have told the story facetiously,
but being awakened and given coffee was nevertheless integral to the way he worked. No doubt he could have done
without the coffee if he had to; but he didn't have to. No
doubt anyone could have performed that service; but, given
the way Trollope worked, it had to be performed.

All artistic work, like all human activity, involves the joint
activity of a number, often a large number, of people.
Through their cooperation, the art work we eventually see or
hear comes to be and continues to be. The work always
shows signs of that cooperation. The forms of cooperation
may be ephemeral, but often become more or less routine,
producing patterns of collective activity we can call an art
world. The existence of art worlds, as well as the way their
existence affects both the production and consumption of art
works, suggests a sociological approach to the arts. It is not
an approach that produces aesthetic judgments, although
that is a task many sociologists of art have set for themselves.
It produces, instead, an understanding of the complexity of
the cooperative networks through which art happens, of the
way the activities of both Trollope and his groom meshed

1

with those of printers, publishers, critics, librarians, and readers in the world of Victorian literature, and of the similar networks and results involved in all the arts.

ART AS ACTIVITY

Think of all the activities that must be carried out for any work of art to appear as it finally does. For a symphony orchestra to give a concert, for instance, instruments must have been invented, manufactured, and maintained, a notation must have been devised and music composed using that notation, people must have learned to play the notated notes on the instruments, times and places for rehearsal must have been provided, ads for the concert must have been placed, publicity must have been arranged and tickets sold, and an audience capable of listening to and in some way understanding and responding to the performance must have been recruited. A similar list can be compiled for any of the performing arts. With minor variations (substitute materials for instruments and exhibition for performance), the list applies to the visual and (substituting language and print for materials and publication for exhibition) literary arts.

The list of things that must be done varies, naturally, from one medium to another, but we can provisionally list the kinds of activities that must be performed. To begin, someone must have an idea of what kind of work is to be made and of its specific form. The originators may get that idea long before actually making the work, or the idea may arise in the process of working. The idea may be brilliant and original, profound and moving, or trivial and banal, for all practical purposes indistinguishable from thousands of other ideas produced by others equally untalented or uninterested in what they are doing. Producing the idea may require enormous effort and concentration; it may come as a gift, out of the blue; or it may be produced routinely, by the manipulation of well-known formulas. The way the work is produced bears no necessary relationship to its quality. Every way of producing art works for some people and not for others; every way of producing art produces work of every conceivable grade of quality, however that is defined.

Once conceived, the idea must be executed. Most artistic ideas take some physical form: a film, a painting or sculpture, a book, a dance, a *something* which can be seen, heard, held. Even conceptual art, which purports to consist solely of ideas, takes the form of a typescript, a talk, photographs, or some combination of those.

The means for the execution of some art works seem to be easily and routinely available, so that part of the making of the art work causes no one any special effort or worry. We can, for instance, have books printed or photocopied with relatively little trouble. Other art works require skilled execution. A musical idea in the form of a written score has to be performed, and musical performance requires training, skill, and judgment. Once a play is written, it must be acted, and that requires skill, training, and judgment too. (So, in fact, does printing a book, but we are less aware of that.)

Another crucial activity in the production of art works consists of manufacturing and distributing the materials and equipment most artistic activities require. Musical instruments, paints and canvas, dancers' shoes and costumes, cameras and film—all these have to be made and made available to the people who use them to produce art works.

Making art works takes time, and making the equipment and materials takes time, too. That time has to be diverted from other activities. Artists ordinarily make time and equipment available for themselves by raising money in one way or another and using the money to buy what they need. They usually, though not always, raise money by distributing their works to audiences in return for some form of payment. Of course, some societies, and some art activities, do not operate within a money economy. Instead, a central government agency may allocate resources for art projects. In another kind of society, people who produce art may barter their work for what they need, or may produce work in the time available to them after they have met their other obligations. They may perform their ordinary activities in such a way as to produce what we or they might identify as art, even though the work is not commonly called that, as when women produced quilts for family use. However it is done, work gets distributed and the distribution produces the means with which further resources for making further work can be gathered.

Other activities that we can lump together as "support" must also take place. These vary with the medium: sweeping up the stage and bringing the coffee, stretching and priming canvases and framing the finished paintings, copy editing and proofreading. They include all sorts of technical activities—manipulating the machinery people use in executing the work—as well as those which merely free executants from normal household chores. Think of support as a residual category, designed to hold whatever the other categories do not make an easy place for.

Someone must respond to the work once it is done, have an emotional or intellectual reaction to it, "see something in it," appreciate it. The old conundrum—if a tree falls in the forest and no one hears it, did it make a sound?—can be solved here by simple definition: we are interested in the event which consists of a work being made *and* appreciated; for that to happen, the activity of response and appreciation must occur.

Another activity consists of creating and maintaining the rationale according to which all these other activities make sense and are worth doing. Rationales typically take the form, however naive, of a kind of aesthetic argument, a philosophical justification which identifies what is being made as art, as good art, and explains how art does something that needs to be done for people and society. Every social activity carries with it some such rationale, necessary for those moments when others not engaged in it ask what good it is anyway. Someone always asks such questions, if only the people engaged in the activity themselves. Subsidiary to this is the specific evaluation of individual works to determine whether they meet the standards contained in the more general justification for that class of work or whether, perhaps, the rationale requires revision. Only by this kind of critical review of what has been and is being done can participants in the making of art works decide what to do as they move on to the next work.

Most of these things cannot be done on the spur of the

moment. They require some training. People must learn the techniques characteristic of the kind of work they are going to do, whether it be the creation of ideas, execution, some one of the many support activities, or appreciation, response, and criticism. Accordingly, someone must carry on the education and training through which such learning occurs.

Finally, to do all this supposes conditions of civic order such that people engaged in making art can count on a certain stability, can feel that there are some rules to the game they are playing. If systems of support and distribution rely on notions of private property, the rights to that property must be guaranteed in some way. The state, pursuing its interest in the ends for which people are mobilized for collective action, must allow the production of the objects and events which are the art, and may provide some support itself.

I have repeatedly spoken in the imperative: people *must* do this, the state *must* not do that. Who says so? Why must any of these people do any of these things? It is easy enough to imagine or remember cases in which these activities have not been carried out. Recall how I began: "Think of all the activities that must be carried out *for any work of art to appear as it finally does.*" That is, the imperatives all operate if the event is to occur in a specific way and no other. But the work need not occur in that way, or in any other particular way. If one or another of these activities does not get done, the work will occur in some other way. If no one appreciates the work, it will go unappreciated. If no one supports its doing, it will go unsupported. If specific items of equipment are not available, the work will be done without them. Naturally, doing without any of these things affects the work produced. It will not be the same work. But that is far different from saying that it cannot exist at all unless these activities are performed. Any of them can be performed in a variety of ways with an equal variety of results.

Poets, for instance, depend on printers, editors, and publishers to circulate their work. But should those facilities not be available, for political or economic reasons, they may find other means of circulating it. Russian poets circulate their work in privately typed manuscripts, readers retyping the manuscript to make further circulating copies, when the government printing houses will not allow official printing or distribution. If the commercial publishers of capitalist countries will not publish a book, poets can, as American poets often do, mimeograph or photocopy their work, perhaps making unofficial use of the equipment of some school or office for which they work. If, that done, no one will distribute the work, they can distribute it themselves, giving copies away to friends and relatives, or just handing it out to strangers on street corners. Or one can simply not distribute the work, and keep it for oneself. Emily Dickinson did that when, after a few unfortunate experiences with editors who altered her "illiterate" punctuation, she decided that she would not be able to publish her work in the form she wanted (Johnson, 1955).

Of course, by using other than the conventional means of distribution or no channel of distribution at all, artists suffer some disadvantages, and their work takes a different form than it might have if regular distribution had been available. They usually see this situation as an unmixed curse, and hope to gain access to regular channels of distribution, or whatever other conventional facilities they find unavailable. But since, as we will see, the regular means of carrying on support activities substantially constrain what can be done, not to have them available, inconvenient or worse as that may be, also opens up otherwise unavailable possibilities. Access to all the regular means of doing things is a mixed blessing.

This is not, then, a functionalist theory which suggests that activities must occur in a particular way or the social system will not survive. The social systems which produce art survive in all sorts of ways, though never exactly as they have in the past. The functionalist suggestion is true in the trivial sense that ways of doing things will not survive exactly as they are unless all the things necessary to that survival continue to aid in it. It is misleading in suggesting that there is any necessity for such ways to survive exactly as they are.

THE DIVISION OF LABOR

Given that all these things must be done for an art work to occur as it actually does, who will do them? Imagine, as one extreme case, a situation in which one person did everything: made everything, invented everything, had all the ideas, performed or executed the work, experienced and appreciated it, all without the assistance or help of anyone else. We can hardly imagine such a thing, because all the arts we know, like all the human activities we know, involve the cooperation of others.

If other people do some of these activities, how do the participants divide up the jobs? Think of the opposite extreme, a situation in which each activity is done by a separate person, a specialist who does nothing but that one operation, much like the division of tasks on an industrial assembly line. This too is an imaginary case, though some arts approximate it in practice. The list of credits which ends the typical Hollywood feature film gives explicit recognition to such a finely divided set of activities. The fine divisions are traditional in the making of large-budget films, partly enforced by union jurisdictional arrangements and partly by the traditional reward system of public credit on which careers in the film industry are based (Faulkner, forthcoming, discusses the role of credits in the careers of Hollywood composers).

There seems to be no limit to the fineness of the division of tasks. Consider the list of technical credits for the 1978 film *Hurricane* (see Chart 1). The film employed a director of photography, but Sven Nykvist did not actually operate the camera; Edward Lachman did that. Lachman, however, did not do all the jobs associated with operating the camera; Dan Myhram loaded it and, when the focus had to be shifted in the course of filming a scene, Lars Karlsson "pulled" the focus. If something went wrong with a camera, camera mechanic Gerhard Hentschel fixed it. The work of clothing and making up the actors, preparing and taking care of the script, preparing scenery and props, seeing to the continuity of the dialogue and the visual appearance of the film, even

CHART 1
HURRICANE, TECHNICAL CREDITS

Directed by	Jan Troell
Produced by	Dino de Laurentiis
Screenplay by	Lorenzo Semple, Jr.
Based on the novel *Hurricane* by	Charles Nordhoff and
	James Norman Hall
Executive Producer	Lorenzo Semple, Jr.
Director of Photography	Sven Nykvist, A.S.C.
Music composed by	Nino Rota
Film Editor	Sam O'Steen
Production, Costumes and Sets designed by	Danilo Donati
Second Unit Director	Frank Clark
1st assistant director	Jose Lopez Rodero
2nd assistant director	Fred Viannellis
3rd assistant director	Ginette Angosse Lopez
Assistant to director	George Oddner
Second unit assistant director	Giovanni Soldati
Second unit assistant manager	Goran Setterberg
Camera operator	Edward Lachman
Second unit & Underwater camera operator	Sergio Martinelli
Focus puller	Lars Karlsson
Second unit focus puller	Sergio Melaranci
Loader	Dan Myhrman
Camera mechanic	Gerhard Hentschel
Gaffer	Alfio Ambrogi
Special effects	Glen Robinson
	Aldo Puccini
	Joe Day
Special effects crew	Jack Sampson
	Raymond Robinson
	Joe Bernardi
	Wayne Rose
Construction Manager	Aldo Puccini

TECHNICAL ASSISTANCE IN THE CONSTRUCTION
OF THE TANK AND VILLA LALIQUE
C.G.E.E. ALSTHOM-PATEETE
UNDER THE SUPERVISION OF MICHEL STREBEL

Choreographer	Coco
Technical consultant	Milton Forman
Art director	Giorgio Postiglione
Illustrator	Mentor Huebner

Make-up artist	Massimo de Rossi
Assistant make-up	Adonellade Rossi
Script supervisor	Nikki Clapp
Hair stylist	Ennio Marroni
Props	George Hamilton
Wardrobe	Franco Antonelli
Sound mixer	Laurie Clarkson
Boom men	John Stevenson
	John Pitt
Key grip	Mario Stella
Stunt co-ordinator	Miguel Pedregosa
Stuntmen	Pablo Garcia
	Roman Ariznavarreta
Still Photographer	Frank Conner
Special Stills	Alfonso Avincola
Unit publicist	Tom Gray
Dialogue coach	Norman Schwartz
Assistant film editor	Bobbie Di
Production Auditor	Brian Gibbs
Assistant Auditor	Rex Saluz
Crane Operator	Dan Hoge
Casting by	McLean/Ebbins/Mansou
Local Casting and Dialogue Coach	John Alarimo
Vehicles	Fiat

the management of financial matters during filming—all these jobs were similarly divided among a number of people whose names appeared on the screen. These credits still do not give full expression to the fineness of the division of labor involved; someone must have typed and duplicated copies of the script, someone else copied the parts from Nino Rota's score, and a conductor and musicians, here unnamed, performed that music.

In fact, situations of art making lie somewhere between the extremes of one person doing everything and every smallest activity being done by a separate person. Workers of various kinds develop a traditional "bundle of tasks" (Hughes, 1971, pp. 311–16). To analyze an art world we look for its characteristic kinds of workers and the bundle of tasks each one does.

Nothing in the technology of any art makes one division of

tasks more "natural" than another, although some divisions are so traditional that we often regard them as given in the nature of the medium. Consider the relations between the composition and performance of music. In conventional symphonic and chamber music in the mid-twentieth century, the two activities occur separately and are seen as two different, highly specialized jobs. That was not always true. Beethoven, like most composers of his time, also performed, both his own music and that of others, as well as conducting and improvising on the piano. Even now, an occasional performer composes, as did the piano virtuosi Rachmaninoff and Paderewski. Composers sometimes perform, often because performance pays a great deal better than composition. Stravinsky, for instance, wrote three pieces for piano, two with orchestral accompaniment, designed to be playable by a pianist of no greater virtuosity than himself (the one without orchestra was written for two pianos, so that he and his son Soulima could play it in towns too small to have a symphony orchestra). Performing these pieces (he reserved performance rights for himself for a number of years) and conducting his own works allowed him to maintain the standard of living he had originally developed on the basis of his professional association with Diaghilev and the Ballets Russe (see White, 1966, pp. 65–66, 279–80, and 350).

The training of classical musicians reinforces this division of labor. Philip Glass, a contemporary composer, has explained that the people who enter the Juilliard School of Music to study composition are usually, when they enter, competent performers on some instrument. Once they enter the school, however, they spend more time composing and correspondingly less time on their instrument, while people specializing in instrumental performance continue to practice full time. Soon the instrumental specialists play so much better than the would-be composers that the latter stop playing; they can write things that are easy for the instrumentalists but that they themselves cannot play (Ashley, 1978).

In jazz, composition is much less important than performance. The standard tunes musicians play (blues and old popular songs) merely furnish the framework for the real creation. When musicians improvise, they use the raw materials of the song, but many players and listeners will not know who actually composed "Sunny Side of the Street" or "Exactly Like You"; some of the most important improvisatory frameworks, like blues, have no author at all. One might say that the composer is the player, considering the improvisation the composition.

In rock music, the two activities are, ideally, carried on by the same person. Fully competent performers compose their own music. Indeed, rock groups who play other people's music get tagged with the derogatory label "copy groups," and a young group comes of age the day it begins to play its own compositions. The activities are separate—performing is not simultaneous with composing, as it is in jazz—but both belong to one person's bundle of tasks (Bennett, 1980).

The same variations in the division of tasks can be found in every art. Some art photographers, like Edward Weston, always made their own prints, regarding printing as integral to the making of the picture; others, like Henri Cartier-Bresson, never made their own prints, leaving that to technicians who knew how they wanted it done. Poets writing in the Western tradition do not ordinarily incorporate their own handwriting into the finished product, leaving it to printers to put the material into a readable form; we see autograph copies of their poetry only when we are interested in the revisions they made in their own hand on the manuscript (see, for instance, Eliot, 1971) or in a rare case such as that of William Blake, who engraved his own plates, on which poems appeared in his own hand, and printed them himself, so that his hand was part of the work. But in much Oriental poetry the calligraphy is as important as the poem's content (see figure 1); to have it printed in mechanical type would destroy something crucial. More mundanely, saxophone and clarinet players buy their reeds at the music store, but oboists and bassoonists buy pieces of cane and manufacture their own.

Each kind of person who participates in the making of art works, then, has a specific bundle of tasks to do. Though the

FIGURE 1. *Page from a set of* **Shokunin-e** *("depictions of various occupations"), Edo period (1615–1868 A.D.), Japan. In Western literature, only the poem's words are important, but in much Oriental literature the calligraphy is equally important, and the calligrapher as important an artist as the poet. Ink and wash on paper. Artist, poet, and calligrapher unknown. The poem reads, "Sounds of hammering continue / Clear moon above / People, listening, wonder. . . ." (Asian Art Museum of San Francisco, the Avery Brundage Collection.)*

allocation of tasks to people is, in an important sense, arbitrary—it could have been done differently and is supported only by the agreement of all or most of the other participants—it is not therefore easy to change. The people involved typically regard the division of tasks as quasi-sacred, as "natural" and inherent in the equipment and the medium. They engage in the same work politics Everett Hughes (1971, pp. 311–15) describes among nurses, attempting to get rid of tasks they regard as tiresome, dirty, or beneath their dignity, seeking to add tasks that are more interesting, rewarding, and prestigious.

Every art, then, rests on an extensive division of labor. That is obviously true in the case of the performing arts. Films, concerts, plays, and operas cannot be accomplished by lone individuals doing everything necessary by themselves. But do we need all this apparatus of the division of labor to understand painting, which seems a much more solitary occupation? We do. The division of labor does not require that all the people involved in producing the art object be under the same roof, like assembly-line workers, or even that they be alive at the same time. It only requires that the work of making the object or performance rely on that person performing that activity at the appropriate time. Painters thus depend on manufacturers for canvas, stretchers, paint, and brushes; on dealers, collectors, and museum curators for exhibition space and financial support; on critics and aestheticians for the rationale for what they do; on the state for the patronage or even the advantageous tax laws which persuade collectors to buy works and donate them to the public; on members of the public to respond to the work emotionally; and on the other painters, contemporary and past, who created the tradition which makes the backdrop against which their work makes sense (see Kubler, 1962, and Danto, 1964, 1973, and 1974 on tradition).

Similarly with poetry, which seems even more solitary than painting. Poets need no equipment, other than what is conventionally available to ordinary members of society, to do their work. Pencils, pens, typewriters, and paper are enough, and, if these are not available, poetry began as an oral tradition and much contemporary folk poetry still exists only in that form (until folklorists like Jackson, 1972 and 1974, or Abrahams, 1970, write it down and publish it). But this appearance of autonomy is likewise superficial. Poets depend on printers and publishers, as painters do on distributors, and use shared traditions for the background against which their work makes sense and for the raw materials with which they work. Even so self-sufficient a poet as Emily Dickinson relied on psalm-tune rhythms an American audience would recognize and respond to.

All art works, then, except for the totally individualistic and therefore unintelligible works of an autistic person, involve some division of labor among a large number of people. (See the discussion of the division of labor in Freidson, 1976).

ART AND ARTISTS

Both participants in the creation of art works and members of society generally believe that the making of art requires special talents, gifts, or abilities, which few have. Some have more than others, and a very few are gifted enough to merit the honorific title of "artist." A character in Tom Stoppard's *Travesties* expresses the idea succinctly: "An artist is someone who is gifted in some way that enables him to do something more or less well which can only be done badly or not at all by someone who is not thus gifted" (Stoppard, 1975, p. 38). We know who has these gifts by the work they do because, these shared beliefs hold, the work of art expresses and embodies those special, rare powers. By inspecting the work we see that someone special made it.

We think it important to know who has that gift and who does not because we accord people who have it special rights and privileges. At an extreme, the romantic myth of the artist suggests that people with such gifts cannot be subjected to the constraints imposed on other members of society; we must allow them to violate rules of decorum, propriety, and common sense everyone else must follow or risk being punished. The myth suggests that in return society receives work of unique character and invaluable quality. Such a belief does not appear in all, or even most, societies; it may be unique to Western European societies, and those influenced by them, since the Renaissance.

Michael Baxandall (1972) pinpoints the shift in European thinking on this point as occurring in the fifteenth century, finding evidence of it in the changes in the contracts made between painters and the purchasers of their work. At one point, contracts specified the character of the painting, the methods of payment, and, especially, the quality of the colors to be used, insisting on the use of gold and the more expensive varieties of blue (some being considerably cheaper than others). Thus, a contract in 1485 between Domenico Ghirlandaio and one client specified, among other things, that the painter should:

> colour the panel at his own expense with good colours and with powdered gold on such ornaments as demand it . . . and the blue must be ultramarine of the value about four florins the ounce. . . . (Quoted in Baxandall, 1972, p. 6)

This resembles the contract one might make with a builder, specifying the quality of steel and concrete to be used.

At the same time, or even earlier, some clients were specifying materials less and skill more. Thus, a contract in 1445, between Piero della Francesca and another ecclesiastical client, while it did not fail to specify gold and ultramarine, put a greater emphasis on the value of the painter's skill, insisting that "no painter may put his hand to the brush other than Piero himself" (Quoted in Baxandall, 1972, p. 20.). Another contract was more detailed:

> The said master Luca is bound and promises to paint (1) all the figures to be done on the said vault, and (2) especially *the faces and all the parts of the figures from the middle of each figure upwards*, and (3) that no painting should be done on it without Luca himself being present. . . . And it is agreed (4) that all the mixing of colours should be done by the said master Luca himself. . . . (Quoted in Baxandall, 1972, p. 23)

This is a very different kind of contract. Here the client wants to be sure that he is getting his money's worth in something rarer than four-florin ultramarine, namely, the unique skill of an artist. "The fifteenth-century client seems to have made his opulent gestures more and more by becoming a conspicuous buyer of skill" (Baxandall, 1972, p. 23).

This shift moves only part of the way to today's fully developed belief that the art work consists mainly of the expression of the skill and vision of a great artist. It recognizes the artist as someone special, but awards artists no special rights. That came later.

Nevertheless, because artists have special gifts, because they produce work thought to be of great importance to a society, and because they therefore get special privileges, people want to make sure that only those who really have the gift, the talent, and the skill get the position. Special mechanisms sort out artists from nonartists. Societies, and media within societies, vary in how they do this. At one extreme, a guild or academy (Pevsner, 1940) may require long apprenticeship and prevent those it does not license from practicing. Where the state does not allow art much autonomy and controls the institutions through which artists get their training and work, access to skills may be similarly restricted. At another extreme, exemplified by such countries as the United States, everyone can learn; participants in the making of art rely on market mechanisms to weed out the talented from the others. In such systems, people keep the idea that artists have a special gift but do not believe that there is any way to tell who has it outside of letting everyone try and then inspecting the results.

Participants in the making of art works, and members of society generally, regard some of the activities necessary to the production of a form of art as "artistic," requiring the special gifts or sensibility of an artist. They further regard those activities as the core activities of art, necessary to make the work art rather than (in the case of objects) an industrial product, a craft item, or a natural object. The remaining activities seem to them a matter of craft, business acumen, or some other ability less rare, less characteristic of art, less necessary to the work's success, less worthy of respect. They define the people who perform these other activities as (to borrow a military term) support personnel, reserving the title of "artist" for those who perform the core activities.

The status of any particular activity, as a core activity which requires special artistic gifts or as mere support, can change. As we have seen, making paintings was once thought of as skilled work, but no more than that, and became defined as something more special in the Renaissance. In a later chapter we will consider how craft activities become redefined as art, and vice versa. Here it will be sufficient to cite the example of the recording engineer and sound mixer, the person who handles the technical end of recording music and preparing the result for commercial reproduction and sale. Edward Kealy (1979) documents the shift in the status of that technical activity. Up to the mid-1940s:

> The sound mixer's skill lay in using to advantage the acoustic design of the studio, deciding upon the placement of a handful of microphones, and mixing or balancing microphone outputs as the musical performance was recorded. Very little editing was possible since the performance was recorded directly on a disc or single track tape. The primary aesthetic question was utilitarian: how well does a recording capture the sounds of a performance? (P. 9)

After World War II, technical developments made "high fidelity" and "concert hall realism" possible.

> The good mixer-craftsman would make sure that unwanted sounds were not recorded or at least minimized, that the desired sounds were recorded without distortion, and that the sounds were in balance. The recording technology itself, and thus the sound mixer's work, was to be unobtrusive so as not to destroy the listener's illusion that he was sitting in Philharmonic Hall rather than his own living room. (P. 11)

With the advent of rock music, musicians whose instruments themselves embodied electronic technology began to experiment with recording technology as part of the musical work. Since they often had learned to play by imitating highly engineered recordings (Bennett, 1980), they naturally wanted to incorporate those effects into their work. Such equipment as multitrack recorders made it possible to edit and combine separately recorded elements and to manipulate electronically the sounds the musicians produced. Rock stars, relatively independent of corporate discipline, began to insist on control over the recording and mixing of their performances. Two things happened. On the one hand, signaled by the prominent credits given to mixers on record albums, sound mixing began to be recognized as an artistic activity requiring special artistic talent. On the other hand, people who had established themselves as musical artists began to take over the job themselves or to recruit ex-musicians to do it. Sound mixing, once a mere technical specialty, had become integral to the art process and recognized as such (Kealy, 1979, pp. 15–25).

The ideology posits a perfect correlation between doing the core activity and being an artist. If you do it, you must be an artist. Conversely, if you are an artist, what you do must be art. This produces confusion when, from either a commonsense point of view or from the standpoint of the art's tradition, that correlation does not occur. For instance, if the idea of gift or talent implies the notion of spontaneous expression or sublime inspiration (as it does for many), the businesslike work habits of many artists create an incongruity. Composers who produce so many bars of music a day, painters who paint so many hours a day—whether they "feel like it or not"—create some doubt as to whether they can be exercising superhuman talents. Trollope, who arose early so that he could get in his three hours of writing before going to work as a civil servant in the British Post Office, was almost a caricature of this businesslike, "unartistic" approach:

> All those I think who have lived as literary men,—working daily as literary labourers,—will agree with me that three hours a day will produce as much as a man ought to write. But then he should have so trained himself that he shall be able to work continuously during those three hours—so have tutored his mind that it shall not be necessary for him to sit nibbling his pen, and gazing at the wall before him, till he shall have found the words with which he wants to express his ideas. It had at this time become my custom,—and it is still my custom, though of late I have become a little lenient to myself,—to

write with my watch before me, and to require from myself 250 words every quarter of an hour. I have found that the 250 words have been forthcoming as regularly as my watch went. (Trollope, 1947, pp. 227–28)

Another difficulty arises when someone claiming to be an artist does not do some of what is regarded as the irreducible core of what an artist must do. Since the definition of the core activity changes over time, the division of labor between artist and support personnel also changes, leading to difficulties. How little of the core activity can a person do and still claim to be an artist? The amount the composer contributes to the material contained in the final work has varied greatly. Virtuoso performers from the Renaissance through the nineteenth century embellished and improvised on the score the composer provided (Dart, 1967, and Reese, 1959), so it is not without precedent that contemporary composers prepare scores which give only the sketchiest directions to the performer (the counter-tendency, for composers to restrict the interpretative freedom of the performer by giving increasingly detailed directions, has until recently been more prominent). John Cage and Karlheinz Stockhausen (Wörmer, 1973) are regarded as composers in the world of contemporary music, though many of their scores leave much of the material to be played to the decision of the player. Artists need not handle the materials from which the art work is made to remain artists; architects seldom build what they design. The same practice raises questions, however, when sculptors construct a piece by sending a set of specifications to a machine shop, and many people balk at awarding the title of artist to authors of conceptual works consisting of specifications never actually embodied in an artifact. Marcel Duchamp violated the ideology by insisting that he created a valid work of art when he signed a commercially produced snowshovel or a reproduction of the Mona Lisa on which he had drawn a mustache (see figure 2), thus classifying Leonardo as support personnel along with the snowshovel's designer and manufacturer. Outrageous as that idea may seem, something like it is standard in making collages, entirely constructed of other people's work.

Another confusion arises when no one can tell which one

FIGURE 2. *Marcel Duchamp,* **L.H.O.O.Q.** *When Marcel Duchamp drew a mustache on a commercial reproduction of the Mona Lisa and signed it, he turned Leonardo into one of his support personnel. (Private collection. Photograph courtesy of the Philadelphia Museum of Art.)*

or ones of the several people involved in the production of the work have the special gift and therefore the right both to receive the credit for the work's ultimate character and to direct the activities of the others. Eliot Freidson (1970) has pointed out that in the cooperative activity of the medical world participants agree that the doctor has that special gift and those special rights. But which of several major kinds of participants in making a film occupies a similarly undisputed leading role? *Auteur* theorists insist that films be understood as the expression of a director's controlling vision, hobbled though it may have been by the constraints imposed by studio superiors or the noncooperation of actors. Others think the writer, when allowed, actually controls the film, while still others think film is an actor's medium. I don't suppose anyone would argue that the production auditor or focus puller has a vision that informs the film, but Aljean Harmetz (1977) makes a good case that E. Y. Harburg and Harold Arlen, the people responsible for the music of *The Wizard of Oz*, provided that film's continuity.

This problem takes a special form in the question that arises over whether we ought, in responding to a work of art, to give some special weight to the maker's intentions, or whether a number of possible interpretations can be made, the maker's not being especially privileged (Hirsch, 1979). We can rephrase this: do we conventionally recognize the author as providing something special in the making of the work, something no one else could provide? If audience members believe the author has done that, they will naturally defer to his or her intentions in their responses. But they may not think so; the performers of and listeners to jazz evidently do not think that the composers of jazz standards merit any special deference with respect to how their songs should be played. Participants in the making of art works may agree as to whose intentions—author's, interpreter's, or audience's—take priority, in which case the issue creates no theoretical or practical difficulty. Those problems arise when participants disagree and standard practice produces unresolvable conflict. The philosophical and aesthetic problem is thus solved by a sociological analysis; such a solution does not, of course, solve the problem. It merely makes it the object of study.

Finally, because the artist's position as artist depends on the production of art works which embody and express his special talents and gifts, participants in art worlds worry about the authenticity of art works. Did the artist supposed to have done this work really do it? Has anyone else interfered with the original work, altered or edited it in some way so that what the artist intended and created is not what we now have before us? Did the artist, once the work was made, alter it in the light of subsequent experience or criticism and, if so, what does that mean with respect to the artist's abilities? If we judge the artist on the basis of the work, we must know who really did the work, and therefore deserves the judgment we make of its worth and the worth of its maker. It is as though making art works is a competition, like a school test, and we have to render a fair judgment based on all the facts. Because of this emphasis on the work-person equation, entire scholarly disciplines devote themselves to establishing who actually painted which paintings and whether the paintings now exhibited under the name of X are actually X's work, whether the scores we hear played were written by the person alleged to have written them, whether the words in a novel were written by the person whose name is on the title page or were plagiarized from someone else who deserves the credit or blame.

Why do these things matter? The work, after all, does not change if we learn that someone else did it; the plays are the same words, whether Shakespeare or Bacon wrote them, aren't they? Yes and no. Borges' (1962) story about Pierre Menard stresses this ambiguity. Pierre Menard, he says, is a French writer who, having written many conventional novels and books, decides to write *Don Quixote*—not a retelling of the story, but the actual *Don Quixote* of Cervantes. After much work, he has managed to write two chapters and a fragment of a third. The words are identical to Cervantes'. But, Borges points out, Cervantes was writing in the language of his time whereas Menard is writing in an archaic language which, furthermore, is not his native tongue. And so on. Who writes the words and when they are written affect our judgment of what the work consists of and therefore of what it reveals about the person who made it. (For further remarks on Borges' story, see Danto [1973], pp. 6–7.)

It matters not only because we appreciate and judge the work differently, but also because artists' reputations are a sum of the values we assign to the works they have produced. Each work that can definitely be attributed to Titian adds to or subtracts from the total on the basis of which we decide how great an artist Titian was. That is why plagiarism evokes such violent reactions. It is not just property that is being stolen, but the basis of a reputation as well.

The reputation of the artist and the work reinforce one another: we value more a work done by an artist we respect, just as we respect more an artist whose work we have admired. When the distribution of art involves the exchange of money, reputational value can be translated into financial value, so that the decision that a well-known and respected artist did not do a painting once attributed to him means that the painting loses value. Museums and collectors have suffered severe financial losses as a result of such changes of attribution, and scholars often find themselves under considerable pressure not to withdraw attributions on the basis of which important investments have been made (Wollheim, 1975).

Trollope found the problem of the importance of the artist's name to the judgment of the work sufficiently interesting to undertake an experiment:

> From the commencement of my success as a writer . . . I had always felt an injustice in literary affairs which had never afflicted me or even suggested itself to me while I was unsuccessful. It seemed to me that a name once earned carried with it too much favour. . . . I felt that aspirants coming up below me might do work as good as mine, and probably much better work, and yet fail to have it appreciated. In order to test this, I determined to be such an aspirant myself, and to begin a course of novels anonymously, in order that I might see whether I could obtain a second identity,—whether as I had made one mark by such literary ability as I possessed, I might succeed in doing so again. (Trollope, 1947, pp. 169–70)

He wrote, and published anonymously, two stories, in which

he tried to disguise both his style and his way of telling a story:

> Once or twice I heard the [stories] mentioned by readers who did not know me to be the author, and always with praise; but [they] had no real success. . . . Blackwood [the publisher], who of course knew the author, was willing to publish them, trusting that works by an experienced writer would make their way, even without the writer's name. . . . But he did not find the speculation answer, and declined a third attempt, though a third such tale was written for him. . . . Of course there is not in this any evidence that I might not have succeeded a second time as I succeeded before, had I gone on with the same dogged perseverance. . . . Another ten years of unpaid unflagging labour might have built up a second reputation. But this at any rate did seem clear to me, that with all the increased advantages which practice in my art must have given me, I could not at once induce English readers to read what I gave to them, unless I gave it with my name. (Trollope, 1947, pp. 171–72)

Trollope concluded:

> It is a matter of course that in all things the public should trust to established reputation. It is as natural that a novel reader wanting novels should send to a library for those by George Eliot or Wilkie Collins, as that a lady when she wants a pie should go to Fortnum and Mason. Fortnum and Mason can only make themselves Fortnum and Mason by dint of time and good pies combined. If Titian were to send us a portrait from the other world . . . it would be some time before the art critic of *The Times* would discover its value. We may sneer at the want of judgment thus displayed, but such slowness of judgment is human and has always existed. I say all this here because my thoughts on the matter have forced upon me the conviction that very much consideration is due to the bitter feelings of disappointed authors. (Trollope, 1947, p. 172)

COOPERATIVE LINKS

Whatever the artist, defined as the person who performs the core activity without which the work would not be art, does not do must be done by someone else. The artist thus works in the center of a network of cooperating people, all of whose work is essential to the final outcome. Wherever he depends on others, a cooperative link exists. The people with whom he cooperates may share in every particular his idea of how their work is to be done. This consensus is likely when everyone involved can perform any of the necessary activities so that, while a division of labor exists, no specialized functional groups develop. This might occur in simple communally shared art forms like the square dance or in segments of a society whose ordinary members are trained in artistic activities. Well-bred nineteenth-century Americans, for instance, knew enough music to perform the parlor songs of Stephen Foster, just as their Renaissance counterparts could perform madrigals. In such cases, cooperation occurs simply and readily.

When specialized professional groups take over the performance of the activities necessary to an art work's production, however, their members develop specialized aesthetic, financial, and career interests which differ substantially from the artist's. Orchestral musicians, for instance, are notoriously more concerned with how they sound in performance than with the success of a particular work; with good reason, for their own success depends in part on impressing those who hire them with their competence (Faulkner, 1973a, 1973b). They may sabotage a new work which can make them sound bad because of its difficulty, their career interests lying at cross-purposes to the composer's.

Aesthetic conflicts between support personnel and the artist also occur. A sculptor I know was invited to use the services of a group of master lithographic printers. Knowing little of the technique of lithography, he was glad to have these master craftsmen do the actual printing, this division of labor being customary and having generated a highly specialized craft of printing. He drew designs containing large areas of solid colors, thinking to simplify the printer's job. Instead, he made it more difficult. When the printer rolls ink onto the stone, a large area will require more than one rolling to be fully inked and may thus exhibit roller marks.

The printers, who prided themselves on their craft, explained that they could print his designs, but the areas of solid color might cause difficulty with roller marks. He had not known about roller marks and talked of using them as part of his design. The printers said no, he could not do that, because roller marks were an obvious sign (to other printers) of poor craftsmanship and they would not allow a print exhibiting roller marks to leave their shop. His artistic curiosity fell victim to the printers' craft standards, a neat example of how specialized support groups develop their own standards and interests (see Kase, 1973).

The artist was at the printers' mercy because he did not know how to print lithographs himself. His experience exemplified the choice that faces the artist at every cooperative link. He can do things as established groups of support personnel are prepared to do them; he can try to make those people do it his way; he can train others to do it his way; or he can do it himself. Any choice but the first requires an additional investment of time and energy to do what could be done less expensively if done the standard way. The artist's involvement with and dependence on cooperative links thus constrains the kind of art he can produce.

Similar examples can be found in any field of art. e e cummings had trouble publishing his first book of poetry because printers were afraid to set his bizarre layouts (Norman, 1958; see figure 3). Producing a motion picture involves multiple difficulties of this kind: actors who will only be photographed in flattering ways, writers who don't want a word changed, cameramen who will not use unfamiliar processes.

Artists often create work which existing production or exhibition facilities cannot accommodate. Try this thought experiment. Imagine that, as curator of sculpture of an art museum, you have invited a distinguished sculptor to exhibit a new work. He arrives driving a flatbed truck, on which rests a giant construction combining several pieces of large, heavy, industrial machinery into an interesting and pleasing shape. You find it moving, exciting. You ask him to take it around to the museum loading dock where the two of you discover that the door on the dock will not admit anything

r-p-o-p-h-e-s-s-a-g-r

who

a) s w (e loo) k

upnowgath

PPEGORHRASS

eringint(o-

aThe) :1

eA

!p:

S   a

(r

rIvInG   .gRrEaPsPhOs)

to

rea (be) rran (com) gi (e) ngly

,grasshopper;

FIGURE 3. *e e cummings, "r-p-o-p-h-e-s-s-a-g-r." e e cummings
had trouble with both audiences and printers because his poetry required them to do things in unaccustomed ways. (Reprinted from*
NO THANKS, *poems by E. E. Cummings, with the permission
of Liveright Publishing Corporation. Copyright 1935 by E. E. Cummings. Copyright © 1968 by Marion Morehouse Cummings. Copyright
© 1973, 1978 by Nancy T. Andrews. Copyright © 1973, 1978 by George
James Firmage.)*

taller than fifteen feet; the sculpture is much larger than that.
The sculptor suggests removing the wall, but by now you
have realized that, even if you got it into the museum, it
would fall through the floor into the basement; it is a museum, not a factory, and the building will not support so
much weight. Finally, disgruntled, he takes it away.

In the same way, composers write music which requires
more performers than existing organizations can pay for.
Playwrights write plays so long that audiences will not sit
through them. Novelists write books that competent readers
find unintelligible, or that require innovative printing techniques publishers are not equipped for. These artists are not
rebellious nuts; that is not the point. The point, rather, is that
the sculptures already in your museum did go through the

door on the loading dock, and did not fall through the floor. Sculptors know the appropriate weight and dimensions of a museum piece, and work accordingly. Broadway plays are of a length audiences will sit through, and the compositions symphony orchestras perform require no more musicians than the organization can pay.

When artists make what existing institutions cannot assimilate, whether the limits be physical or conventional (the weight of sculpture versus the length of plays), their works are not exhibited or performed. That is not because the managers of those organizations are conservative fuddy-duddies, either, but because their organizations are equipped to handle standard formats and their resources will not permit the substantial expenditures required to accommodate nonstandard items, or to sustain the losses involved in presenting work audiences will not support.

How do nonstandard works ever get exhibited, performed, or distributed? I will go into this question later, and here just mention that there often exist subsidiary, nonstandard distribution channels and adventurous entrepreneurs and audiences. The former provide methods of distribution, the latter take a chance on the result. Schools often provide such an opportunity. They have space and more-or-less free personnel in their students, and thus can muster forces more commercial presentations could not afford: real crowds for crowd scenes, outlandish assortments of instrumentalists and vocalists for musical experiments.

More artists adapt to what existing institutions can handle. By accommodating their conceptions to available resources, conventional artists accept the constraints arising from their dependence on the cooperation of members of the existing cooperative network. Wherever artists depend on others for some necessary component, they must either accept the constraints they impose or expend the time and energy necessary to provide it some other way.

CONVENTIONS

Producing art works requires elaborate cooperation among specialized personnel. How do they arrive at the terms on which they cooperate? They could, of course, decide everything afresh on each occasion. A group of musicians could discuss and agree on which sounds would be used as tonal resources, what instruments might be constructed to make those sounds, how those sounds would be combined to create a musical language, how the language would be used to create works of a particular length requiring a given number of instruments and playable for audiences of a certain size recruited in a certain way. Something like that sometimes happens, for instance, in the creation of a new theatrical group, although in most cases only a small number of the questions to be decided are actually considered anew.

People who cooperate to produce a work of art usually do not decide things afresh. Instead, they rely on earlier agreements now become customary, agreements that have become part of the conventional way of doing things in that art. Artistic conventions cover all the decisions that must be made with respect to works produced, even though a particular convention may be revised for a given work. Conventions dictate the materials to be used, as when musicians agree to base their music on the notes contained in a set of modes, or on the diatonic, pentatonic, or chromatic scales, with their associated harmonies. Conventions dictate the abstractions to be used to convey particular ideas or experiences, as when painters use the laws of perspective to convey the illusion of three dimensions or photographers use black, white, and shades of gray to convey the interplay of light and mass. Conventions dictate the form in which materials and abstractions will be combined, as in music's sonata form or poetry's sonnet. Conventions suggest the appropriate dimensions of a work, the proper length of a performance, the proper size and shape of a painting or sculpture. Conventions regulate the relations between artists and audience, specifying the rights and obligations of both.

Humanistic scholars—art historians, musicologists, and literary critics—have found the concept of the artistic convention useful in explaining artists' ability to make art works which evoke an emotional response in audiences. By using such a conventional organization of tones as a scale, composers can create and manipulate listeners' expectations as to what sounds will follow. They can then delay and frustrate the satisfaction of those expectations, generating tension and release as the expectation is ultimately satisfied (Meyer, 1956, 1973; Cooper and Meyer, 1960). Only because artist and audience share knowledge of and experience with the conventions invoked does the art work produce an emotional effect. Barbara H. Smith (1968) has shown how poets manipulate conventional means embodied in poetic forms and diction to bring poems to a clear and satisfying conclusion, in which the expectations produced early in the lyric are simultaneously and satisfactorily resolved. E. H. Gombrich (1960) has analyzed the visual conventions artists use to create for viewers the illusion that they are seeing a realistic depiction of some aspect of the world (see figure 4). In all these cases (and in others like stage design, dance, and film), the possibility of artistic experience arises from the existence of a body of conventions that artists and audiences can refer to in making sense of the work.

Conventions make art possible in another sense. Because decisions can be made quickly, plans made simply by referring to a conventional way of doing things, artists can devote more time to actual work. Conventions make possible the easy and efficient coordination of activity among artists and support personnel. William Ivins (1953), for instance, shows how, by using a conventionalized scheme for rendering shadows, modeling, and other effects, several graphic artists could collaborate to produce a single plate. The same conventions make it possible for viewers to read essentially arbitrary marks as shadows and modeling. Seen this way, the concept of convention provides a point of contact between humanists and sociologists, being interchangeable with such familiar sociological ideas as norm, rule, shared understanding, custom, or folkway, all referring to the ideas and understandings people hold in common and through which they effect cooperative activity. Burlesque comedians could stage elaborate three-man skits without rehearsal because they had only to refer to a conventional body of skits they all knew, pick one, and assign the parts. Dance musicians

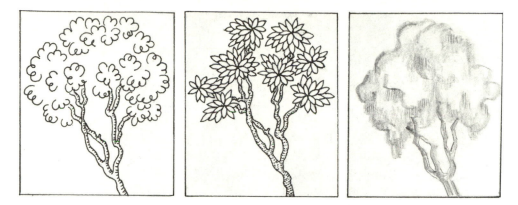

FIGURE 4. Three realistic drawings of a tree. The conventions of visual art make it possible for artists to render familiar objects in a shorthand knowledgeable viewers can read as realistic. These three ways of drawing the same tree (using conventions of the European sixteenth-century, European early twentieth-century, and classical Indian painting) are all easily understood as a tree. (Drawings by Nan Becker.)

who are total strangers can play all night with no more pre-arrangement than to mention a title ("Sunny Side of the Street," in C) and count off four beats to give the tempo; the title indicates a melody, its accompanying harmony, and perhaps even customary background figures. The conventions of character and dramatic structure, in the one case, and of melody, harmony, and tempo, in the other, are familiar enough that audiences have no difficulty responding appropriately.

Though standardized, conventions are seldom rigid and unchanging. They do not specify an inviolate set of rules everyone must refer to in settling questions of what to do. Even where the directions seem quite specific, they leave much to be resolved by reference to customary modes of interpretation on the one hand and by negotiation on the other. A tradition of performance practice, often codified in book form, tells performers how to interpret the musical scores or dramatic scripts they perform. Seventeenth century scores, for instance, contained relatively little information; but contemporary books explained how to deal with questions, unanswered in the score, of instrumentation, note values, extemporization, and the realization of embellishments and ornaments. Performers read their music in the light of all these customary styles of interpretation and could thus coordinate their activities (Dart, 1967). The same thing occurs in the visual arts. Much of the content, symbolism, and coloring of Italian Renaissance religious painting was conventionally given; but a multitude of decisions remained for the artist, so that even within those strict conventions different works could be produced. Adhering to the conventional materials, however, allowed viewers to read much emotion and meaning into the picture. Even where customary interpretations of conventions exist, having become conventions themselves, artists can agree to do things differently, negotiation making change possible.

Conventions place strong constraints on the artist. They are particularly constraining because they do not exist in isolation, but come in complexly interdependent systems, so that one small change may require a variety of other changes. A system of conventions gets embodied in equipment, materials, training, available facilities and sites, systems of notation, and the like, all of which must be changed if any one component is (cf. Danto, 1980).

Consider what changing from the conventional Western chromatic musical scale of twelve tones to one including forty-two tones between the octaves entails. Such a change characterizes the compositions of Harry Partch (1949). Western musical instruments cannot produce these microtones easily, and some cannot produce them at all, so conventional instruments must be reconstructed or new instruments must be invented and built. Since the instruments are new, no one knows how to play them, and players must train themselves. Conventional Western notation is inadequate to score forty-two-tone music, so a new notation must be devised, and players must learn to read it. (Comparable resources can be taken for granted by anyone who writes for the conventional twelve chromatic tones.) Consequently, while music scored for twelve tones can be performed adequately after relatively few hours of rehearsal, forty-two-tone music requires much more work, time, effort, and resources. Partch's music was often performed in the following way: a university would invite him to spend a year. In the fall, he would recruit a group of interested students, who would build the instruments (which he had already invented) under his direction. In the winter, they would learn to play the instruments and read the notation he had devised. In the spring, they would rehearse several works and finally would give a performance. Seven or eight months of work finally would result in two hours of music, hours which could have been filled with more conventional music after eight or ten hours of rehearsal by trained symphonic musicians playing the standard repertoire. The difference in the resources required measures the strength of the constraint imposed by the conventional system.

Similarly, conventions specifying what a good photograph should look like embody not only an aesthetic more or less accepted among the people involved in the making of art photographs (Rosenblum, 1978), but also the constraints built into the standardized equipment and materials made by major manufacturers. Available lenses, camera bodies, shutter speeds, apertures, films, and printing paper all constitute a tiny fraction of the things that could be made, a selection that can be used together to produce acceptable prints; with ingenuity they can also be used to produce effects their purveyors did not have in mind. The obverse of the constraint is the standardization and dependability of mass-produced materials that photographers prize; a roll of Kodak Tri-X film purchased anywhere in the world has approximately the same characteristics and will produce the same results as any other roll.

The limitations of conventional practice are not total. You can always do things differently if you are prepared to pay the price in increased effort or decreased circulation of your work. The experience of composer Charles Ives exemplifies the latter possibility. He experimented with polytonality and polyrhythms early in the 1900s before they became part of the ordinary performer's competence. The New York players who tried to play his chamber and orchestral music told him that it was unplayable, that their instruments could not make those sounds, that the scores could not be played in any practical way. Ives finally accepted their judgment, but continued to compose such music. What makes his case interesting is that, though he was also bitter about it, he experienced this as a great liberation (Cowell and Cowell, 1954). If no one could play his music, then he no longer had to write what musicians could play, no longer had to accept the constraints imposed by the conventions that regulated cooperation between contemporary composer and player. Since his music would not be played, he never needed to finish it; he was unwilling to confirm John Kirkpatrick's pioneer reading of the *Concord Sonata* as a correct one because that would mean he could no longer change it. Nor did he have to accommodate his writing to the practical constraints of what could be financed by conventional means, and so wrote his *Fourth Symphony* for three orchestras. (That impracticality lessened with time; Leonard Bernstein premiered the work in 1958, and it has been played many times since.)

In general, breaking with existing conventions and their manifestations in social structure and material artifacts increases artists' trouble and decreases the circulation of their work, but at the same time increases their freedom to choose unconventional alternatives and to depart substantially from customary practice. If that is true, we can understand any work as the product of a choice between conventional ease and success and unconventional trouble and lack of recognition.

ART WORLDS

Art worlds consist of all the people whose activities are necessary to the production of the characteristic works which that world, and perhaps others as well, define as art. Members of art worlds coordinate the activities by which work is produced by referring to a body of conventional understandings embodied in common practice and in frequently used artifacts. The same people often cooperate repeatedly, even routinely, in similar ways to produce similar works, so that we can think of an art world as an established network of cooperative links among participants. If the same people do not actually act together in every instance, their replacements are also familiar with and proficient in the use of those conventions, so that cooperation can proceed without difficulty. Conventions make collective activity simpler and less costly in time, energy, and other resources; but they do not make unconventional work impossible, only more costly and difficult. Change can and does occur whenever someone devises a way to gather the greater resources required or reconceptualizes the work so it does not require what is not available.

Works of art, from this point of view, are not the products of individual makers, "artists" who possess a rare and special gift. They are, rather, joint products of all the people who cooperate via an art world's characteristic conventions to bring works like that into existence. Artists are some subgroup of the world's participants who, by common agreement, possess a special gift, therefore make a unique and indispensable contribution to the work, and thereby make it art.

Art worlds do not have boundaries around them, so that we can say that these people belong to a particular art world while those people do not. I am not concerned with drawing a line separating an art world from other parts of a society. Instead, we look for groups of people who cooperate to produce things that they, at least, call art; having found them, we look for other people who are also necessary to that production, gradually building up as complete a picture as we can of the entire cooperating network that radiates out from the work in question. The world exists in the cooperative activity of those people, not as a structure or organization, and we use words like those only as shorthand for the notion of networks of people cooperating. For practical purposes, we usually recognize that many people's cooperation is so peripheral and relatively unimportant that we need not consider it, keeping in mind that such things change and what was unimportant today may be crucial tomorrow when events suddenly have made that kind of cooperation difficult to obtain.

Art worlds do not have clear boundaries in another sense.

To the sociologist studying art worlds, it is as clear as, but no clearer than, it is to the participants in them whether particular objects or events are "really art" or whether they are craft or commercial work, or perhaps the expression of folk culture, or maybe just the embodied symptoms of a lunatic. Sociologists, however, can solve this problem more easily than art world participants. One important facet of a sociological analysis of any social world is to see when, where, and how participants draw the lines that distinguish what they want to be taken as characteristic from what is not to be so taken. Art worlds typically devote considerable attention to trying to decide what is and isn't art, what is and isn't their kind of art, and who is and isn't an artist; by observing how an art world makes those distinctions rather than trying to make them ourselves we can understand much of what goes on in that world. (See Christopherson, 1974a and b, for an example of this process in art photography.)

In addition, art worlds typically have intimate and extensive relations with the worlds from which they try to distinguish themselves. They share sources of supply with those other worlds, recruit personnel from them, adopt ideas that originate in them, and compete with them for audiences and financial support. In some sense, art worlds and worlds of commercial, craft, and folk art are parts of a larger social organization. So, even though everyone involved understands and respects the distinctions which keep them separate, a sociological analysis should take account of how they are not so separate after all.

Furthermore, art worlds provoke some of their members to create innovations they then will not accept. Some of these innovations develop small worlds of their own; some remain dormant and then find acceptance from a larger art world years or generations later; some remain magnificent curiosities of little more than antiquarian interest. These fates reflect both the judgments of artistic quality made by contemporary art worlds and the perhaps chance operations of a variety of other factors.

The basic unit of analysis, then, is an art world. Both the "artness" and the "worldness" are problematic, because the work that furnishes the starting point for the investigation may be produced in a variety of cooperating networks and under a variety of definitions. Some networks are large, complicated, and specifically devoted to the production of works of the kind we are investigating as their main activity. Smaller ones may have only a few of the specialized personnel characteristic of the larger, more elaborate ones. In the limiting case, the world consists only of the person making the work, who relies on materials and other resources provided by others who neither intend to cooperate in the production of that work nor know they are doing so. Typewriter manufacturers participate in the small worlds of many would-be novelists who have no connection with the more conventionally defined literary world.

In the same way, the cooperative activity may be carried on either in the name of art or under some other definition, even though in the latter case the products might seem to us to resemble those made as art. Because "art" is an honorific title and being able to call what you do by that name has some advantages, people often want what they do to be so labeled. Just as often, people do not care whether what they do is art or not (as in the case of many household or folk arts—cake decorating, embroidery, or folk dancing, for instance) and find it neither demeaning nor interesting that their activities are not recognized as art by people who do care about such things. Some members of a society can control the application of the honorific term *art*, so not everyone is in a position to have the advantages associated with it, if he wants them.

For all these reasons, it is not clear what to include in an analysis of art worlds and what to leave out. To limit the analysis to what a society currently defines as art leaves out too much that is interesting: all the marginal cases in which people seek but are denied the name, as well as those in which people do work that outside observers can see might meet the definition but whose makers are not interested in that possibility. That would allow the process of definition by members of the society, which ought properly to be the subject of our study, to set its terms. On the other hand, to study everything that might meet a society's definition of art includes too much. Almost anything might meet such a definition, if we applied it ingeniously enough. I have not accepted standard definitions of art in the analysis to come. I have also not included everything, sticking to the marginal cases in which the label is in dispute or people do something that seems to have a substantial resemblance to things called "art," so that the process of definition comes into focus as a major problem.

As a result, I have given much attention to work not conventionally thought to have artistic value or importance. I have been interested in "Sunday painters" and quiltmakers as well as in conventionally recognized fine art painters and sculptors, in rock-and-roll musicians as well as in concert players, in the amateurs not good enough to be either as well as in the professionals who are. In doing so, I hope to let the problematic character of both "artness" and "worldness" permeate the analysis, and avoid taking too seriously the standards of those who make the conventional definitions of art for a society.

Though art worlds do not have sharp boundaries, they do vary in the degree to which they are independent, operating in relative freedom from interference by other organized groups in their society. Put another way, the people who cooperate in the work being studied may be free to organize their activity in the name of art, as is the case in many contemporary Western societies, whether they make use of that possibility or not. They may, however, find that they must take into account other interests represented by groups organized around other definitions. The state may exercise such control over other areas of society that major participants in the making of art works orient themselves primarily to the concerns of the state apparatus rather than to the concerns of people who define themselves as interested in art. Theocratic societies may organize the making of what we, from the perspective of our society, would recognize as works of art as an adjunct of activity defined in religious terms. In frontier societies subsistence may be so problematic that activities which do not contribute directly to the production of food or other necessities may be seen as un-affordable luxuries, so that work we might define, from a contemporary vantage point, as art gets done in the name of household necessity. What cannot be justified that way is not done. Before people can organize themselves as a world explicitly justified by making objects or events defined as art, they need sufficient political and economic freedom to do that, and not all societies provide it.

This point needs emphasis, because so many writers on what is ordinarily described as the sociology of art treat art as relatively autonomous, free from the kinds of organizational constraints that surround other forms of collective activity. I have not considered those theories here because they deal essentially with philosophical questions quite different from the mundane social organizational problems with which I have concerned myself (see Donow, 1979). Insofar as what I have to say questions the assumption of freedom from economic, political, and organizational constraint, it necessarily implies a criticism of analytic styles based on it.

. Art worlds produce works and also give them aesthetic value. This book does not itself make aesthetic judgments, as the preceding remarks suggest. Instead it treats aesthetic judgments as characteristic phenomena of collective activity. From this point of view, the interaction of all the involved parties produces a shared sense of the worth of what they collectively produce. Their mutual appreciation of the conventions they share, and the support they mutually afford one another, convince them that what they are doing is worth doing. If they act under the definition of "art," their interaction convinces them that what they produce are valid works of art.

2 • Conventions

Consider this note: 𝄞 , middle C, *do*. It is the first note of a melody I have in mind. Solve this problem: What is the second note?

Some people will guess ══ , D above middle C, *re*. Others will say it is ══ , E above middle C, *mi*. Others will be suspicious, thinking I have something trickier in mind, and try C-sharp or, seeing that there is no necessity for my melody to move up, B below the staff. In fact, of course, the problem is not soluble; you do not have enough information. It might be any of those or any other note of the chromatic scale.

Suppose I give you another clue, the second note of the melody. It is the first one guessed, D above middle C. What is the third note? Most people will now, with much more assurance, guess E, *mi*. Or suppose the second note isn't D, it's E. Then most people will know that the third note is G, *sol*. In neither case can they be 100 percent sure, but they feel that the probability of being right is certainly much greater than in the first case.

Why is the original question so difficult? Why is it so much easier to answer when you know two notes instead of one?

The answer is interesting not because it is hard to get, but because it leads to an understanding of the social organization of art worlds.

It is easier to tell the third note when you know the first two because once you know two notes you can guess at a pattern, something that is impossible if you know only one note. If the first two notes are ▬▬▬ , C-D, the suggested pattern is the diatonic scale, *do-re-mi-fa*, etc., and the likely candidate for the third note is *mi*, the third note of the scale, following the first two "logically." In the same way, if the first two notes are ▬▬▬ , C-E, *do-mi*, the pattern suggested is the major triad, Č-E-G, *do-mi-sol*, and the likely candidate for the third note is *sol*, the third note of the triad, following the first two with equal "logic." We can answer the question because we have identified a pattern which, if continued, gives us the missing note. (See Meyer, 1973.)

How do we know the pattern? That takes us out of the realm of gestalt psychology and into the operations of art worlds and social worlds generally, for it is a question about the distribution of knowledge, and that is a fact of social organization. We know these patterns—the diatonic scale and the major triad—because anyone who has grown up in any Western country, lived as a child there, and, especially, gone to its schools, will know them. From our earliest days in a culture which uses such scales and harmonies, we hear songs—lullabies, nursery rhymes, and, later, popular songs of all kinds—based on these ubiquitous conventional building blocks of Western music. When we enter school, we learn the names of those notes (in the conventional *do-re-mi* notation and in conventional notation on the staff, with the letter names C, D, E, and so forth), and learn to sing them on cue when we see the notes.

We can answer the question, then, because we learned the materials needed to solve the problem years ago. Any competent member of a Western society could answer the question, having learned the same materials as a child. (That is why I have dared to use a musical example in a book intended for nonmusicians.) People who grew up in a completely different musical tradition might not understand the question, and would not know the answer if they did, never having learned the conventions necessary for the problem's solution.

We have already seen how conventions provide the basis on which art world participants can act together efficiently to produce works characteristic of those worlds. Different groups of participants know different parts of the total body of conventions used by an art world, ordinarily what they need to know to facilitate the portion of the collective action in which they take part.

Every art world uses, to organize some of the cooperation between some of its participants, conventions known to all or almost all well-socialized members of the society in which it exists. Sometimes an art world uses materials deeply embedded in the culture quite apart from the history of that art medium, as when classical ballet relies on our conventionalized understanding of the roles of men and women and the character of romantic attachments between them as the skeleton on which to construct a series of dances in which the man supports the woman, woos her, is spurned, and eventually wins her (see figure 5). The dances have whatever modicum of plot they contain because we already know almost all of the story, having acquired it much as we learned *do-re-mi*, and need only the barest cues to inject the rest of the drama into the action we see.

Sometimes the art world relies on conventions of the art itself, but ones which everyone has experienced so early and so often that they are as much part of the culture as the sex roles ballet depends on for its sense. Imagine that you have been watching a feature film for ninety minutes and you now see one of the chief characters slowly walk away from the camera while the camera simultaneously pulls farther and farther back. What is happening? The film has ended, and people in the theater are getting up, throwing away their popcorn boxes, and putting on their coats as they prepare to leave. Freeze frames and swelling music similarly indicate the ending in a conventional way.

The conventions of stick-figure drawing make use of the commonsense knowledge we all have of what constitute the

FIGURE 5. *Jim Sohm and Diana Weber in the San Francisco Ballet production of Prokofiev's* Romeo and Juliet. *Classical ballet relies on our conventionalized understanding of the roles of men and women and the character of romantic attachments between them to provide much of the dances' sketchy stories. (Photo courtesy of the San Francisco Ballet.)*

FIGURE 6. *Conventional symbols for men's and women's toilets. Conventional understandings of human anatomy, clothing, and stick-figure drawing make it possible to use these signs to mark men's and women's toilets so that no one will make a mistake.*

essential portions of the human anatomy for pictorial purposes. We add our conventional understanding of men's and women's clothing to create, for instance, signs for men's and women's toilets in public places, assuming that anyone will understand them well enough not to go into the wrong room (see figure 6).

Verbal art forms use a mixture of conventions which are part of the culture, independent of the art medium itself, and conventions of the art so well known that they are also part of the culture every well-socialized person knows. Poetry and other verbal arts rely heavily on the associative and evocative materials embedded in language as it is used in ordinary speech as well as in literature. Phonemes take on, in the development of a language, meanings signaled by their sounds, just because so many words in a given meaning family already use those sounds. Thus, in English the initial sound *gl-* has a connotation of phenomena of light; many words describing such phenomena begin that way: *gleam*, *glow*, *glitter*, *glint*, *glare*, and so on. (All words beginning this way need not have the connotation for the point to stand; *glide* and *gland* have the beginning, but no connotation of light. Nevertheless, English speakers ordinarily hear the notion of light in that family of initial sounds.) Similarly, words ending in *-ump* connote awkwardness and heaviness: *dump*, *bump*, *rump*, *lump*, *stump*, *grump*, and so on (Bollinger, 1950). Poets control the feel of a passage in part by controlling the way these "meaningful" sounds enter into it, adding to or modifying the more overtly expressed meanings. We can see the point clearly enough in invented words ("'Twas brillig, and the slithy toves"—think about *brillig* and *slithy* and what we understand by them). We can create a humorous effect by combining sounds with contradictory connotations: *glump*, for instance, suggests a heavy, awkward phenomenon of light. The computer slang word *glitch* gets its effect this way.

Poetry and other forms of literature also use devices that gained their effect through the development of the medium. Smith (1968) has analyzed a large variety of such devices which produce a feeling of finality and closure in a poem. Some forms end in a characteristic way; we know a sonnet has ended when we finish fourteen lines, rhymed in a particular way. Less formal customary procedures produce the same effect of closure. The topic the poem treats may be dealt with in some way that seems definitive. The last line or two may complete some argument or witticism. The last lines may be mostly or entirely monosyllabic, or use words which themselves refer to ending in one form or another: *last*, *finished*, *end*, *rest*, *peace*, or *no more*, or such ending-related events as sleep, death, or winter. Experienced readers of poetry may not identify the elements consciously, but respond to them as closural.

Music uses many technical devices sufficiently well known to all well-socialized members of a society to be usable resources for artists. Composers can, for instance, take for granted that audiences will understand and respond, as expected, to a minor key as "sad" or to certain rhythm patterns as "Latin American."

Conventions known to all well-socialized members of a society make possible some of the most basic and important forms of cooperation characteristic of an art world. Most important, they allow people who have little or no formal acquaintance with or training in the art to participate as audience members—to listen to music, read books, attend films or plays, and get something from them. Knowledge of these conventions defines the outer perimeter of an art world, indicating potential audience members, of whom no special knowledge can be expected. Art forms designed to reach the maximum number of people in a society take most advantage of these resources. Some—popular television shows, for instance—do that in an established way. Others use these resources more unconventionally in an attempt to reach a large number, as with political street theater. One of the classic street-theater pieces of the anti-Vietnam War movement consisted of a group of men dressed as U.S. soldiers, carrying rifles, who chased someone dressed as a civilian Vietnamese woman down a crowded New York street, caught her, and shot her; when the expected crowd gathered, the group began a discussion of the political meaning of the war. The crowd gathered because what they saw was immediately intelligible, making use as it did of materials known to any adult living in the country at that time.

Some nonartistic knowledge available to only a segment of the population can serve as the basis for art works aimed at that segment. Books and films intended for adults can assume knowledge of some matters children do not know; children then have difficulty responding to works adults understand immediately. Baxandall gives the example of fifteenth-century Italian merchants, who learned, as training for business, geometrical methods for gauging quantities of goods and formulas for manipulating ratios and proportions, the same devices painters used to analyze solid forms pictorially. Businessmen, who were among the people who paid for paintings, thus knew how to appreciate what painters were doing visually; they knew mathematics and:

> used it in important matters more often than we do, played games and told jokes with it, bought luxurious books about it,

and prided themselves on their prowess in it. . . . this specialization constituted a disposition to address visual experience,
in or out of pictures, in special ways: to attend to the structure
of complex forms as combinations of regular geometric
bodies and as intervals comprehensible in series. Because
they were practiced in manipulating ratios and in analysing
the volume or surface of compound bodies, they were sensitive to pictures carrying the marks of similar processes. . . .
The status of these skills in his society was an encouragement
to the painter to assert them playfully in his pictures. . . . he
did. (Baxandall, 1972, pp. 101–2)

Some knowledge common to everyone is thought to be too
vulgar to be used as the basis of an art work. Mikail Bakhtin
(1968) suggests that Rabelais' great contribution to literature
was to bring the language of the marketplace—bawdy, vulgar, and irreverent—into art, and thus to help topple the
constraining styles of thought, along with the social structures, of feudalism. He argues that most art is inevitably, by
virtue of its sponsorship by the people who control the
society, couched in a serious and official language which
takes at face value official claims to authority. Beneath this,
however, runs an irreverent, gross stream of folk culture
mocking what is officially serious, degrading it with scatol-
ogy, blasphemy, and erotic humor. That folk culture, embodied in the talk and practice of the marketplace and the
popular fairs, persisted through the Middle Ages, even
though it found almost no place in the official, religious art of
the time. As the feudal order came to an end, the images and
language of the folk culture increasingly found a place in
literature, culminating in Rabelais' bawdy book.

Other conventions arise in the art world itself and are
known only to people who have some dealings with it. We
generally recognize the distinction Hume made in his discussion of the standard of taste (1854 [1752]) when he remarked that while what made art great was a matter of
opinion, some opinions were better than others because their
holders had more experience of the works and genres in
question and so could make finer and more justifiable dis-
criminations. They had a greater awareness of the conventions that informed the making of those works, gained by

their more continuous presence in the audience for them. Someone who has seen many productions of the same play, by different companies and in different theaters, with different costumes, scenery, and lights, directed differently, embodying different interpretations, has a more complete awareness of what the conventional designations in the script make possible, as well as of what scripts like it make possible.

This knowledge distinguishes the occasional member of the audience from the steady patron, the serious listener or reader whose attention artists hope for, because that serious reader will understand most fully what they have put into the work. Knowing the conventions of the form, serious audience members can collaborate more fully with artists in the joint effort which produces the work each time it is experienced. Further, steady patrons of art events—those who attend performances and exhibitions or those who read serious literature—provide a solid basis of support for those events and objects and for the activity that produces them. Such serious and experienced audience members belong to the art world, more or less permanent parties to the cooperative activity that makes it up.

What do these people know that differentiates them from those who respond simply as well-socialized members of the society? The list includes such things as: the history of attempts to make similar works in that medium or genre; characteristic features of different styles and periods in the history of the art; the merits of different positions on key issues in the history, development, and practice of the art; an acquaintance with various versions of the same work; and the ability to respond emotionally and cognitively to the manipulation of standard elements in the vocabulary of the medium. It probably also includes gossip of the art world, both contemporary and past, items of interest about the personal affairs of participants in that world, independent of their works; whether such material is relevant to an understanding of those works is perennially debated.

What serious audience members know about an art often conflicts, because of innovative changes, with what well-

FIGURE 7. *Oberlin Dance Collective performing* Format III. *Contemporary dance makes use of movements—stumbling and falling, for instance—that classical ballet (and classical ballet audiences) define as mistakes. (Photograph courtesy of the Oberlin Dance Collective.)*

socialized members of the society know. Many arts have a lengthy tradition of formalization, in which they stylize the materials they use, divorcing them from the things people do and the objects they make in "real life." Artistic innovators frequently try to avoid what they regard as the excessive formalism, sterility, and hermeticism of their medium by exploiting the actions and objects of everyday life. Choreographers like Paul Taylor and Brenda Way use running, jumping, and falling down as conventionalized dance movements, instead of the more formal movements of classical ballet, or even of traditional modern dance (see figure 7).

Photographers Robert Frank, Lee Friedlander, and Gary Winogrand use the cut-off heads, tilted frame, and banal everyday subject matter of the amateur snapshot to replace the conventional formalisms of art photography. Composers Terry Riley and Philip Glass use the simple repetition of children's music to replace the complex melodic and harmonic developments of more traditional serious music. In all these cases, however, less involved audiences look precisely for the conventional formal elements the innovators replace to distinguish art from nonart. They do not go to the ballet to see people run, jump, and fall down; they can see that anywhere. They go instead to see people do the difficult and esoteric formal movements that signify "real dancing." The ability to see ordinary material as art material—to see that the running, jumping, and falling down are not just that, but are the elements of a different language of the medium—thus distinguishes serious audience members from the well-socialized member of the culture, the irony being that these materials are perfectly well known to the latter, although not as art materials.

Serious audience members, however, do not know all the things that other more professionalized participants in art worlds know. They know no more than they need to know to play their part in the cooperative activity, which is to understand, appreciate, and support the activities of those called artists in that world.

The distribution of conventional knowledge changes. What everyone once knew can cease to be part of the equipment of an ordinary, well-socialized member of society and become something that only better-prepared, more serious participants in art activities know. Baxandall (1972) shows how the details of the religious stories which provided the texts for Renaissance Italian paintings were common knowledge to the ordinary citizen and churchgoer when they were painted. Painters could count on their audience understanding, from small conventional signs, what phase of the Annunciation story was depicted in a painting (see figure 8), and experiencing it accordingly. That kind of Christian knowledge is now restricted to serious students of the medium.

FIGURE 8. *Master of the Barberini Panels,* Annunciation: Reflection. *Painters of the Italian Renaissance used conventional signs to indicate which phase of the story of the Annunciation they were picturing. This picture shows the moment of "Reflection" (Cogitatio), in which the Virgin, disquieted by the Angel Gabriel's salutation ("Blessed art thou among women"), reflects on what the angel may have to tell her. (Photograph courtesy of the National Gallery of Art, Washington, D.C., Samuel H. Kress Collection.) (See Baxandall, 1972, 49–56.)*

Bakhtin (1968) points out that few people can read Rabelais today, finding him disgusting on the one hand and boring on the other, because we have lost touch with the folk culture which alone could make one feel and see the humor (and thus the political message) of the work. Conversely, what is at first known only to a small circle of innovators and aficionados can, like the ability to experience atonal music, spread to wider and wider circles with time.

Another group overlaps with the serious audience members: students of the arts. Professions which have more or less formal training programs may lose some proportion of their trainees during the training period and some further fraction after the novices begin to practice. Not all trained physicians practice medicine, and a much larger proportion of Americans trained in law never practice. The proportion of trainees who never practice varies greatly between occupations, as well as between countries.

In the present-day United States, enormous numbers of people study the arts seriously and semiseriously, taking courses, practicing difficult disciplines, devoting large amounts of time and other resources, often making substantial sacrifices and requiring them of their families and friends as well. Few of them ever become full-time professional artists. No art has sufficient resources to support economically or give sympathetic attention to all or any substantial proportion of those trainees in the way customary in the art worlds for which they are being trained. This is an important proviso. If the arts were organized differently— less professional, less star-oriented, less centralized—that support might be available. The problems arise when thousands of students hope to become Broadway stars, premier ballerinas in a major company, or winners of the Nobel Prize in literature. But the arts might be, and have at times been, organized so that these were not the available or reasonable goals to aim at.

Nevertheless, large numbers train for careers in the arts; even more begin such training without completing it, not necessarily because they do not still desire such careers but because they believe that formal training is neither necessary nor desirable for such a career. They may be right. Theodore Hoffman (1973) argues that few successful commercial actors come from the hordes of students who graduate from drama programs every year. He also suggests that these trained and semitrained people are important to the economy of the art world, providing the backbone of support for the commercial theater (and especially its avant-garde segment) in New York. As much as 15 percent of all theater tickets sold in New York are sold to people studying drama at the time; they are especially likely to support experimental works which would have trouble attracting the general public, less attuned to the conventions of new work.

Those who have received training and now do something else may be an additional, substantial portion of the public for any art form. The audience for ballet, and especially for modern dance, probably consists in large part of dancers, dancers-in-training, and people who once studied dance. Look at the audience at any dance event. No equivalent sample of theater- or concertgoers displays such erect carriage, such self-conscious placement of feet and legs, such well-maintained bodies.

Similarly, the thousands of people who study photography every year produce few professional photographers, people who make a living from the practice of photography. Nor do they produce many art photographers (the distinction is necessary because many serious, contributing members of the photographic art world do not earn a living in it, and even those who do usually manage by teaching and lecturing rather than by selling photographs). But these people buy photographic books, take classes and workshops, and attend lectures, providing most of the economic base for the world of art photography. In addition, they provide a large part of the educated audience to whom photographic artists can address their work with some hope of being understood. Hans Haacke's polls of contemporary gallerygoers show that between 40 and 60 percent are either artists or art students, students constituting between 10 and 15 percent (Haacke, 1976, pp. 17, 42).

What conventions do these people know and respond to?

What part can they therefore play in the patterned cooperation that makes up an art world? In addition to what well-socialized members of the society and serious audience members know, this inner circle of the audience knows the technical problems of the craft and the difficult problems, distinguishable from those of technique and craft, of utilizing technical means and abilities to provoke an emotional and aesthetic response from an audience. Having been on the other side of the line that separates performers and creators from consumers, as those roles are conventionally distinguished, they can respond to the work with a fuller understanding of what has been attempted and how even a failure might be interesting. They are the most understanding and forgiving audience, on whom the riskiest experiments may be attempted.

The three groups so far distinguished all participate in the art world primarily as consumers of art works, purchasers of objects and books, and audiences at performances, and secondarily as students and trainees of varying seriousness. They provide the material support of money spent and the aesthetic support of understanding and response. The three groups are related. The innermost circle, present and ex-students, serves as a distant, early-warning system for less advanced audience segments. They will risk more, make a greater effort to learn new conventions proposed by innovators, experience a higher number of failures and disasters, and waste more time on experiences that turn out to be of no interest. They provide both kinds of support for the widest variety of attempts the art world spawns, and thus encourage experimentation. They also help less adventurous audience segments catch up with newer developments by weeding out the grossest and most obvious failures, the attempts which, even by their own standards, do not succeed. They thus assure others that what has survived this preliminary sorting is worth a look; the assurance is just what the others want. In this way, less involved participants see just a few carefully selected innovations and new conventions, guaranteed in a way that makes them seem worth learning to appreciate.

We know little about how critical assessments of art are passed around among various audience segments. Elihu Katz and Paul Lazarsfeld (1955) proposed a general two-step model of influence, based on studies of the distribution of mass-media messages: certain influential people paid more attention to the media, forming firmer opinions, and others in the community paid attention to them, taking messages from and about the media filtered through these more knowledgeable types. The same model applied to doctors learning to prescribe a new drug: a few influential doctors in the community would try the drug out; if they had no trouble and found it useful, other doctors, influenced by them, would then begin using it (Coleman, Katz, and Menzel, 1966). We need studies which tell us how, in specific art worlds, assessments of styles, genres, innovations, artists, and particular works are circulated. Who tries things first? Who listens to and acts on their opinions? Why are their opinions respected? Concretely, how does the word spread from those who see something new that it is worth noticing? Why does anyone believe them?

An entirely different set of conventions creates the basis for the cooperative activities of the people who create art works and their support personnel. Many of the production conventions which make cooperation possible are simple forms of standardization which exemplify the philosophical notion of convention analyzed by David K. Lewis (1969). Lewis uses a technical language not really necessary here; readers who find his analysis worth pursuing should consult the original text. Briefly, Lewis wants to understand how people manage to coordinate their activities, how (in situations in which all the actors have a common interest but it is not clear which of the possible ways of achieving it they should use) they manage to choose the same one and thus get what they want done with little wasted motion. The easiest way would be for the people involved to discuss the problem and agree on the procedure to be used. We often do that. But we even more often find it unnecessary because, we might say, "it's obvious what to do," or "the most natural thing to do is *X*," or "if everyone does what seems easiest it will all work out OK," or some similar formula. We find that we can achieve the desired coordination without communication. How do we do it? By referring to a past solution to the problem, well known to all the participants and known by them to be well known to all the others. Given those conditions and everyone's desire to coordinate his own activity, the easiest thing, and therefore the most likely, is for everyone to do what everyone knows is the way everyone already knows. This is easy to do because everyone knows that everyone will know this . . . and so on through as long a hierarchy of such nested expectations (usually not a very long one) as is required for everyone to convince himself that is what he ought to do.

If the people involved all do the most likely thing, they will achieve the result they want, and thus increase the likelihood that the next time a problem they define as similar arises, they will all use the same solution, and that will still further increase the likelihood that they will use the solution in the future . . . and so on. The means everyone adopted to solve the problem of coordination is what Lewis means by a "convention," and it aptly describes those standardized means of doing things characteristic of all the arts. Many of the things artists and support personnel do in coordinating their activities are chosen from among a range of possible ways of accomplishing the same thing, any one of which would be acceptable as long as everyone used it.

There is no logical reason, for instance, to tune musical instruments to a concert A that is 440 vibrations per second, no reason why that note should be called A instead of Z, and no reason why those notes should be written on a staff of five lines instead of four, six, or seven. But everyone does it that way and thus any one participant can be sure that what he does that way will be intelligible and easy to coordinate with. Reason enough.

Some of the conventions which coordinate activity among artists and support personnel consist of just such simple standardization. When a particular convention can be taken for granted, when almost everyone involved almost always does things that way, the understandings that shape the convention can be embodied in permanent equipment. The existence of such permanent equipment (expensive, it goes without saying) makes it more likely that the conventional ways of doing things will continue, because any change will be expensive.

When conventions are standardized in this way, and embodied in practices and equipment that are totally taken for granted, anyone with experience in the art can be counted on to know that basic minimum. It becomes the automatic basis on which the production of art works can proceed, even among people deeply devoted to not doing things in the conventional way. Thus, most modern dance, designed *not* to be like conventional ballet, ends up presupposing that recruits will have had some ballet training and have acquired the muscles, habits, and understandings that come with such training. Even when you don't want to do what is conventional, what you do want to do can best be described in the language that comes from the conventions, for it is the one language everyone knows.

Equipment, in particular, produces this kind of universal knowledge. When the equipment embodies the conventions, the way a conventional thirty-five-millimeter camera embodies the conventions of contemporary photography, you learn the conventions as you learn to work the machinery. Thus anyone who can handle the machinery will know how to do the things necessary for coordinated activity. The same is true of many of the understandings associated with conventional music; you learn them as you learn to manipulate the instrument.

Many conventions grow up through an interaction of technical and other considerations. For many years (roughly the years covered in Alec Wilder's *American Popular Song: 1900–1950*), the American popular song used, almost exclusively, a thirty-two-bar form organized in eight-bar phrases with the themes arranged A-A-B-A and melodies restricted to a range of a tenth or less with intervals restricted to those contained in the diatonic scale and the harmonies related to it; most performances of those songs consisted of two to three choruses. The eight-bar phrases and thirty-two-bar format were arbitrary; the range and intervals used catered to the limited training of the vocalists who sang them and of the lay public, which was supposed to be able to sing them too; the number of choruses reflected what could be contained on the standard ten-inch seventy-eight-rpm record.

Using extremely standardized conventions, artists can coordinate their activity under the most difficult circumstances. When I played the piano in Chicago nightclubs in the 1940s, we typically played seven or eight hours a night. Toward the end of an evening, players got quite tired and sleepy. I discovered that the extreme conventionalization of the popular songs we played meant I could play when I was half, or more than half, asleep. I would often wake up in the middle of a song, getting lost only when I realized that I had been asleep and consequently had no idea where I was. Until then, I must have made use of my knowledge that all the phrases of the song were eight bars long, that they used only a few chords from the many possibilities available, and that those were arranged in a few standardized ways. David Sudnow (1978) has described the way these understandings get built into the performer's physical reactions as well as his cognitive equipment, so that playing while asleep becomes understandable and unremarkable.

Because equipment comes to embody one set of conventions in such a coercive way, artists frequently exercise their creativity by trying to make equipment and materials do things their makers never intended. Photographic equipment has become increasingly standardized as the industry becomes concentrated in the hands of a few corporations, and art photographers devote more and more time and ingenuity to devising ways to make the materials still available (not the only kinds that could be made, but the only kinds the corporations involved market in an easily accessible and relatively inexpensive form) do things they were not made to do. They manipulate films—designed to be used with a standard exposure to produce a standard negative that can be printed easily with conventional techniques—to produce a quite different negative which can only be printed by using exotic darkroom techniques. Musicians make sounds inventors and teachers of their instruments never had in mind; one example is playing directly on the strings of the piano rather than hitting the keys.

Standardized conventions built into equipment mediate the cooperation of those segments of the art world concerned with equipment and materials. Since everyone knows the kinds of materials and equipment available, a simple reference to a catalogue number produces the desired result. Manufacturers, suppliers, and repair people constitute a stable and quite conservative segment of any art world, as do those people who manipulate equipment under the direction of the artists: bricklayers (under the direction of architects), electricians (under the direction of stage and film directors), or printers (under the direction of authors).

Artists learn other conventions—professional culture—in the course of training and as they participate in the day-to-day activities of the art world. Only people who participate regularly in those activities, practicing professionals (however the particular world circumscribes that group), know that culture. Conventions represent the continuing adjustment of the cooperating parties to the changing conditions in which they practice; as conditions change, they change. Schools teach a version of that adjustment that was once current; it is seldom fully up-to-date, except when, rarely, the training institution is an integral part of the art world (that might be true of innovative modern music in some music schools and university music departments). So you can only learn current conventions by participating in what is going on.

Worlds vary in how much cooperation they require between the artists themselves. Poetry requires almost none. Poets rely on other poets primarily as critics, fellow experimenters, and audience; they can produce their work without any help from other poets, and rely primarily on technical personnel like printers and distributors for such help as they need. Orchestral music, ballet, drama, and other group arts, on the other hand, necessarily involve the cooperative efforts of a variety of artists; these working groups have the most fully developed systems for quickly developing and transmitting new conventions.

Since conventions do not change all at once, much of what

artists learn in their initial training will continue to be useful in coordinating activity with others. Young jazz musicians learn early in their (largely informal) training that the standard popular songs on which many jazz numbers are based have an eight-bar middle section (the "bridge") that takes one of two harmonic forms, each named after the well-known song in which it appears: an "I Got Rhythm" bridge, consisting of the following chords for two bars apiece—III7 (in the key of B flat, a D7 chord), VI7 (G7), II7 (C7), V7 (F7)—or a "Honeysuckle Rose" bridge—I7 (in the key of F, F7), IV (B flat), II7 (G7), V7 (C7). Knowing that, anyone playing an unfamiliar tune can quickly learn eight of its bars by being told which sort of bridge it has, if it is one of those standard types. Dance musicians in general learn, more or less by heart, a large number of well-known songs, so that they can immediately produce a passable ensemble version of any of them, without written music, on request. I realized I was outdated as a pianist for weddings, bar mitzvahs, supermarket employees' Christmas parties, and the other engagements at which dance musicians perform when I discovered that it was no longer enough to know songs. I learned one night, when a bandleader called, not a song but "My Fair Lady"—I was required to know the entire score of all the current Broadway musical comedies, complete with key changes. Having been away from the business for a while, I had fallen behind in my stock of what was then conventional knowledge, and could no longer hold my own on jobs that required that knowledge. Younger players, coming into the business later, presumably had learned all that just as I had acquired the stock of songs sufficient in my youth.

The matters to be coordinated in the production and preparation of a specific performance are seldom so cut-and-dried. Even quite standardized performances allow optional methods of doing some things. Violinists have to decide how a passage they are playing together should be bowed and what kind of attack should be used. Brass players who play in both dance bands and concert groups have to establish how groups of connected eighth notes will be played: given even value, as in conventional concert performance (♫♫ ♫♫) or with the first note of each pair slightly longer as in jazz (♪♪ ♪♪ ♪♪ ♪♪). A conventional language allows these matters to be discussed and settled expeditiously.

Matters of interpretation—matters allowing more than one mode of performance—play an even larger role in drama than in music, since a typical script specifies much less of what is to be done than does a typical musical score. In establishing an interpretation, actors and directors use a conventional language, largely methodological, that furnishes the terms in which such matters as where actors should move, how long they should delay before proceeding with the next speech or action, where they should look while others are speaking or moving, and so on can be discussed and settled (the relevant terms are *blocking*, *beats*, and *focus* [Lyon, 1975]).

Art worlds sometimes splinter and turn into relatively autonomous subgroups. When that happens, participants in each of the splinters know, and become responsible for knowing, somewhat different sets of conventions. People who play what has come to be called "new music" find that composers want them to make sounds not conventionally made on their instruments. Most players originally learn these from, or work them out in consultation with, the composer or someone with whom they have personal contact. But as performance of the music becomes more widespread, players who have not had personal access to composers confront scores using unfamiliar and unconventional notation (see figure 9) to denote effects that were known, though not usually notated, or were previously unused. Thus, clarinet players might find in their part notes marked half-open and half-blacked-in, denoting quarter tones, (like this: ♩ or ♩) or marked with wedges (▾) or other devices to indicate a slap-tongue effect. They can create those sounds, but players must know or be taught what is wanted so that the notation is mutually understood. Then composers can use the notation to get the sound they want, players can know they are making the sounds wanted, and the two parties to the performance can coordinate their activity. (See Rehfeldt, 1977, a

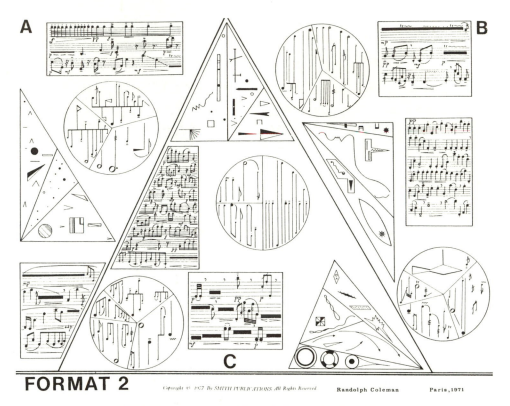

FORMAT 2   Randolph Coleman   Paris, 1971

FIGURE 9. Score of Randolph Coleman's Format II. *Contemporary composers use forms of notation that are not widely known. Players who can play works written in conventional notation without trouble require special explanations and training to play such "new music." (Score courtesy of the composer and Smith Publications. Copyright © 1977 by Smith Publications, all rights reserved.)*

handbook trying to bring some order into new notations and effects for instrumentalists.)

The mechanisms which produce and maintain a professional culture can break down, and when that happens, the ability of professionals to work together breaks down as well. Robert Lerner shows how such simple matters as penmanship and spelling needed standardization in the Middle Ages before literature could be a practical activity:

> After the fall of Rome, regional diversity in handwriting had become extreme, and writing had become difficult to read

because scribes in some areas preferred to write very esoterically, using difficult signs and swirls, and because in others they became careless and sloppy. Communication and education could not spread until this tendency was reversed. . . . Though the then current cursive scripts increased speed in writing by the use of ligatures between letters, they were all but illegible and gradually in the late eighth century were replaced by a script known as Carolingian miniscule, characterized by small, separate and highly legible letters. . . . Soon all Western Europe was using the same script, and manuscripts became easier to read not only because the new script was so legible but because spaces and phrases were initiated by capitals in contrast to the older Roman practice of omitting spaces and punctuation. (Lerner, 1974, pp. 182–84)

Without that simple standardization, literary art would be impossible. We will see later how the spread of such standardization makes the boundaries of an art world.

Knowledge of professional culture, then, defines a group of practicing professionals who use certain conventions to go about their artistic business. Most of what they know they learn in the course of their daily practice, and, as a general rule, none of the art world's other participants need to know such things to play their parts. These understandings facilitate getting the work done, but one need not know them to understand the works themselves. The group defined by knowledge of these working conventions can reasonably be thought of as the inner circle of the art world.

Smaller groups form within the broad outlines of an art world. Every art work creates a world in some respects unique, a combination of vast amounts of conventional materials with some that are innovative. Without the first, it becomes unintelligible; without the second, it becomes boring and featureless, fading into the background like music in supermarkets and pictures on motel walls. The variations may be so small that only an aficionado would notice them, or so obvious no one could ignore them. In either case, given the world they are made in and the audience they are presented to, there will be more or less—but usually some—new material to be learned, material specific to the piece itself.

Artists usually develop their own innovative materials over a period of time, creating a body of convention peculiar to their own work. (Groups of artists frequently collaborate in the development of innovations so that schools and artistic sects develop characteristic conventions as well.) Those who collaborate with them, especially audiences, learn these more particular, peculiar, and idiosyncratic conventions in the course of experience with individual works and bodies of work. The artist may be learning them in the same way, in the course of the production of a work or body of work, or may have developed them in experiments never made public.

So each work, and each artist's body of work, invites us into a world defined in part by the use of materials hitherto unknown and therefore not at first completely understandable. People who continue to attend to the new work, despite its initial unintelligibility, may learn enough to interpret it. The new materials then become conventional in the technical sense used above, being mutually understood by the parties involved so that they can assume that everyone involved knows and will use them in interpreting and responding to the works in question. This involves fewer people than the more general cases previously discussed, the participants being restricted to the producer of the works and those audience members who have made the effort and expended the time necessary to learn the conventions peculiar to the work or to the larger body of the artist's work. This is what it means to be a Mozart buff or a Charlie Parker fan.

Audiences learn unfamiliar conventions by experiencing them, by interacting with the work and, frequently, with other people in relation to the work. They see and hear the new element in a variety of contexts. The artist teaches them what it means, what it can do, and how they might experience it by creating those contexts. Thus, Robert Frank is widely credited with introducing a new iconography into contemporary photography, giving a new symbolic value to flags, crosses, automobiles, and other commonplace elements of the urban landscape (see figure 10). By consistently showing the American flag being treated casually, even contemptuously—as a decoration in a recruiting center manned

FIGURE 10. *Robert Frank*, Navy Recruiting Station, Post Office—Butte, Montana. *Artists teach their audiences a new language. Robert Frank taught a generation of photographers and viewers to see in such objects as cars, flags, and crosses the special symbolism he gave them in the context of his book,* The Americans. *(From* The Americans, *1959; undated black and white photograph, courtesy of the artist.)*

by an employee whose feet are on the desk, or as part of the apparatus of a commercial sign—he teaches us to experience, when we see it, something other than the patriotic sentiments it ordinarily evokes. That use of flags and similar secular and religious symbols, more or less original with Frank and unfamiliar to viewers at first, is now part of the standard language of contemporary "socially conscious" photography. Originally Frank's language, to be learned from him in order to interpret and understand his work, it is now common parlance.

Each work in itself, by virtue of its differences (however small or insignificant) from all other works, thus teaches its audiences something new: a new symbol, a new form, a new mode of presentation. More important, the entire body of work by a single artist or group gradually, as innovations develop (perhaps through an artist's entire career), teaches the new material to so many people that we can speak of the training of an audience. A trivial example: the audiences of popular radio and television programs learn to anticipate remarks and jokes they have learned will appear sometime during each performance. When Fibber McGee finally opened his closet door and everything in it fell, and fell, and fell . . . the audience had begun to laugh long before the closet door opened and the falling began, having learned to laugh at the very possibility. A more serious example: serious composers teach their audiences new harmonic usage and new forms, as Debussy taught listeners to hear and respond to the "orientalism" of the whole-tone scale and Webern taught them to hear melodic fragments distributed, note by note, among a complex of instruments instead of being played in entirety by one.

The group which understands these artist-specific conventions may be quite ephemeral, may not even merit being called a group: all the people who have learned to read Dickens cannot be called a group; they never act together. They have just made the same choice from easily available literary materials. They may not be able to make the conventions of Dickens' fiction explicit—may not be able to explain how he makes characters into caricatures and back again—but they know how to respond to those well-known conventions.

On the other hand, when the conventions of a piece or a body of work are truly innovative, never widely known or known at all, people who become interested in the new work are not simply choosing among known reputations, but are engaging in an action that demands something more of them. They often cannot simply follow an impulse or satisfy a curiosity but must act in concert with others who share their interest, or else the material that interests them will not be available at all. They may find it necessary, desirable, or useful to join organizations which promote their interest in modern dance, subscribe to quarterlies specializing in experimental fiction, show up for the one occasion on which a new film can be viewed, and so on. It would be extravagant to say that the people who do this constitute a group which routinely acts together, but they are not an aggregate of totally unconnected individuals. They are, in some sense, engaged in a joint effort to make the conventions whose innovative character interests them more widely known or at least viable as one of the resources of an art.

To summarize, various groups and subgroups share knowledge of the conventions current in a medium, having acquired that knowledge in various ways. Those who share such knowledge can, when the occasion demands or permits, act together in ways that are part of the cooperative web of activity making that world possible and characterizing its existence. To speak of the organization of the art world—its division into audiences of various kinds, and producers and support personnel of various kinds—is another way of talking about who knows what and uses it to act together.

3 · Mobilizing Resources

IT WAS Monsieur Tuttin who was always given Pablo [Picasso]'s work to print, since Pablo's disregard for conventional lithographic processes created all kinds of problems for the printers. The difficulty was, Monsieur Tuttin did not like Pablo's work. In fact, he detested it.

Pablo had done a lithograph of one of his pigeons in a highly unconventional way. The background coat was in black lithographic ink and the pigeon itself had been painted on top of that in white gouache. Since lithographic ink has wax in it, gouache normally wouldn't "take" very well but in spite of that fact, Pablo had carried it off brilliantly on the lithographic paper. When Mourlot [proprietor of the lithographic print shop] came to the Rue des Grands-Augustins and saw what Pablo had done, he said, "How do you expect us to print that? It's not possible." He pointed out to Pablo that in theory, when the drawing was transferred from the paper to the stone, the gouache would protect the stone and the ink would run only onto those parts where there was no gouache; but, on the other hand, on contact with the liquid ink the gouache itself would surely dissolve, at least in part, and run.

"You give it to Monsieur Tuttin; he'll know how to handle it," Pablo told him.

The next time we went to Mourlot's shop, Monsieur Tuttin was still fussing about the pigeon. "Nobody ever did a thing like that before," he fumed. "I can't work on it. It will never come out."

"I'm sure you can handle it," Pablo said. "Besides, I have an idea Madame Tuttin would be very happy to have a proof of the pigeon. I'll inscribe it to her."

"Anything but," Monsieur Tuttin replied in disgust. "Besides, with that gouache you've put on, it will never work."

"All right, then," Pablo said. "I'll take your daughter out to dinner some evening and tell her what kind of a printer her father is." Monsieur Tuttin looked startled. "I know, of course," Pablo went on, "that a job like that

*might be a little difficult for most of the people around
here, but I had an idea—mistakenly, I can see now—
that you were probably the one man who could do it."
Finally, his professional pride at stake, Monsieur Tuttin
gave in grudgingly.*

GILOT AND LAKE, 1964, p. 86*

Making art works of any kind requires resources. *What*
resources depends on the medium and the kind of work
being made in it. Lithography, as anyone practices it, requires lithographic stones, inks, and crayons. As Picasso
practiced it, it also required M. Tuttin's virtuoso skills. Poetry
requires very little: pencil and paper and, in the extreme case
of orally preserved works, not even that, just a good memory.
Grand opera (as usually performed) requires vast amounts
of material resources—costumes, stage sets, lights, musical
scores and copied parts, theaters with elaborate technical
apparatus—and personnel—musicians, singers, production
technicians, and people to handle finances. Every art form
requires some such mixture, simple or complex, large or
small, most falling somewhere between the extremes of
opera and poetry.

As artists contemplate the making of a work, they think
about where and how they can get such resources. Are such
resources available at all? Does anyone make that material?
Are there any people trained to do what I want done? If the
resources exist, can I get them? How much will it cost? Will
those people work with me? What have I got that they want,
or what can I get that they want? How are art worlds organized so that artists can routinely find the resources they
need to do what they want to do?

However artists get resources, the distribution system, by
making available some kinds of materials and personnel and
not others, makes the works which rely on easily gotten
resources more likely than those for which resources are

more difficult to get. These systems, moreover, do not necessarily provide just what artists need, because the people who run them have their own needs, ambitions, and organizational imperatives. The requirements of artists figure in their calculations without necessarily determining the result. Cooperative links with the people who furnish resources, both material and human, are a characteristic feature of any art world.

Eleanor Lyon (1974) has suggested the idea of a pool of resources as a way of thinking about these processes. If people who work in a particular medium need paints, instruments, or photographic paper, or actors, musicians, cameramen, or dancers, they will find, more or less available, a pool of such materials or people from which they can choose what they want. How much choice the pool affords them, the quality of its members, and the terms on which they are available all vary. Resource pools grow up in response to a real or imagined demand for those resources. Factories manufacture paints and merchants stock them in the belief that they can be sold, just as young people learn to play the tuba or dance on their toes in the belief that someone will want them to exercise those skills professionally. In both cases the belief may be unfounded, the paints unsold, the young artists disappointed in their ambitions.

Manufacturers and distributors of materials, and the personnel in talent pools, do not act simply to satisfy the requirements of artists. They have their own preferences and requirements. If rising interest rates raise a merchant's cost of maintaining an inventory, you may not be able to find a complete selection of colors easily, or at all. Young peoples' interest in guitars and drums may mean the symphony orchestras do not have as many string players to choose from as they would like. More generally, the people who control the content of a resource pool must contend with their own constraints and exigencies, which affect what artists have to work with. Because the formation of personnel pools takes longer and involves such different investments, I will consider them separately from pools of material resources.

MATERIAL RESOURCES

Whether artists need specialized materials that no one else has any use for, or whether they can use standard materials already easily available, affects the work they do. What materials are available, and on what terms, depends on the way the society organizes productive economic activity. In what follows, I will talk mostly about the markets characteristic of many contemporary societies.

Some media require goods designed and manufactured especially for them: oil paints in small tubes, musical instruments and their accessories, ballet shoes. The manufacture of such items is frequently so technical a specialty that the artists who use them cannot produce the items themselves (though some make it their business to do just that and such items as bassoon reeds are typically made by their users). Other media require raw materials that can be extracted from nature by anyone who wants to bother: wood sculptors look for felled trees people will let them haul away. Still others require nothing more than materials easily available to anyone, ordinary stuff routinely furnished for other purposes. So poets use typewriters and paper available for routine business and personal use, sculptors use welding equipment and metal available for routine manufacturing purposes, and visual artists occasionally take advantage of the availability of ordinary household furnishings and foodstuffs in their work.

When artists use materials manufactured for nonartistic purposes and widely used by nonartists, they are least constrained by the conventions of art worlds. On the other hand, they are stuck with what other people need for other purposes and thus make easily available. Because this is usually the cheapest way to get work materials, artists who have little or no money often use it, for such materials are everywhere to beg, borrow, or steal. When the Tactile Art Group (a seminar led by Philip Brickman and myself at Northwestern which undertook to invent a new art form) produced its first works, almost every tactile artist used stuff found in the average graduate student apartment, especially food: flour, Jello, beans, fruits and vegetables in various mixtures, contained in ordinary kitchen containers, designed to be felt by audience members. Other works went a little farther afield and used sandpaper and other basement and garage items.

No special apparatus need be constructed to provide these materials for art works. The ordinary workings of the consumer economy produce its typical products, usually a sizable variety from an artist's viewpoint. Consumer demand in the United States for various kinds of writing and typing paper produces as much variety of color, size, and quality as any visual artist might ordinarily need for use in collages and constructions, and certainly a greater variety than even the most neurotic novelist or poet might need to stimulate literary invention. (Papers made specifically for the use of visual artists are another story.) The resource pool available for ordinary activities includes whatever these artists need.

Something similar occurs when artists use resources created for industrial or commercial use, although here the pool may be more limited, either because industrial applications do not demand as great a variety of materials or because artists are not aware of where they can be found. The photographic industry does not produce materials primarily, or even secondarily, for art photographers. On the contrary, it produces primarily for either the commercial market (commercial photographs or a variety of industrial applications) or the home snapshot market, neither of which requires the variety artists might like to have easily available. But the same industry produces materials that photographers have only recently discovered can be used to color images in ways that do not require elaborate darkroom equipment or procedures. In short, industrial-commercial demand produces a varied resource pool, but artists may not be as aware of it as they are of ordinarily available household goods.

Many items, of course, are made specifically for art uses, musical instruments and paper made for the visual arts being clear examples. Manufacturers of these items are integral parts of the music and art worlds. They manufacture for an art world and are sensitive to what they think its members want, and artists rely on their products, having learned in their formative years to do what can be done with the materials available. Instrument makers are permanent members of the art world. While sensitive to what artists need, they also constrain artists by what they provide. What they make ordinarily satisfies most of the workers in a medium, just because those workers are used to working with those materials.

At the same time, and for the same reasons, what manufacturers make typically fails to meet the needs of people who are trying to create something new (or, for that matter, something old) in a medium. The more materials and equipment are adapted to doing one kind of thing well, the less adapted they are to doing some other things. If you construct a musical instrument like a saxophone to play the tones of the chromatic scale, it is ill-adapted to playing quarter tones or microtones; for that purpose, you must design and build entirely new instruments. Some artists, similarly, have found that the suppliers of papers do not make what they want for their work, so they have taken up the craft of papermaking. In the process, they have learned to exploit the artistic possibilities of paper in new ways, incorporating into the body of the paper itself some of what they might otherwise have applied to its surface.

How much conventional materials constrain an artist depends in part on how monopolistic the market is. If only one or a few manufacturers dominate the market (in the most extreme case the state controls manufacturing, so that all production decisions are centralized), such monopolists may be relatively insensitive to what artistic minorities want or need. Take the manufacture of photographic materials. George Eastman, the founder of Eastman Kodak, had a gift for discovering potentially competitive processes and getting commercial control of them (Jenkins, 1975). This has had serious consequences for art photographers. Only a few companies make the paper on which photographers print, and they often discontinue materials artists use for reasons having to do with their own internal operations. For example, many photographers learned to take advantage of the emotional and aesthetic effects made possible by Record Rapid, a warm-toned, brownish paper, the only such paper to have survived the increasing concentration of manufacturing in the hands of a few firms. When Agfa stopped making it, they had to develop new artistic strategies which did not require that product.

How much dependence on manufacturers and suppliers in an art world constrains an artist depends, too, on how similar the works in that world are. If artists agree on what sort of work is good and ought to be done, available materials will probably be limited to what is needed to do that kind of work. If the art world's repertoire is more varied, manufacturers will probably cater to that variety. If the economy permits and rewards such activity, some entrepreneurs will find it worth the risk to cater to even a small, minority market. These suppliers often provide the basic materials needed to manufacture what more conventional workers might buy, and sell to people prepared to do some of the work ordinarily done for artists by larger manufacturers. The flavor of such an enterprise appears in this quotation from the catalogue of a small firm which sells chemicals to photographers who want to use printing materials not commercially available:

> the ability to work these processes, from home made preparations, enables you to exercise more control *and to ensure that your particular working method isn't discontinued by the manufacturer.* . . . Beyond that, you will have become the kind of person who can improvise something new, perhaps something better. These processes, not particularly difficult, are in that spirit of creativity, self-determination, and self-reliance. . . . (*Photographer's Formulary: Chemical and Laboratory Resources*, Catalog III, 1979, my emphasis)

Suppliers of materials do not always constrain what artists do. From time to time inventors create new kinds of equipment and materials which, when made available to artists, create new artistic opportunities. The Xerox and 3-M Color-in-Color machines, and machinery designed to transmit images over telephone lines, have made possible a new kind of visual image. Artists can now, for instance, produce color by the direct application of heat to paper, and then transform those colored images by manipulating a machine's filters. They can create vertical and horizontal transformations of imagery by manipulating the speeds at which they run the receivers and transmitters of a teleprinter. These electronic imaging machines, designed for commercial use, have spawned a new field of visual art called "generative systems." (Thompson, 1975, describes this development and gives a number of examples of the kind of work produced.) Computer programs which produce a graphic output will no doubt be exploited similarly.

Whether materials are made expressly for artistic uses or are made for other uses and then adapted, artists get materials and equipment through whatever mechanisms a society has for distributing goods. Where a market economy does the allocating, artists can buy or rent what they need, if they have the money. (How they get it is another question, taken up later.) Artists without money can steal; successful artists often admit, or brag, that they stole in their less successful days. The teacher of my beginning photography class told us not to try to save paper when trying to make a good print from a negative: "Use it all up, then buy some more, and if you don't have any money, steal it!" Artists can also barter for what they need. Suppliers will sometimes take art works in return for materials, or other kinds of arrangements can be worked out, as Lyon describes in the case of a small avant-garde theater:

> Some material resources became available through negotiated exchanges. Props and costumes were donated by local stores in return for credit on the program. Costumes were also obtained from the (local) university drama department because the summer shows were sponsored by the school. However, what was available through these sources limited what could appear on the stage; for example, some scenes had to be revisualized because the available appropriately sized costume did not fit the initial image. (Lyon, 1974, p. 89)

If the materials and equipment you want or need have not been manufactured by anyone for any purpose, you can still make them yourself. Many artists have. Doing that, they have all the troubles, described later, of mavericks and isolates.

FIGURE 11. *Performance of Harry Partch's* Oedipus. *Harry Partch, writing for a forty-two-tone scale, had to build his own instruments and teach people to play them. Here students at Mills College play Partch's Harmonic Canon I, Diamond Marimba, and Cloud-Chamber Bowls in a performance in March 1952. (Photograph courtesy of the Mills College Library.)*

Insisting on nonstandard equipment, they have to devote time that might otherwise be spent making art to making its material precursors. Furthermore, what they make often requires knowledge participants in their art world do not conventionally need, so that other people who cooperate in the realization of a work will not know what to do or how to do it. Harry Partch, composing for a forty-two tone scale, had to build his own instruments and create his own notation, because no one in the music world knew how to do what had not been possible to do until he created the possibility (see figure 11).

PERSONNEL

It is unfeeling to speak of the people who cooperate in the production of art works as "personnel" or, worse yet, "support personnel," but that accurately reflects their importance in the conventional art world view. In that view, the person who does the "real work," making the choices that give the work its artistic importance and integrity, is the artist, who may be any of a number of people involved in its production; everyone else's job is to assist the artist. I do not accept the view of the relative importance of the "personnel" involved that the term connotes, but I use it to emphasize that it *is* the common view in art worlds.

It is even useful to carry the dehumanization of artistic support personnel one step further and think of them as resources, assembled in resource pools like material resources, and ask how such pools are assembled and how the people in them get connected to particular art projects in a support role.

The people who make up a pool of potential personnel for art projects belong to that pool because they can do some specialized task required in the making of the art works in question and they make themselves available to do it. The numbers and kinds of people and the conventional terms on which they make themselves available differ from medium to medium and place to place. The Broadway theater world has available to it perhaps ten times as many (or more) people with extensive dramatic training, who could perform adequately in a variety of roles and vehicles, than are actually working as actors at any given time. On the other hand, few people have the odd combination of skills called for in making theatrical props, and even fewer make themselves available for theatrical work. There will usually be an oversupply of people for the roles thought to contain some element of the "artistic"—in theater, that includes playwrights, actors, and directors—and a short supply of people with technical skills to do support work that does not share in that charisma. More people want to write novels than design them for the printer, be great musical performers than repair instruments, draw on lithographic stones than print from them.

People enter a pool of personnel resources by learning how to do what people who perform a function in an art world do, by learning to do one of the support tasks that world's artists need. Whether they study in a school, teach themselves, or pick up a skill on the job, they learn some operating conventions of the art world, and learn to apply them in actual situations of artistic production. When called on, then, they can step in as more or less interchangeable parts capable of doing the job to be done as well as any other member of their category. One of the most important things an art world provides its artistic members is a supply of interchangeable human parts. When you can count on replacing people with others just as good, you can carry on artistic work in a routine way. That is why the cooperative networks and conventions that make up an art world create opportunities as well as constraints. In fact, as we will see later, the ability of art world participants to perform interchangeably defines, in an important sense, the boundaries of an art world. Of course, artists recognize that there are substantial differences in the ability of support personnel to deliver, and working artists know who can be trusted with standard tasks and who cannot—which actors take direction quickly and intelligently, which dancers can successfully perform the steps and sequences the choreographer has in mind, which cameramen can create the visual effects the director desires, and which will not be able to do these things and therefore will necessitate adjustments and compromises in the original idea.

How do people learn these basic skills? In an important sense, art world members teach themselves. Whatever instruction they receive, they must internalize the lessons through such mental rehearsals and exercises as Sudnow (1978) describes in his analysis of how he learned to play the piano. Some people learn only in this way. H. Stith Bennett (1980) describes how young rock musicians in the Colorado mountains teach themselves to play by imitating what they hear on recordings, without benefit of lessons or instruction books; it is a hard way to learn, but they become very proficient, Bennett says, at using the recording as a score, imitating what they hear so successfully that they can learn the entire contents of a twelve-inch record (as much as forty minutes of music) in a day. In teaching themselves, novices incorporate into their methods of operation the conventions of the art world they are aiming at, using available works as a guide. If they teach themselves successfully, they then can offer their services as practitioners of whatever support activity they have trained for, and join that resource pool.

Some people learn on the job, as apprentices or occupants of an unofficial position which allows them to observe full-fledged practitioners at work, or just by being put in a position to do the job whether they know it or not. The "Leonardo da Vinci" of music copyists, according to the *New York Times*, learned his trade this way:

> One day I was walking down the street and I ran into the music librarian of Paramount Publix Corporation. [He had violin training but was working as a chemist.] They ran Twentieth-Century Paramount and also ran 52 weeks of musical attractions around the country. "Look," the guy said, "You have a musical education. Come with me." That was in 1925, and he gave me a job at $60 a week, not bad for that time. I walk into a big room, with maybe 40 people copying music. I looked. All my life I had trouble copying a G clef. But I learned. The boss said, "You have music at home? Go copy it." So I learned by a little bit, a little bit more, a little bit more. Mostly I copied nightclub music, acts arranged for combos. There were lots of movie scores, too. (Schonberg, 1978)

An apocryphal story says that Gypsy musicians give six-year-old boys a small violin and set them down in the middle of a Gypsy orchestra while it is playing. The boys get no instruction, but can play what they like while the rest of the group performs; whatever odd, mistaken sounds they make presumably are covered up by the others' playing. They attempt to match what they hear and in a relatively short time learn to play a part in the collective musical production. Once someone has learned to perform some portion of what is required, he can learn still more and can offer himself as a member of the pool of competent technicians.

Many people learn the trades of support personnel in a

school. Although in a real sense these are trade schools, some of their students learn to be "artists." By going to film school, for instance, one might learn to be a cameraman or a lighting technician, or to be a director or a screenwriter, the film business being so confused about which people are artists and which support personnel that the latter often think of themselves, and are sometimes thought of, as artists in their own right. The confusion is chronic in music schools, for almost all the students who hope to become violin or piano virtuosi will end up as, at best, members of the violin section of a symphony orchestra, and most likely will be teachers of those instruments somewhere, if they don't drop out of the business altogether or drift into such more lucrative occupations as film-score recording (Faulkner, 1971).

Art schools vary similarly in their emphasis, some defiantly setting out to train only artists. (My first photography teacher told us, the first day of class, "The name of this school is San Francisco *Art* Institute; if you are here to learn anything besides art, you're in the wrong place. Get your money back before it's too late!") Others deliberately set out to train people to do what the art world they might serve seems to require (Pevsner, 1940). British schools of visual art have typically, with a few exceptions, taught such trades as printing, design, and commercial photography, intending their students to work in the printing trades, advertising, and related industries. Though these schools emphasize commercial and industrial work, their emphasis is not very different from that of state schools which train people to dance in state-supported ballets or of similar schools for the training of musicians, singers, and other performers in England, Scandinavia, and elsewhere. These institutions provide a pool of people for established art worlds, and usually inadvertently also provide a pool of well-trained rebels to staff alternative art projects which do not fit into the established ways of those worlds. (As I suggested earlier, ballet schools teach people classical ballet technique, whose vocabulary is basic to the development of nonballet dance styles, being the one vocabulary all participants can be counted on to know.)

What does an artist do when he cannot find anyone in the pool of available personnel who can do what is needed? Typically, artists whose work differs that much from what is conventional train their own personnel, just as people who need materials and equipment that are not easily available make their own. They may start a school or a performing company, or take on apprentices or employees to whom they teach what their support people must know. If they work in a sufficiently unconventional way, they may not take on people who have had any exposure to more conventional ways of doing things or been trained in conventional schools or companies, on the (probably correct) ground that such people will have too much to unlearn. Conventionally trained personnel have job and career possibilities which make them less willing to undergo privations, accept strict and unusual professional discipline, and ignore a total lack of conventional professional success.

Given that a pool of interchangeable support personnel exists, how do its members get connected to the particular art projects to which they contribute their services? Consider two basic principles involved in most systems, which generally occur in all kinds of mixed forms. At one extreme, members of the pool work for an organization which carries on art world projects; their career within the organization provides the mechanism by which they are allocated to particular jobs. At the other extreme, pool members contract separately for each project, in what might be called a freelance system. In either case, successful members of the pool have a career, in an organization or a series of them or by virtue of building up a network of connections which assures them of steady work. The two systems vary in the permanence of the relation between the support personnel and the artists for whom they work.

Established organizations with permanent members produce the characteristic works of many art worlds. People frequently spend many years with the same symphony orchestra, ballet company, repertory theater, or lithographic print shop. When they move, they move along well-defined career tracks to a similar organization with which they will spend many more years. When organizations dominate the allocation of personnel in this way, people orient what they do to the needs of those organizations and the kinds of career contingencies they create for their employees. At first, they worry about simply getting in: Can I get a job playing horn in an orchestra? In a major orchestra? Later they may try to move to a "better" organization of its kind; their craft culture usually defines some jobs as more desirable and worth trying for. The organization in which they eventually find themselves determines what they do, telling them what is needed for any particular project. A repertory actor plays year after year, or at least for a year or two, in some of the plays his theater does; a symphony player plays whatever the conductor chooses for that year's programs. When hiring and firing are dominated by bureaucratic rules, the tenure protection imposed by a union contract or a governmental or private organization's own rules make the connection more permanent.

Support personnel with permanent positions in a stable organization develop motives different from those of the artists with whom they work. While the artists worry about the work's aesthetic effect, as well as its effect on their reputations, support personnel consider their activity on a given project in the light of its overall effect on their long-term organizational interests. Support personnel, hired for their ability to perform one function, spend all their time doing that one thing and develop a guild pride or a protectionist attitude about it which conflicts with the production of the overall work; as long as they have done their chore properly, they don't worry much about the rest of it. Conversely, they may feel trapped in that function, the way ambitious symphony players fear being trapped as section players, who never have a chance for more expressive and creative performances (Faulkner, 1973a and 1973b), or repertory actors fear being typecast in character roles. Technicians probably fear this trap less than those who once had artistic aspirations. Organizations likewise find themselves trapped by the presence of permanent personnel whose mediocre skills and abilities limit what can be done.

Support personnel often act in ways calculated to maintain or improve their position in the organization. When the permanent employees of a publishing house decide how much time to invest in the editing of a book or how much money to invest in its promotion and distribution, they think not only of how the individual work might best be served but also of how the house's resources might best be divided among the several similar projects in hand at the moment and of how a mistaken judgment on those questions might affect their careers. That is why so many novelists' books die the day they are released (Hirsch, 1972): the publisher's promotional expert (a classic example of a support position) decides that, although the book is now printed, disappointing advance sales show there is no point in putting any more money into it, so it is allowed to appear without the advertising or other activities through which new books are called to the special attention of reviewers and others who might keep it from disappearing among the mass of other material published simultaneously.

Two other typical motives, which usually occur together, are a desire for a better job with another organization and craft pride. You serve both ends by seeing that your part is done well, no matter what the fate of the larger project, and even though seeing that your part is done well may interfere with its success. Composers fear that symphony players will deliberately (or so the aggrieved composers feel) play their new works badly in rehearsal, alleging that the parts are unplayable or that there are too many mistakes in the copying, so that they will not have to struggle with difficult parts that might not show their talents to advantage. The perpetrators of these acts may want to look good for some other potential employer (Faulkner, 1973a and 1973b, describes these aspirations in symphony players) or simply may want to preserve their reputation among other members of the occupation.

Support personnel also get connected with artists through free-lance systems, in which personnel are assembled for each project as the need arises. As with material goods, artists use whatever resources they have, financial or otherwise, to induce people to participate. In the usual free-lance system, support personnel participate for just as long as they are contracted for and no longer. They may regret not being able to devote more time to a project they find particularly interesting, but the dynamic of a financially based free-lance system pushes them on to the next one. Lillian Ross (1969 [1952]) describes how John Huston, having finished directing *The Red Badge of Courage*, then left to go to work on *The African Queen*. Much work remained to be done by others. Higher-ups at MGM, having decided the picture would fail unless it was drastically changed, altered it substantially, over the strong objections of producer Gottfried Reinhardt, who tried to preserve what he understood to be Huston's original vision. He lost the fight when the new head of the studio, Dore Schary (who had just replaced Louis B. Mayer, in a move that shocked and surprised the film world), took a personal interest in redoing the film (as well he might have, since Nicholas Schenk, the president of the company that owned MGM, had encouraged him to take full responsibility, as vice-president in charge of production, for what others in the studio thought to be an impossibly arty film). All through the bitter struggle Huston, who would get the artistic blame or credit for the result, was in Africa, taking no part in the events that led to the redoing of his film (see figure 12). When he got the final news about what had happened, his only reaction was a cable to Reinhardt: "DEAR GOTTFRIED. JUST GOT YOUR LETTER. KNOW YOU FOUGHT GOOD FIGHT. HOPE YOU NOT TOO BLOODY MY ACCOUNT." Although Huston had left the picture behind, he was lucky. The critics, at least, thought the picture an artistic success. The film's opponents were right too; it didn't make any money.

To recur to the theme of how decisions may be made for reasons extraneous to the actual project in hand, consider Schenk's reason for allowing Schary to make *The Red Badge*. Intending to replace Mayer with Schary, he wanted to make Schary happy with his new job and simultaneously to teach him a lesson about what the organization he was about to head would require of him:

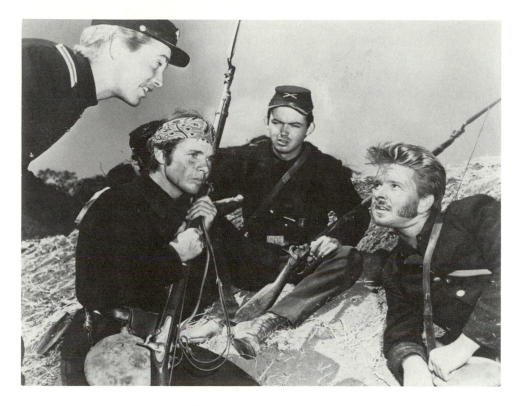

FIGURE 12. Scene from The Red Badge of Courage, *directed by John Huston. In free-lance systems support personnel work only as long as they are contracted for. John Huston, director of* The Red Badge of Courage, *allowed studio executives to alter his film drastically after he had finished shooting it and gone to Africa to do* The African Queen. *(Photograph courtesy of the Museum of Modern Art/Film Stills Archive.)*

Dore is young. He has not had this job very long. I felt I must encourage him or else he would feel stifled. It would have been so easy to say no to him. Instead, I said yes. I figured I would write it off to experience. You can buy almost anything, but you can't buy experience.

How else was I going to teach Dore? I supported Dore. I let him make the picture. I knew that the best way to help him was to let him make a mistake. Now he will know better. A young man has to learn by making mistakes. I don't think he'll want to make a picture like that again. (Ross, 1969 [1952], p. 220)

The head of a permanent organization might have such motives: to tame a talented but slightly unruly subordinate so that he will never forget the interests of the firm for the temptation of art again. Of course, the chief's motives need not be so commercial; in another setting he might want to teach someone not to subordinate the claims of art to commerce.

In a free-lance system, people get jobs on the basis of their reputations. As Hollywood composers told Robert Faulkner (forthcoming), "You're only as good as your last picture." Workers have no contract to protect them from the consequences of a bad job. Nevertheless, some manage to work regularly, moving from one project to another with little wasted time. They do this partly because they can deliver the job the artist they work for wants done. A film composer must be able to deliver a score that does the job the director or producer wants done—produces the mood or effect desired, at the minimum necessary cost, and quickly enough that no time or money is lost waiting for the result. But, remember, support work can in principle be done by any competent technician, unlike the core artistic work, which participants think only the gifted few can do. Support personnel are not unique; they are interchangeable. Therefore, artists who need someone for a particular project can choose from a number of competent workers in the resource pool; they all meet the specifications.

You need ability, then, for free-lance success, but it is not enough. Successful free-lancers also need a network of connections, so that a large number of people who might need their services have them in mind, and in their telephone book, to be called when the occasion arises. Reputation helps. If you have delivered successfully on earlier projects, other people will take a chance, not only on using you but on recommending you to third parties. Hollywood composers much in demand systematically recommend to their clients less well-known composers they feel sure will handle the job competently. A network of connections consists of a number of people who know you and your work well enough to trust the well-being of some portion of their project to you. The key element of the network is trust. When I first became active as a weekend musician in Chicago in the 1940s, an older musician, about to recommend me for a one-night job, interrogated me about my ability to handle it: "Are you sure you can do it? Because if you can't it's my ass. In fact, it's not just my ass, it's three or four different asses." (He was recommending me to someone who was recommending me to someone else, through a chain of several links [Becker, 1963, p. 107].) Through interlocking trust and recommendations, workers develop stable networks which furnish them with more or less steady work.

Faulkner (forthcoming) shows the stability of the system for people at the top: less than 10 percent of Hollywood's composers score 46 percent of the films using original music, less than 8 percent of all filmmakers produce 36 percent of those films, and 30 percent of all films are made by combinations of the top composers and producers. At the bottom, a large number of producers and composers make one film, but cannot manage to get a second credit. A composer in the top group explained: "The whole idea is to keep the thing moving, to get more work and better work, the more projects you're associated with the more people know you and, hopefully, know what you can do for their films."

Support personnel provide evidence that they are trustworthy by performing adequately for the artist-employers in whose work they participate. They have difficulty doing that when the employer does not use technical language sufficiently precise to describe what he wants the technician to do; he will know if the result is not what he wants, but cannot give positive directions. Faulkner (forthcoming) describes the serious difficulties composers of film scores have with producers who know nothing about music, and suggests that successful composers must be able to understand what producers really want, given an incoherent and inaccurate description. He quotes some composers' stories of the difficulties of communicating with nonmusician producers:

> You can get up against some directors who will open up with something like, "Give me something real, real modern!" And you're trying to figure out what they mean and it turns out the guy thinks Tchaikovsky is modern, as the old story goes. You know, the producer who says, "I must have something new, something fresh, different, it's got to be different, like Bela Barstock (sic)."

It seems likely that the more the support job is thought to be integral to the success of the project, the less the people who do it are thought of as interchangeable. They may still be treated as interchangeable—filmmakers do not give up a project if they cannot get the composer they want, though they might if they could not get the right actors or director, but they devote more time to finding a replacement and take the problem more seriously than if they cannot get the first accountant or best boy they ask for (to choose two of the more unlikely titles that appear in motion-picture credits).

Participants in free-lance systems, both the artists and other overseers who do the hiring and the support people they hire, may also have motives more or less extraneous to the production of the work at hand. Pauline Kael gives the particularly egregious example of the executive producer who "packaged the deal" for the film version of Mary McCarthy's novel *The Group*:

> [his] enthusiasm for the project had little to do with the literary qualities or dramatic potential of Miss McCarthy's work, but on [*sic*] the gorgeous possibility of getting options on a bunch of inexpensive, luscious young nobodies [the main characters in the story are eight college women], building them up into stars, and then having them available for his own films and for handsome loan-out deals. . . . with a property featuring eight young girls, surely he would get his own Capucines and [Ursula] Andresses; and with a stable of young beauties under option, a modern movie packager-producer could be richer than the greatest whoremasters of history. (There are even directors in Hollywood who make more money from the pieces they own of the stars they gave their first break to than from directing.) (Kael, 1968, pp. 68–69)

We might think of systems of securing support personnel as ways of getting their attention and interest. The two systems, organizational hiring and free-lancing, evoke different styles of attention. Employees of organizations can, if their employers think it important, devote some portion (even all) of their attention to a work for as long as the employers think necessary; they often work on many projects at once. Free-lancers typically work in spurts, one solid chunk of undivided attention given to a project they then forget, for better or for worse. Brecht could rehearse the Berliner Ensemble for months on end, but, as we have seen in the case of Huston and *The Red Badge of Courage*, Hollywood can command people's attention only for the short period during which they are actually paid. Since budgets are always smaller than they might be, people are seldom paid for anything that does not contribute directly to the project. Pauline Kael has always had an interest in why movies are so much worse than they need be for strictly commercial reasons; her investigation of the making of *The Group* suggests a couple of reasons. For instance, she found it shocking that no one connected with the making of the movie knew anything about Mary McCarthy, her life, or her work, and thus could not bring that kind of knowledge to bear in making the film. The workings of a free-lance system make the lack understandable. Filmmakers cannot be experts on the enormous variety of writers and topics they may find themselves working with in the course of a career; their time is taken up with their current project's most pressing details. They have no time, and would not be rewarded for spending it that way if they had it, to acquire the kind of general culture Kael acquired in the normal routine of her work. They prepare for their work by learning how to make movies; she prepares for hers by reading the works of Mary McCarthy. Free-lancing teaches you to devote all your attention to what is most immediately at hand.

Kael heard a mistake on the sound track of the semi-finished film: one of the girls was supposed to say that all the members of her group had voted for Roosevelt, except one who forgot to vote; instead, she said that all the members of her class had done so, destroying the meaning of the line and some important meanings of the story. When Kael heard this on the set, she mentioned it to both the producer and the director, as something to be fixed during rerecording. It wasn't, so she pointed it out again:

> Each assured me that I must be hearing wrong. Neither apparently took the trouble to check or listen, because when the film was screened for the press, there it was again. By then, Lumet [the director] was in London working on his next film, Buchman [the producer] was back on the Riviera.
>
> Thinking that *someone* might care about the blooper, I called around, and after three people involved in the production had assured me that if the Sydneys [Lumet and Buchman] had had Helena say "class" that must have been what they wanted, I finally got hold of the editor, Ralph Rosenblum, who realized at once that it was an error. But he had enough other problems to worry about: in the absence of the Sydneys, he was left to argue the cuts the National Catholic Office for Motion Pictures . . . wanted. (Kael, 1968, pp. 96–97)

Here the principle works in reverse. Since no one demanded that these free-lancers give their attention to this detail, they didn't.

What if artists have no money? Even in a money economy, a lack of money is not fatal, although it creates serious constraints. Lyon (1974) found that the small, penniless theatrical company she studied bartered extensively for personnel as well as materials. One form of barter consisted of making people "members" of the theater, with some say over what was done and some claim to a share of the credit for the result. Perhaps more important, "The actors expected the Western Theater to provide them with opportunities to act" (p. 85) and, more troublesome, many people volunteered to do technical and other less desirable work only because they hoped it would eventually lead to a chance to act. That created obligations such that "the director sometimes felt compelled to fulfill this implicit expectation. Unfortunately, a few poor actors had thus landed small parts, leading the theater to the unpleasant task of discouraging future acting aspirations in these participants" (p. 88). Furthermore, the plays the group could put on were limited in part by the kind of actors who had volunteered to become members: "Since there were only three experienced actresses in the company, a play with many demanding female parts would have to be discarded" (p. 86). Finally, they could not do plays with very small casts; as one actor explained, "How would you like to be an actress with a company with nothing to do for eight weeks? Nobody enjoys that. So we have to find plays where there's something for everybody to do" (p. 86).

A large number of support personnel, as we have seen, either once had or still do have the idea that what they do is in itself art. It is an exaggeration to say that everyone in an art world is support personnel for someone else, and it is not true that everyone or almost everyone thinks of himself as an artist. But these overstatements point to something important: every function in an art world can be taken seriously as art, and everything that even the most accepted artist does can become support work for someone else; furthermore, in many arts it is not at all clear who is the artist and who are the support people. When Rauschenberg erased a DeKooning drawing, or Duchamp drew a mustache on the Mona Lisa, were the authors of the originals merely support personnel? If not, why not? What of the people whose work, in reproduced form, becomes part of someone else's collage?

John Cage said that music is the moral evaluation of sound. We might generalize his remark: when we speak of art, we make a moral evaluation of the relative worth of the various contributions to a work. It is no surprise that many of the participants differ with more conventional evaluations and rank their own contribution as more important than that of the artist as conventionally defined. (See the film editor's point of view in Rosenblum and Karen, 1979, pp. 230–1.) If we remain neutral on this question, we may find it difficult to sympathize with the notion that "interference" by some of the participants in the production of an art work necessarily means that the work is less valuable artistically; perhaps that intervention is just what the work needed. We have seen that critics thought *The Red Badge of Courage* pretty good, even though others than the director had grossly interfered with it. Similarly, the composers Faulkner interviewed complained of the way directors and producers tampered with their scores and ideas; yet the point of a movie is not its musical score, which must be subsidiary to the images on the screen (at least in feature films, even unconventional ones).

To summarize, artists use material resources and personnel. They choose these out of the pool of what is available to them in the art world they work in. Worlds differ in what they make available and in the form in which they make it available. The patterns of economic activity characteristic of a society shape what artists can get to work with and who they can get to work with them. Such facts as the degree of monopolization of production materials, the profitability of minority markets, and the degree to which artists need items specially designed and manufactured for them all affect what is available and thus what artists can do. Similarly, the organizations through which support personnel find the projects they work on create organizational, professional, and career motives which may run counter to the intentions of the artists who employ them.

What is available and the ease with which it is available enter into the thinking of artists as they plan their work and into their actions as they carry out those plans in the real world. Available resources make some things possible, some easy, and others harder; every pattern of availability reflects the workings of some kind of social organization and becomes part of the pattern of constraints and possibilities that shapes the art produced.

4 • Distributing Art Works

PROFESSIONALLY marginal artists. . . . encounter an excruciatingly trying problem. As each year passes, their studios grow increasingly crowded with paintings that no one wants to buy, starkly visible evidence which reminds them daily of their inability to win (or regain) acceptance of their work. . . . some grow despairing of ever achieving a modest degree of success, or of finding a new style as salable as their previous one, and quit painting. As one artist said of them: "When you can't sell your paintings and you continue to produce you can't help but become bitter unless you're a very strong person, and most artists are not."

LEVINE, 1972, pp. 306–7

Artists, having made a work, need to distribute it, to find a mechanism which will give people with the taste to appreciate it access to it and simultaneously will repay the investment of time, money, and materials in the work so that more time, materials, and cooperative activity will be available with which to make more works. Artists can work without distribution. Many works, once made, have been hidden by their makers or ignored by the publics they were meant for. Many, perhaps most, artists never realize any money from their work and cannot support further work on the proceeds from what they have already done.

Fully developed art worlds, however, provide distribution systems which integrate artists into their society's economy, bringing art works to publics which appreciate them and will pay enough so that the work can proceed. These distribution systems, like other cooperative activities which make up an art world, can be manned by artists themselves. More commonly, specialized intermediaries do the work. The interests of the intermediaries who operate distribution systems frequently differ from those of the artists whose work they handle. Because they are in business, distributors want to

93

rationalize the relatively unstable and erratic production of "creative" work (Hirsch, 1972): dealers must have work to show in their galleries, producers need theatrical events to fill a season. And they need these even when artists want to produce, not the kind of work thought to be needed, but some other kind the system cannot handle as well. Distributors want to make a messy process more orderly, ensuring the stability of their own businesses and also creating stable conditions under which art can be produced on a regular basis. This often leads them to deal with works on some basis other than their artistic merit, however that is judged (Moulin, 1967).

Since most artists want the advantages of distribution, they work with an eye to what the system characteristic of their world can handle. What kinds of work will it distribute? What will it ignore? What return will it give for what kind of work? Distribution systems vary in the kind of intermediaries who handle the movement of work and money between artists and audiences, and in the immediacy of the communication and influence between the two groups. Art works always bear the marks of the system which distributes them, but vary in how that happens. When artists support themselves from nonart sources, the distribution system has minimal influence; when they work directly for a patron, it is maximized; when they create works for unknown audiences, the influence comes through the constraints imposed by the intermediaries who operate the necessarily more complex and elaborate distribution system. Artists experience these influences as constraints when the distributors have independent ideas about what the art works ought to be like or when they have insufficient knowledge of the conventions of the art to make choices and demands the artists regard as knowledgeable. Conversely, they accept patrons or intermediaries who have that knowledge as partners in the work's production.

Art works, then, come to be what the art world's distribution system can handle because, for the most part, work that doesn't fit doesn't get distributed, when it is made at all, and most artists, wanting their work distributed, do not make what the system will not handle. To say that artists work with an eye to these matters does not mean they are completely bound by them. Systems change and accommodate to artists just as artists change and accommodate to systems. Furthermore, artists can secede from the contemporary system and create a new one, or attempt to, or do without the constraining benefits of distribution. Art worlds often have more than one distribution system operating at the same time. Contemporary painting has elements of a dealer-gallery system coexisting with patronage relationships, and that was true of seventeenth-century Italian painting as well. Contemporary poetry combines self-support and government and private patronage. As a result, artists can choose from such combinations the distribution system which serves them best or constrains them least.

Distribution has a crucial effect on reputations. What is not distributed is not known and thus cannot be well thought of or have historical importance. The process is circular: what does not have a good reputation will not be distributed. This means that our later consideration of what constitutes great or important art will have to keep in mind the way distribution systems, with their built-in professional biases, affect opinion about what belongs in those categories.

SELF-SUPPORT

Many art worlds—for example, contemporary poetry and photography, for most of their participants—produce so little income for their practitioners that most work is produced through a system of self-support. Artists who lack substantial financial resources cannot do work which requires costly materials, equipment, personnel, or space. Media like poetry and photography, requiring relatively small investments, thus attract many practitioners. That makes it even more difficult for any one of them to support full-time artistic activity on the proceeds from art work itself. Most artists in these media, then, provide their own support from some source outside the workings of the art world or tangential to the actual creation of art works. Some artists have been supported by a well-to-do or working spouse. Some artists have made or inherited enough to live on, freeing their time for art work. Some artists simply have whatever jobs are available to them by virtue of their social position or other training. Many poets support their work this way: T. S. Eliot worked in a bank and then for a publisher, Wallace Stevens was an executive of an insurance company, and William Carlos Williams was a practicing physician. Other artists have jobs which are part of the art world, though not as artists. Painters may work as framers, composers as orchestrators, novelists and poets as editors. In a common arrangement, they teach the art they practice, in elementary and secondary schools, in professional art schools, and as private teachers.

How much time do these jobs leave for serious art work? Artists frequently complain that their "day job" (the expression is common in the performing arts, where the "art job" usually occurs at night) interferes with their work. It takes up so much time that none is left for art or it overlaps enough in content to interfere with creating original art works. (Photographers who do commercial work sometimes say that the commercial attitude influences their "personal" work, making it hard for them to see and photograph in a way that does not embody the restraints of the advertising mentality.) Artists may prefer professional work as teacher, doctor, or lawyer because it lets them allocate their own time. Alternatively, they may prefer less prestigious work that demands less attention, even though it is physically more difficult, time-consuming, and tiring.

Artists who finance their own work can be free of the existing distribution system for their medium: they need not distribute their work at all, certainly not for monetary return. If they are sufficiently isolated or alienated from the art world, they will experience this as a liberation rather than a deprivation. If they need not produce for distribution within the constraints of a system, they can ignore its requirements and make works as big or small, short or long, comprehensible or unintelligible, performable or not as they like, for those constraints typically originate in the rigidity of a distribution system, which cannot handle work of the wrong specifications. (This possibility finds its fullest expression in the case of maverick and naive artists, discussed later.)

Most artists remain sufficiently oriented to the art world to need its distribution system to bring the finished work to an audience, if not for economic support. Some simply use the regular distribution channels available to people who make their living at art work, publishing, exhibiting, and performing in the same places professionals do, differing from them only in not needing to put up with the system's constraints if they don't want to. For this reason, self-support provides the greatest freedom to artists. In fact, with sufficient outside resources, they can create their own distribution system. Visual artists frequently establish cooperative galleries, sharing the expenses and doing much of the gallery's work in return for the chance to exhibit every year. Aspiring musicians and singers not yet of interest to concert managements and recording executives often subsidize their own recitals.

If an established distribution system rejects enough people who would like its benefits, someone may organize a self-supported alternative to handle their work: for example, the *Salon des Refusés* was organized in Paris in the 1860s to show paintings rejected by the "real" *Salon*, and vanity presses publish at the author's expense work refused by commercial publishers. As the examples suggest, participation in the established distribution system is one of the important signs by which art world participants distinguish serious artists from amateurs. People who use alternative systems created for those rejected by the regular system, whatever their reason, may mark themselves as non-serious.

Michal McCall (1977, 1978) studied women painters in St. Louis, a provincial art world where, because it is provincial, they found it hard to demonstrate their artistic seriousness. They had to show it in ways other than painting. Some managed to get jobs teaching in the art departments of local colleges and universities, a local sign of seriousness; in fact, some took the jobs to demonstrate seriousness, as an interviewee explained to McCall:

> She's married to a *very* rich man who's only too happy to
> support her "hobby." But she wants to be self-supporting—or
> at least to support her art work. She says she won't feel
> grown-up until she does. You have to have your head really
> straight to be able to do serious work if you aren't self-sup-
> porting. (McCall, 1978, p. 307)

McCall notes that "selling art is a solution to this problem. It
not only provides an income, it proves to self and others that
art is an occupation, and not an avocation." Another painter,
who did not teach, told her:

> It isn't possible to support yourself selling in St. Louis. But I
> would like to sell some things. Just as a kind of proof that I'm
> an artist. So I could say I earned something when my husband
> teases me. I didn't used to want to sell anything, but now that
> I have a body of drawings, I could imagine selling some. . . .
> (McCall, 1978, p. 307)

These women want, among other things, to distinguish
themselves from the world of what McCall calls "picture
painters," people who paint but not within the organizations
or on the basis of the ideologies and aesthetics of the established world of painting. Picture painters, for example, emphasize how quickly they can produce a finished painting,
often painting several at once:

> First I put the washes on all of the canvases. Then I do all the
> backgrounds. Then I spend about two hours on each one,
> putting in all the details and the foreground. (McCall, 1977,
> p. 38)

Most telling, they exhibit and sell their work at shows organized by the amateur art associations they belong to, and
compete in contests at the association meetings:

> We all bring a painting. There's a theme—maybe a snow scene
> in January or flowers in the Spring. Everyone has to do a
> painting using that theme. Then we judge them at the meet-
> ings. We all vote and you get a certain number of points if you
> win. (McCall, 1977, p. 39)

Picture painters may produce paintings no worse than professional artists' (McCall does not deal with that question, and it is not a judgment to accept *a priori*), but they exhibit in a way members of the "serious" art world see as amateurish and therefore to be avoided. (Compare the world of camera clubs described in chapter 10.)

Self-support, then, solves some but by no means all of the problems posed by art world distribution systems. You need not use the system to provide economic support for your work if the medium does not require extensive expenditures, if you have sufficient resources to cover even high expenses, or if you can get what you need by barter. But you may still want to bring your work to the attention of an appropriate audience. If you can mainly, or only, reach that audience through the established distribution system, you must still deal with it, devise an alternative way of accomplishing the same end, or do without such audience appreciation. Artists may not want the audiences that can be reached through the conventional system, because those audiences use that system precisely because it brings them the work they prefer and know how to appreciate; they have no interest in the unconventional works it does not handle.

PATRONAGE

In a patronage system, some person or organization supports the artist entirely for a period during which the artist contracts to produce specific works, or a specified number of works, or even just possibly to produce some works. The people who can afford to support artists this way come from the wealthy classes of a society. They have had the leisure to acquire substantial knowledge of the complicated conventions which govern the production of works of high art and can, being knowledgeable, exert detailed control over the works whose production they support, if they so desire. The patron may be a government, which commissions paintings or sculptures for specific public spaces or puts the artist on a permanent salary, in return for specific services to be performed from time to time, as with a poet laureate. The patron may be a church; popes, cardinals, and Italian religious orders from the Renaissance on have supported artists while they produced major paintings and sculptures or even decorated whole churches. Churches still dispense patronage, but corporations more commonly play that role now, paying for works which decorate their headquarters and other buildings or can be displayed publicly as part of their effort at image building (Haacke, 1976, 1978). Rich people still commission work for their own collections or for gifts to civic or religious organizations, or simply send the artist a stipend with no strings attached.

The artist with a patron need only please that patron. Patronage arrangements may be totally private, although once the artist has been supported the resulting work may be published, exhibited, or distributed widely. What pleases patrons depends on their taste and judgment alone, although the judgments of others may eventually influence them. If enough people think the artist's work does not merit support, the patron may stop sending checks. But not necessarily. Stubborn patrons, sure of their own judgment, often ignore public criticism, and have supported much innovative and unpopular work. In any event, politically, financially, and socially powerful patrons often control opportunities to exhibit or to have performed the works they commission. In that way, they partially shape the taste of others.

The stratified societies which produce patrons exhibit a complex relationship between wealth, knowledge, taste, patterns of support for artists, and the kind of work produced. Patrons want artists to make what they have learned to appreciate and prize as the elements of fine art, so how the wealthy and powerful are educated becomes an important determinant of what they will pay artists to produce. The ability to pick the best artists and commission the best work shows the nobility of spirit and character the powerful and wealthy think they possess, so that being a good patron supports the claim to high rank.

These relationships, traced out in detail for Italian painting of the seventeenth century by Francis Haskell (1963), suggest the general dimensions and problems of patronage systems. During this period, the major patrons were the

successive popes, the cardinals they appointed (quite frequently relatives, so that the patronage might be said to
come from families), and religious orders. Patrons commissioned work, intended to glorify themselves or the groups
they represented, in the form of large-scale decorations for
churches—for the ceilings or walls of a chapel or even for the
main body of a large church (the greatest commission, perhaps, was for the decoration of St. Peter's)—or the architecture and sculpture of a new church. They often played an
active role in the planning and design of the work, suggesting
topics, themes, and details that used the conventional language of contemporary art to further political and family
aims. Thus, when Pope Urban VIII commissioned a major
work in St. Peter's from Bernini, he

> probably played a direct part in outlining the iconographical
> scheme: certainly he made sure that he should be closely
> identified with it. The Barberini [the Pope's name had been
> Maffeo Barberini] bees crawl up the columns and hang
> down on bronze leaves from the cornice; the Barberini sun
> blazes above the rich capitals; an elementary knowledge of
> botany makes it clear that the leaves on the columns are those
> of the laurel—another Barberini emblem—and not the tradi-
> tional vine. From now on their family history was to be indel-
> ibly linked with that of the great church. (Haskell, 1963, p. 35)

Urban VIII was the ideal patron. He paid well and on time;
not all patrons did. Being cultivated, familiar with the elaborately coded meanings of the period's painting, he could
participate in planning decorative schemes like the above,
which celebrated appropriate religious subjects while expressing secular, political, and dynastic meanings, the icon-
ographic games which marked a man of wit and learning. A
good patron also had access to the best places to paint—the
most important churches and the most important parts of
those churches, places where everyone would see one's
work. That helped artists develop a reputation, which freed
them from tiresome or difficult patrons. When an artist had a
good reputation, others would be eager to pay him to paint
their palaces and churches. Families and religious orders

competed for Bernini's services, and his work appeared in the most spectacular places.

To pay well and on time, a patron had to be personally rich or have access to the wealth of the church; popes were superior patrons, often combining family and Vatican wealth so that they could continue spending and paying even when the Roman economy declined. Of course, when the pope died and was replaced by one from a different family, nephews and relatives of the late pope often lost the ability to pay so well and so promptly, along with their church offices.

The importance of a patron's taste and learning becomes clear when we consider people who did not have it and did not behave in the ways envisioned in the conventional arrangements. As the power and wealth of the papal state declined, wealthy businessmen took up the prerogatives of patronage: "It was, indeed, looked upon as a necessary appurtenance of aristocratic status, and may often have had little to do with appreciation or understanding" (Haskell, 1963, pp. 247–48). But these *nouveaux riches* differed from the older patrons. Lacking the older patrons' traditional culture, the new patrons did not want pictures based on mythology and elaborate religious symbolism, requiring an education they may not have had. They preferred pictures of everyday life, and Haskell notes that:

> a desire for the more picturesque aspects of "reality" in art has linked the uninitiated connoisseurs of many different civilizations, and has been met by artists ranging from the sublime to the abysmal. (Haskell, 1963, p. 132)

To look at realistic pictures of the life around you requires no special training, for it relies on knowledge any competent member of the society has. You can admire the skill with which that life is rendered, the vitality and truthfulness of the representation. Instead of paintings of the Fates, the Virtues, the Doctors of the Church, and little angels, the new patrons preferred topics like these:

> Men at work—the cakeseller with his ring-shaped loaves; the water-carrier outside the walls of the town; the tobacconist filling the pipes of resting soldiers; the peasant feeding his

horses; the smith. Men at play—gulping down a quick drink at the inn but still on horseback to save time; dancing the tarantella before a group of admiring spectators; playing *morra* in an old cave; dressed in brilliant costumes for the carnival procession. Or a sudden glimpse of violence as the dandified brigand—plumed hat gay against the stormy sky, pistol about to fire—rides into the farm and terrorizes the stable lad and his dog. (Haskell, 1963, p. 132)

Painters in this popular style did not appeal to the more conservative and traditional noble patrons. But there were fewer such patrons and they spent less of the money being spent for paintings, so paintings based on their class-bound cultivation and learning attracted talented painters less and less.

In short, a patronage system makes an immediate connection between what the patron wants and understands and what the artist does. Patrons pay, and they dictate—not every note or brush stroke, but the broad outlines and the matters that concern them. They choose artists who provide what they want. In an efficient patronage system, artists and patrons share conventions and an aesthetic through which they can cooperate to produce work, the patrons providing support and direction, the artists creativity and execution.

The Italian example gives us the basic dimensions within which patronage systems vary in different societies. Many wealthy classes share no body of values and traditions of the kind that informed the Italian baroque. Their members can express their "nobility" by supporting artists, but cannot cooperate in the production of works which express, justify, and celebrate their position and class. The patron who supported Marcel Duchamp supported the production of a series of esoteric objects which, whatever their meaning, provided no easily understood support for the patron's social position. It gave the patron entry into the otherwise closed and esoteric world of contemporary art and access to rank, or at least participation, in a world whose own system of rank was independent of the larger society's, depending instead on the shared taste of practitioners of the art, and perhaps only a small segment of those. Rockefellers and Guggenheims use their economic and social resources to erect monuments to themselves, in the form of major museums of contemporary avant-garde art. But the art in those museums embodies the ideologies of contemporary art movements, and the patrons show their rank in those systems by a cultivated knowledge of art esoterica. (Remember, in contrast, that in baroque Italy painters learned the ideology, symbolism, and aesthetic of people who, at the top of the social hierarchy, could afford to support them.)

Patronage differs in the performing arts, where the costs of contemporary performing arts organizations—symphonies, operas, repertory theaters, and ballet—are so great no one patron can cover them. As a result, the people who might patronize individual painters or writers collaborate to support these organizations, and the coordination of that collaboration necessitates an elaborate paraphernalia of boards and auxiliaries to carry on the required fund raising. Patrons of these major cultural enterprises give enough to maintain a continuous flow of performances and the preparation of new productions. They get no collectable objects to display as evidence of their taste and seriousness, but their names appear in programs, and they sometimes get credit for financing a new production (e.g., of an opera or ballet), and thus receive a certain amount of status honor.

Contemporary private patrons, then, can afford to be the models of enlightened generosity Haskell describes as the ideal patron. They have the money, and most of them have acquired the esoteric knowledge of contemporary art necessary to be enlightened in how they spend it. They may not, however, control the best places to display work for maximum public effect unless they are, as many major collectors of modern art are, major officers of and donors to important museums. Some collectors—Guggenheim, Whitney, Hirshorn—have even opened their own museums. (Joseph Hirshorn, while he spent enormous amounts of money on contemporary art, did so in a way that cast doubt on whether he fully participated in and understood the aesthetic involved; he might, for instance, buy the entire contents of an artist's studio in a twenty-minute visit.)

Governmental patrons, on the other hand, can display

work in important and accessible places. When governments commission art works for purposes of display or commemoration, artists can sometimes depend on officials as a source of support. But in government many items have a higher priority than art, so this is a shaky source. In addition, government officials usually have to answer to superiors, who (especially if they are popularly elected) may not have sophisticated tastes or, if they do, may answer to constituencies which do not. For these reasons, official commissions generally go to those practicing artists who most clearly represent established values and artistic styles. (See Moulin, 1967, pp. 265–84.) As a result, work defined as politically radical, obscene, sacrilegious, or too different from conventional definitions of what constitutes art receives little government support anywhere.

Despite these constraints, many governments have been responsible for major contemporary works. In such cases, specialized officials, "enlightened" in Haskell's sense, sharing the conventions and aesthetic of artists in the contemporary painting and sculpture world, take over the day-to-day workings of the bureaucracies which administer funds appropriated for art. They insulate artists from some, though not all, direct political pressure. André Malraux, while he was minister of culture in the French government, exemplifies the type.

Something similar happens in business patronage of the arts, although there, as Hans Haacke (1976, 1978) has shown, choices are made and justified as exercises in public relations and corporate image building and therefore are usually quite conservative, designed to produce a positive effect on the greatest number of people. The thinking that informs corporate patronage is exemplified in these quotations Haacke gleaned from the remarks of some important officials about the relations between art and business:

> My appreciation and enjoyment of art are esthetic rather than intellectual.
>
> I am not really concerned with what the artist means; it is not an intellectual operation—it is what I feel.
>
> Nelson Rockefeller

But the significant thing is that increasing recognition in the business world that the arts are not a thing apart,
    that they have to do with all aspects of life, including business—
that they are, in fact essential to business.

Frank Stanton

EXXON's support of the arts serves the arts as a social lubricant.
    And if business is to continue in big cities, it needs a lubricated environment.

Robert Kingsley,
Department of Public Affairs, EXXON Corporation
(Quoted in Haacke, 1976, pp. 116, 117, and 120)

When contemporary patrons have such ideas about art, they come into frequent conflict with artists and other contemporary art world participants, who, more liberal politically, typically view the correct relation between government, business, and the arts differently. Haacke's polls of people visiting an avant-garde New York gallery show that they are more left in their politics and more adventurous in their taste than the people who provide the major support for public art. Seventy percent of the visitors to a typical contemporary art gallery have a professional interest in art. Seventy-six percent think artists and museum staff should be represented on the board of trustees of art museums (an idea such boards have resisted strongly). Seventy-four percent supported McGovern in the 1972 U.S. election. Sixty-seven percent think the interests of profit-oriented business are incompatible with the common good. Sixty-six percent have incomes below $20,000 a year and 81 percent think U.S. taxation policy favors large incomes. No more than 15 percent think that any New York art museum would exhibit works critical of the present U.S. government. Forty-nine percent consider themselves liberal, and 19 percent, radical (Haacke, 1976, pp. 14–36). In short, the public for contemporary art believes that the work it is most interested in is ultimately controlled by people who have a view of the art enterprise contradictory to their own.

Government patronage, discussed later, differs with the character of the regime. I only want to note here that the government may have a monopoly over the means of making and distributing work. In that case, the state is no longer one of several possible sources of financing; it is the only one, and work does not get done without its help. In a number of countries, while literature and music are in the hands of privately owned firms, the state controls the film industry, directly or through financial support. The regime may think films a greater threat to political stability, since they reach more people than written materials, or only the state may be able to aggregate enough money to finance a respectable-looking film. In some countries, of course, the state maintains as a matter of course a monopoly over all forms of communication and enterprise. One might then describe the arts as a state-controlled industry rather than speak of state patronage.

PUBLIC SALE

Under this kind of system, artists make works which are sold or distributed publicly. Typically, professional intermediaries operate organizations which sell works or tickets to performances to anyone with the money to buy them. Some relatively simple statements suggest the basic workings of public-sale systems. (1) Effective demand is generated by people who will spend money for art. (2) What they demand is what they have learned to enjoy and want, and that is a result of their education and experience. (3) Price varies with demand and quantity. (4) The works the system handles are those it can distribute effectively enough to stay in operation. (5) Enough artists will produce works the system can effectively distribute that it can continue to operate. (6) Artists whose work the distribution system cannot or will not handle find other means of distribution; alternatively, their work achieves minimal or no distribution.

We can apply the three criteria painters applied to patrons to public-sale systems. What kind of financial support do they provide for people making art works? How do they bring together audiences who share the conventions and taste that enter into the making of the works? How do they provide for the public display of the artist's work, thus contributing to the building of reputations and careers? Remember that the intermediaries who run these organizations intend to keep the process of production and distribution more or less orderly and predictable, so that they can continue their operations and thus continue to serve both audiences and artists while profiting themselves. The operating public-sale systems serve some artists well, providing support, contact with an audience with taste, and opportunities for the effective public display of their work. They do less well for artists whose work doesn't quite fit the system, and very badly for artists whose work doesn't fit at all.

In some systems an entrepreneur invests in a stock of work by one or more artists and provides a place where prospective buyers can inspect it and possibly buy it. In the performing arts variant, an entrepreneur invests in the production of performances, usually by investing in their preparation or, alternately, by guaranteeing a minimum take, and then sells tickets. In either case, intermediaries make enough on some of what they offer to enable them to continue to offer a variety. We can call relatively small-scale versions of this system a gallery-dealer type or, speaking of the performing arts, an impresario system. These small-scale systems typically distribute works conceived as unique. At the other extreme, an entrepreneur invests in the production of many copies of a work intended for mass distribution, in a way typical of the recording industry, films, and book publishing. We can call these systems, following Paul Hirsch (1972), culture industries.

Dealers

Haskell (1963) and Harrison and Cynthia White (1965) describe the shift from systems of patronage to systems dominated by dealers, galleries, and critics. In eighteenth- and nineteenth-century Italy and France, large numbers of wealthy merchants and other business people became interested in acquiring paintings for their own enjoyment and as marks of the cultivation and taste appropriate to the social position they aspired to. Simultaneously, many people had become artists, hoping for the successful careers patronage made possible. Under patronage, public exhibits were not common and, when held, brought together enormous numbers of canvases for a relatively short time so that potential patrons could see whom they wanted to take on as proteges; in the case of the Paris Salon, the state awarded prizes which helped patrons make their choices.

But more painters wanted patrons than the system could accommodate. White and White (1965) estimate that in France, around 1863, three thousand recognized male painters in Paris and another thousand in the provinces turned out, every ten years, approximately two hundred thousand reputable canvases (p. 83).

> the system never developed, within its own confines, the ability to place this hoard of unique objects for pay. Not all paintings had to be placed, of course, nor were they placed by the alternative system of dealers and critics that was evolving. But enough of them had to be placed to give the artist some semblance of the regular income necessitated by his own middle-class view of himself.
>
> . . . .
>
> A much larger market for paintings was needed and could be mobilized. . . . The dealers recognized, encouraged, and catered to new social markets. . . . There were enough, and sufficiently varied, potential buyers so that one had to think in terms of markets rather than individuals (White and White, 1965, pp. 88, 94)

Visual art is now sold almost entirely through an international network of such dealers. Dealers (according to Moulin's classic [1967] study of the art market, on which the following discussion heavily relies) integrate the artist into the society's economy by transforming aesthetic value into economic value, thus making it possible for artists to live by their art work. Dealers usually specialize in either "consecrated" art or contemporary art. Their style of doing business and the economic contingencies of their operations vary accordingly:

> Whether these dealers [in consecrated art] specialize in Old Masters or in modern painting, from the masters of impressionism to the masters of the 20th century, the works put on sale possess, on the cultural plane, the status of legitimacy and, on the economic plane, the status of assured value. . . .
>
> Their artistic choices have as a basis the choices already made by history. Errors of judgment occur only at the level of the identification and authentication of works. (Moulin, 1967, pp. 99–100, my translation)

Even if such works fall out of critical favor, their undeniable importance in the history of art assures their continuing value. That value is further supported by the forever limited supply; a dead artist will paint no more canvases, although more may be discovered and further dead artists may be (and often are) added to the list of those whose work has historic importance (see Moulin, 1967, pp. 424–41).

In contrast, the supply of contemporary paintings has no limit. Dealing in contemporary work requires an entrepreneur, someone willing to take risks: "The innovative dealer bets on an unknown work; his objective is to give it a public existence and impose it on the market" (Moulin, 1967, p. 118, my translation). But how can the entrepreneur know whether the work and artist he bets on, and recommends to others, will be accepted by the public? No one can know for sure, until history has spoken through the actions of others which sustain his judgment and cause an increase in the prices of the work. Innovative dealers thus find that their aesthetic and financial judgments and activities are thoroughly mixed. Further, they cannot, and do not, wait for history to speak; they actively try to persuade the others whose actions will make history. They do this through their galleries.

A gallery consists of: a dealer, who ordinarily has a permanent location in which to display art works to prospective buyers; a group of artists (often referred to as the dealer's "stable"), who produce the work to be sold; a group of buyers, who support the gallery through regular purchases; a critic or critics, who help, through published explanations and evaluations, to build up an interest in and a market for the works of the gallery's artists; and a large group of gallery-goers, who attend openings, come to see shows, and generally diffuse interest in the gallery's artists by talking about them and recommending shows to others. Potential buyers of the work do not share an aesthetic and body of conventional knowledge with artists, both because they come from less cultured classes than patrons and because the culture of the art world has become increasingly esoteric and professionalized, devoted to the exploration of problems growing out of its own tradition (see Kubler, 1962).

Dealers typically specialize in a style or school of art. "Their" artists have something in common, so that people who come to the gallery can expect to see work which depends more or less on the same or related assumptions and conventions. Steady attendance at a gallery's exhibitions teaches you how to appreciate that style—what its possibilities are, what experiences you can have in viewing it, facts about the artists and their background, and its philosophical or aesthetic intentions and underpinnings (contained in wall labels and catalogues). Gallerygoers who identify themselves as potential purchasers get personalized lessons from the gallery staff, who analyze the work of individual artists and even individual paintings or sculptures, suggest their relationship to other important or current styles or schools, and discuss the aesthetics of the work, simultaneously perhaps discussing where you might put a particular work in your home, how you might want to pay for it, and how it would fit in with other works you already own.

These lessons in how to appreciate the work of a gallery's artists build on a groundwork laid by critics and aestheticians. Aestheticians (as the next chapter shows) deal with the basic philosophical positions which justify work of one or another kind as legitimate art, suitable for appreciation. Critics operate at a more mundane level, discussing the day-to-day affairs of the art world they are part of, current events—shows, major acquisitions, and changes of style—which affect reputations and the prices of work, and particular theories of painting which inform some picture or group of them. White and White (1965) cite a representative example of the criticism which explained impressionist painting to the French art-buying public:

> In the field of color, they have made a genuine discovery whose origin cannot be found elsewhere. . . . The discovery properly consists in having recognized that full light decolorizes tones, that sunlight reflected by objects tends, by virtue of its clarity, to bring them back to the luminous unity which dissolves its seven spectral rays into a single colorless refulgence, which is light. From intuition to intuition, they have succeeded . . . in splitting the light into its beams, its elements, and in recomposing its unity by means of the general harmony of the colors of the spectrum which they spread on their canvases . . . (Edmond Duranty, cited in White and White, 1965, p. 120)

Such remarks would help a person who still valued Academic history painting to see what there was to like in paintings which had no famous people in them, commemorated no important events, and expressed no important patriotic or religious values.

Critical writing is especially influential when it explains clearly what the previous standard was, and how the new work now shows that that standard was too constricted and that there are in fact other things to enjoy. John Szarkowski, an important tastemaker in photography, thus explains why Robert Frank's book, *The Americans*, was disliked when it first appeared in 1958 and what one might see in it by giving up the then conventional view:

> the angriest responses to *The Americans* came from photographers and photography specialists . . . who recognized how profound a challenge Frank's work was to the standards of photographic style—photographic *rhetoric*—that were in large part shared even by photographers of very different philosophical postures. These standards called for a precise and unambiguous description of surface, volume, and space; it was in these qualities that the seductiveness, the physical beauty, of photography lay. (Szarkowski, 1978, p. 20)

The Americans—Frank's searing personal view of this country during the Eisenhower years—was . . . based on a sophisticated social intelligence, quick eyes, and a radical understanding of the potentials of the small camera, which depended on good drawing rather than on elegant tonal description (Szarkowski, 1978, p. 17)

Critics frequently make the same discoveries gallery owners make, and the two groups collaborate to promote those painters and sculptors whose innovations they find attractive and critically acceptable. The dealers show the work, and the critics provide the reasoning which makes it acceptable and worth appreciating. Both groups often purchase the new work they are interested in for their own collections. It would be surprising if they did not, since they originally chose it, at least in part, because they found it attractive and thought it likely to be important in the development of painting, as well as because they wanted to help the as yet relatively unknown artists by buying their work.

Dealers need people who will not only appreciate the work they present, but also buy it and keep it—collectors. Most people who like contemporary art do not actually buy it. One of Haacke's polls of gallerygoers shows that only 18 percent have spent more than two thousand dollars buying art (Haacke, 1976, p. 46). Dealers try to train appreciators to be collectors. That means adding to appreciation of the work such elements as pride and confidence in displaying one's taste, the confidence showing in the expenditure involved and the willingness to let others know you have made it. Raymonde Moulin (1967, pp. 190–225) outlines the diversity of collectors' motives, from cultural snobbery and sheer financial speculation to a deep engrossment in painting for its own sake, as well as the collecting mania described in fictional detail by Evan S. Connell, Jr. (1974). She points out how the confounding of economic and aesthetic values appears even in the behavior of the speculator:

> The speculator makes two bets, intimately connected in the short run, one on the aesthetic value, the other on the economic value of the works he buys, each of the two guaranteeing the other. To win this double bet is to confirm oneself simultaneously as an economic actor and a cultural actor. (Moulin, 1967, p. 219, my translation)

Playing on such mixtures of motives, dealers (aided by the writings of critics) attract an audience, a clientele interested in the work they show. The buyers, enjoying the works as they have learned to, communicate to others, both in their talk and by the example of their own acquisitions, the possibilities of the new style or school, thus making the dealer's arguments more persuasive.

Art works are now universally regarded as an important means of investment. Wisely chosen art works appreciate substantially, sometimes doing better than more conventional alternatives. But, as Moulin (1967, pp. 462–76) shows, when the U.S. stock market dropped dramatically in 1962, American collectors sold off their paintings and produced an even more dramatic depreciation in the prices of contemporary paintings, both in New York and in Paris. The prices of historically legitimated paintings dropped much less.

As a result, investing in contemporary art requires expert advice if it is to be done wisely. Successful critics and dealers, reputed to have a good eye for aesthetic (and therefore economic) value, shape their clients' taste and, by so doing, ensure that their own investments in artists who are not fully established become and remain profitable. The more people they convince of the artistic merits of "their" artists, the more valuable their own holdings. Dealers thus find it advantageous to hold on to the work of artists just becoming known. It will be worth more as the painter's reputation grows.

Because art works have economic value, some of the distribution system's work deals directly with the problems that creates. One crucial problem is establishing the authenticity of the work being sold. This matters little when the artist is contemporary and unknown—who would fake the work?—but becomes very important when larger sums are involved, or when the artist is dead or cannot remember for sure creating the work in question. In such situations, experts collaborate with dealers, applying the methods of art historical research to authenticate particular works and the methods of aesthetics to decide the relative worth of artists, works, and entire schools. They use methods of stylistic an-

alysis to decide whether a Titian is a real Titian. The construction of a provenance, a step-by-step tracing of the ownership of a work, can serve the same purpose. Such experts
as Bernard Berenson collaborated with dealers like Joseph
Duveen to persuade a generation of rich Americans who
knew little about art to spend fortunes on works the expert
guaranteed as authentic; at the same time, Berenson was
putting the methods of systematic attribution on a sound and
defensible basis. These scholarly techniques are now a standard part of the value-creating activity of a community of
dealers, critics, scholars, and collectors.

In short, dealers, critics, and collectors develop a consensus about the worth of work and how it can be appreciated.
When that happens, we may say that the dealer has created
or trained an audience for the work he handles, an audience
as cultivated with respect to that body of work as an Italian
nobleman or pope was with respect to baroque painting.
They know and understand it, and the painter can paint for
them, sure in the knowledge that they will appreciate his
insights, wit, and technical achievements.

Such a dealer, of course, must also have artists who create
the work. A dealer actively collects artists, and encourages
them to produce sufficient work to allow him to build up an
interest among the gallery's steady clientele. Marcia Bystryn
(1978) has suggested a division of labor among galleries in
the contemporary New York painting world. One type spon-
sors large numbers of relatively unknown artists, giving them
a first chance at being seen by serious critics and collectors.
The second type chooses from this group those who have
received some encouragement, whose work has been well
received critically and bought by a few important collectors.
Dealers, and their requirements for a steady supply of work to
be shown and sold, create some important constraints on
artists. They often suggest the kinds of work that might constitute an appropriate next step for the artist, and are a
certain source of pressure to produce work in sufficient
quantity to sustain both the gallery (the gallery's artists together must produce sufficient work to allow for a continuous schedule of exhibitions) and the artist's career (an

artist who is not producing much work is no longer, in some sense, a practicing artist, at least not one who can play a serious role in a gallery's operations). The two types of galleries, between them, produce a steady supply of artists willing to risk their time, energy, and reputations making work that may or may not be taken seriously, develop an audience sufficient to support the artists' work, and produce reputations that ratify a position in the system of esteem of the art world. Between them, they weed out aspiring artists, encouraging some to greater production and more confidence in their own work, suggesting to others that they have gone as far as they are likely to go. (A more complex typology of galleries can be found in Moulin, 1967, pp. 89–149.)

Although dealers have little trouble recruiting aspiring artists (in fact, it is aspiring artists who have trouble finding dealers), they often have trouble keeping them. As with all relations with support personnel, artists find dealers a mixed blessing. On the one hand, dealers do things most artists would like someone else to do. Moulin quotes a French painter:

> To be honest, I have to say that we're always on the lookout for a dealer, in order to get away from the administrative work, the publicity that the dealer takes charge of, in order to protect myself, in order not to have to entertain collectors. It's a lost day when a collector comes, three hours lost beforehand from anxiety; then, if he doesn't like things, you're annoyed, or if he does, you're excited. A painter can't be everywhere. (Moulin, 1967, p. 333, my translation)

More important, because a young painter may be regarded as a good investment, well-established dealers make artists "theirs," acquire a monopoly on the sale of their work by contracting for their entire output in return for a monthly stipend on which the painter can live, work, and buy materials. Finally, the dealer, by virtue of his specialized business skills and connections in the market, knows, as the artist does not, how to translate aesthetic value into economic value. Moulin cites the case of Jacques Villon. Although well known and respected, his work did not sell. When he was almost seventy the dealer Louis Carré began to handle his work and, through a carefully organized series of shows, raised the price of Villon's paintings from hundreds to hundreds of thousands of francs (Moulin, 1967, pp. 329–33).

On the other hand, dealers do not always pay what they owe. Their business is sensitive to the fluctuations of the economic situation, and when things get bad they may cancel contracts. Dealers who are not well established may have trouble paying artists; artists may have trouble recovering unsold work (see the detailed account of such an incident in Haber, 1975). More important, as Moulin points out, the economic interests of artist and dealer often diverge. A dealer will often want to hold a work for years while its value grows, but the painter wants the work shown, purchased, and placed where he can benefit from its being discussed by an audience which appreciates what he is doing and can contribute useful ideas and criticism. Finally, the artist wants his reputation to grow as much as possible as quickly as possible, but the dealer may find it more advantageous to wait for the work's long-term appreciation. Artists with good reputations may look for other dealers who will make better terms.

The gallery-dealer system is intimately connected to the institution of the museum. Museums become the final repository of the work which originally enters circulation through dealers, final in two senses: (1) work that enters a museum collection usually stays there, either because the gift or bequest which brought it there requires that or because, having staked their reputations as connoisseurs on the acquisition of certain works, museum officials do not want to admit they were wrong by selling the work, at least not until sufficient time has gone by so that they are not the ones responsible; (2) When a museum shows and purchases a work, it gives it the highest kind of institutional approval available in the contemporary visual arts world; no more can happen that will make that work more important or allow it to add more than it already has to the artist's reputation.

The ultimate control of museums rests in the hands of the trustees, who provide much of the money with which they operate. Even public museum trustees, in political systems that allow for private accumulation of wealth and property, usually represent the wealthiest classes, because they can assist the museum with gifts of money and art, and usually do, in return for positions of control. Vera Zolberg (1974) has shown, in her analysis of the development of the Chicago Art Institute, that rich patrons originally exerted direct control over the museum's affairs, taking a hand in acquisitions, displays, and other artistic matters. They later put control into the hands of academically trained art historians, who had better information about what was "really" valuable and important than could part-time connoisseurs. Finally, as museums became increasingly large and complicated, and as the notion that administration is an art transferable from one situation to another gained ground, patrons (and the Chicago Art Institute exemplifies the trend) put control into the hands of trained administrators, who may have had no previous experience in the arts.

These shifts in the control of museums do not mean that artists have no trouble with museums. Like dealers, museum directors, and the trustees they work for, have interests which may differ from those of the artists; to make matters more complicated, museum staff may act in what they think are the trustees' interests, even though the trustees may have no such interests. Thus, many museums showed obvious reluctance (especially during the Vietnam War and related events of the 1960s) to exhibit openly political contemporary art, at a time when artists were becoming more openly political. In an exemplary case, on the invitation of a curator of the Guggenheim Museum, Hans Haacke had prepared a piece which traced and displayed the pattern of ownership of slum properties on New York's Lower East Side. The director of the museum, insisting that the work was "political," canceled the show; this led to the firing of the curator involved, a boycott of the museum by many contemporary artists, and (perhaps) to Haacke's later piece detailing the corporate connections and activities of the museum's trustees. (See Haacke, 1976, for the details.) The case was an odd one, since none of the trustees had any interest in slum properties or the kind of people who owned them, and presumably would not have objected to the exposure of those activities in the work. The professionals who administer these institutions are apparently more wary of offending trustees than they need be, preferring not to run unnecessary risks.

The control of museums by wealthy people has more subtle effects on their contents, though these effects are not easy to pinpoint. The authors of the *Anti-Catalog* (Catalog Committee, 1977) produced an analysis of the Whitney Museum's exhibition of the private collection of Mr. and Mrs. John D. Rockefeller III (shown in 1976, as part of the U.S. celebration of the national bicentennial), emphasizing the degree to which this collection (and, by extension, the many museum collections it resembles) glorified wealth, and business and ignored social conflict, minority groups, and other matters uncongenial to the interests and taste of wealthy patrons.

Impresarios

Since the performing arts do not produce objects which can be stored, exhibited, and sold, they distribute art differently from gallery systems. They resemble them in that an entrepreneur invests time, money, and energy in assembling materials and bringing them to potential audiences. They differ in selling the audience not objects, but tickets to see something done. Objects can be sold after potential buyers see them; performances must be presold. The impresario undertakes to sell enough tickets for the performance to bring profit to him and a living to the performing artists (or at least an income sufficient to allow more work to be done) and to create an audience which will appreciate the work and reward the artists with an increased reputation.

Impresarios undertake to do whatever is necessary to gather an audience in an appropriate place for the performance to occur. They rent the space the performance will take place in, do the necessary advertising, sell tickets, handle finances, and make sure that necessary auxiliary personnel (e.g., technicians and ushers) are there. They typically guarantee artists a certain minimum fee, perhaps against a percentage of the gross, which is where the risk comes in; if the performance does not draw a large enough audience, the entrepreneur loses the difference between the artist's fee plus his costs and what he has actually taken in.

Much of what has been said about dealers and galleries applies to impresarios. They provide the opportunity to display work to an informed and appreciative audience which shares the perspective and conventions that inform the artist's work, and thereby produce sufficient revenue to let the work continue. Of necessity, they operate somewhat differently. It takes more people to support performing art institutions than galleries, and impresarios cannot count, as gallery owners can, on a few buyers to pay the expenses for exhibitions attended by many. So they must create a larger audience trained to enjoy what they intend to present. This is one reason they try to sell tickets to a series of events, rather than just to isolated concerts or plays. People who purchase season tickets will not only have paid before they receive what they are paying for, but also place themselves in a position to receive a series of lessons in what the impresario offers, whether it be avant-garde music or dance, classical theater, light musical comedies, chamber music, symphony, or opera. One component of what an audience needs in order to appreciate particular works is experience in the genre they represent, and audience members get this when they buy a season ticket.

The impresario need not be a Sol Hurok or a Bill Graham. The entrepreneurial function may be performed by an organization—a regional theater, a symphony association, or a quasi-governmental organization. Performers often act as their own impresarios, especially in smaller operations. A local theater may do all its own production work and take all the financial risks (see Lyon, 1974 and 1975). Such groups, expecting a relatively small audience, make a corresponding investment.

With larger investments, the performance becomes a project to which people commit themselves for varying kinds and durations of work via the free-lance system discussed in the last chapter. Here the impresario, who makes the commitments necessary to assemble the cooperating parties, is necessary. With the commitments made, the project proceeds, coming to fruition in a series of performances which recoup the original investment.

Some of these organizations have a permanent existence: for example, theatrical and dance companies, or symphony and opera associations. Making up the bulk of their programs from well-known works audiences learned to like long ago, they have no problem assembling an audience with appropriate tastes. Their difficulties arise when the artists who make up the group, or choose the repertoire, want to respond to currents of change in the world of their art and perform more contemporary or experimental works, which have no presold audience. That desire arises because artists think that by doing works of this kind they can make better reputations for themselves among the peers and specially knowledgeable laypeople to whom they are most responsive. But because the work is unknown and experimental, the audience that ordinarily supports the organization will complain that it is unfamiliar and difficult. Every large, permanent performing arts group has this problem. Smaller groups, with fewer expenses, can specialize in such work and draw a concomitantly smaller but dedicated presold group of aficionados.

An established and well-known group can provide the opportunity for appropriate display of works and performing talents just because it has an established audience. Whatever is done at a concert of the New York Philharmonic or some similar orchestra will have achieved the best possible opportunity a symphonic work has to be heard.

Audience members who pay for a ticket before they have seen or heard what they are paying for may feel that they did not get the kind of thing they paid for, that they did not get enough of what they paid for, or that what they got was not as good as they expected. All of these complaints, in one way or another, rest on an assumed shared basis of conventional artistic standards and on similarly shared assumptions about what constitutes one's money's worth. An audience which pays the ordinary full price for a concert or theater piece which runs only thirty minutes complains that they have been cheated; when an understudy replaces a star a large portion of the audience wants its money back; a work that is too avant-garde for its audience causes trouble. American audiences are polite to mediocre performers, but audiences in other countries can be very noisy when what they hear or see is not up to the expected standard; the rudeness of Italian opera audiences is legendary.

Impresarios have a less personal relationship with the audiences to which they bring performances than do dealers with their clients. But they work in a similar way to teach willing pupils what must be known to appreciate the work they distribute. They cannot depend on an audience which, like royal patrons of an earlier era, not only supported performers, but knew enough of the art's conventions to perform along with them. Contemporary artists and audiences do not share such a class culture. But, as with galleries and paintings, ability to appreciate the performing arts signifies a culture and sophistication which many socially mobile people have not acquired elsewhere and must learn, if they are to learn it, from the people who distribute art. In that way, the intermediaries who manage the public sale of art provide opportunities for display to an audience whose taste they have trained, and thus provide the integration into the society's economy which allows artists to live from their work. (See Zolberg, 1980, for a comparison of distribution systems and their effects in music and the visual arts.)

Culture Industries

Paul Hirsch (1972) used the term *culture industries* to refer to "profit-seeking firms producing cultural products for national [we could add "international"] distribution" and spoke also of "the cultural industry system, comprised of all organizations engaged in the process of filtering new products and ideas as they flow from 'creative' personnel in the technical subsystem to the managerial, institutional and societal levels of organization" (p. 642). To paraphrase his analysis, these organizations deal with very large audiences that are almost totally unknown to them and that therefore are unpredictable, despite the efforts of market researchers to fathom that obscurity. No one knows with any assurance what conventions this mass audience appreciates and accepts, what class or professional artistic cultural understandings might inform their choices. As a result, artists cannot produce or intermediaries order work to suit an audience's taste. Hirsch quotes a spokesman for the recording industry, a classic example of a culture industry:

> We have made records that appeared to have all the necessary ingredients—artist, song, arrangements, promotion, etc.—to guarantee they wind up as best sellers. . . . Yet they fell flat on their faces. On the other hand we have produced records for which only a modest success was anticipated that became runaway best sellers. (Brief, 1964, quoted in Hirsch, 1972, p. 644)

Hirsch notes, finally, that these industries adopt a number of strategies to deal with this uncertain environment, including a "proliferation of contact men"—who distribute products to retailers and people in the mass media who can influence sales—"overproduction and differential distribution of new items," and "cooptation of mass-media gate keepers." The most characteristic culture industries in contemporary societies are book publishing, the record business, the film industry, and radio and television.

We tend to think of these industries as recent, the results of the technical inventions that made most of them possible. In fact, all the major features of the type can be found in the English publishing industry of the middle and late nineteenth century. (I have relied heavily in what follows on Sutherland, 1976.) Victorian publishers developed a system of distribution based on high prices and low volume, much of any novel's sale going to the giant circulating libraries of the period. Novels appeared in three volumes (commonly known as "threedeckers") and retailed for a guinea and a half, a very high price, which allowed the publisher to break even on minimal sales to booksellers and jobbers at large discounts. Sutherland cites the case of "an obscure and unsuccessful novel of the period, *Zaidee* by Mrs. Oliphant, which Blackwood's brought out in 1856. They had 1578 copies of this work printed at a cost of £358. A paltry 496 were sold [which] yielded £535 10s. So with just two-thirds of the stock still on hand (1031 copies) [the publisher] had covered his costs." He goes on to say that one reason for "the golden age of the English novel . . . was the sheer super-abundance of the novel in the period—the fact that publishers could offer so large an invitation to ambitious literary talents" (Sutherland, 1976, p. 17). That is, it was so easy to at least break even that publishers could afford to publish a great many books, and did. The encouragement that gave would-be novelists led to a proliferation of discovered talent.

This system changed as people discovered ways of exploiting the growing literacy and taste for fiction of the English public. Sutherland mentions a number of methods, including the development of large lending libraries and prompt reissue of "collected editions" of authors' work. Two other methods—magazine serialization and publication of the book in monthly parts—allowed a book to be printed and distributed to the public before it had been completely written. The author and publisher could then take account of the public response in the book's further construction. At an extreme, a badly received book could be killed, the remaining parts never written, printed, or distributed. Publishers knew when a book was doing badly, because the sale of the serialized parts, or the magazine in which they were appearing, would drop off precipitously, beyond the expected drop-off of readers who had given the book a try and not found it interesting. Further, as the book progressed, those involved in its marketing could suggest, based on their experience in the trade, how to proceed with the work. In that way they exemplified Sutherland's generalization that:

> Many of the great novels of the period which appear to be the unaided product of creative genius were often. . . . the outcome of collaboration, compromise or commission. (Sutherland, 1976, p. 6)

All three represented influential interactions with the novelist's publisher. As we will see, the results of those interactions shaped, and can be seen in, the novels' style and construction.

Consider some of the major features of this distribution system. The audience is unpredictable, and the people who produce and distribute the artistic work have no real contact with it. They market the work in large quantities, as with books and records, or through a mechanical system, as with radio and television, so that they could not, if they tried, know audience members personally. They thus do not have the immediate communication with an audience that characterizes patronage and the gallery-dealer arrangement. In those systems, makers and distributors talk directly to audience members, sometimes while the work is in progress, and know in detail what they think, what they respond to, and what they like and don't like. In contrast, what culture industries' audiences think, what really moves them in what ways, is something no one knows in such a quick and direct way; in fact, for all the devices of audience research, it is something no one at all knows for sure.

Not knowing who the audience is, artists necessarily make work without knowing who will consume it under what circumstances and with what results. As Charles Newman remarked, "No serious fiction writer in America today can tell you who he is writing *for*" (Newman, 1973, p. 6). Neither can any other writer for a mass market, or any maker of films. He may have an audience in mind, but he does not know if the one he has in mind is the one that will read or see the work. Rather, artists (and the distributors who handle their work) construct an imaginary audience out of fragments of information they assemble by various means. Retailers' customers may tell them what they like and don't like. Retailers may report that information to a salesman, who calls on them periodically and who in turn reports it to his superior, who reports it to the people in charge of production, who may then pass on some version of it to the artist who produced the work. It is unlikely that the information passed along that long chain is accurate or usable when it finally reaches the artist. It suffices, because it has to.

Since no one knows what the mass audience will approve and support, culture industries encourage everyone and anyone to propose ideas for them to distribute. Most of the cost of developing ideas is borne by artists who hope the industry will take them up and distribute them. The industry selects some of these numerous proposals for use. As Hirsch points out, "cultural organizations ideally maximize profits by mobilizing promotional resources in support of volume sales for a small number of items" (Hirsch, 1972, pp. 652–53). They promote items by selective advertising and other promotional devices, and note the effect of these measures on sales. As that information comes in, they drop some of the distributed items from the actively promoted list, effectively killing their chances of success. Where so many items are available, those that do not receive some special attention do not get known well enough to reach those who might want them. (Bliven [1973] describes, in the words of a book salesman, how publishing firms continually readjust their plans for new books.)

Works reach the public with varying amounts of promotion and availability. The system thus provides varying amounts of money (in some cases, enormous amounts), an opportunity (smaller or larger) for display of one's work, and a relatively small chance of reaching an audience which shares the taste and perspective which produced the work. Because they do not connect with an audience directly, artists whose work is distributed through the culture industries come to depend on and are responsive to the immediate feedback and judgment of their professional peer groups, on the one hand, and of the people who manage the distribution system on the other.

The system affects the art work through the interaction between the managers of the culture industries and the artists. Take as simple a matter as the length of a work. Writers learn to think and plan in the lengths that are commercially suitable. Trollope (1947 [1883], p. 198), writing in the days of the triple-decker, said, "An author soon becomes aware of how many pages he has to fill." Sutherland gives further examples. The serialized form in which novels appeared, and the possibility that the series might be cut off abruptly, led novelists to avoid spending much time planning a novel that might never be finished, or setting up elaborate effects in early chapters that could not be fully realized until much later in the book. Instead, authors used the picaresque form, as in *Pickwick Papers*, which they could stop at any time with no great loss to the continuity. When a novelist, however, became well enough known to the public that a pretty good sale was assured just by his name, he could drive a harder bargain with the publisher, including the demand for a guarantee that the entire work would be published no matter what the early sales were. Thus, as Dickens became better known, he began to experiment with more tightly plotted novels like *Bleak House*.

Sutherland cites Thackeray's *Henry Esmond* as a case in point. While *Vanity Fair* began as a series of sketches, and was paid for month by month, the contract for *Henry Esmond* not only allowed the author to take a more comprehensive view, it insisted on it. Several features of the contract produced this result. Thackeray was paid in three installments, the first for signing the contract, the second for completing the manuscript, and the third on publication. The delay of the second payment until the manuscript was done meant that Thackeray could write what the contract also stipulated (and Sutherland notes that this was unusual in contracts of the time), a "continuous" narrative. The novel's elaborate plot culminates in a final scene in which many themes and details are knit together, resolving tensions built up from the beginning. Compared with Thackeray's earlier novels—"No one, I fancy, hurries through the final chapters of [*Vanity Fair* and *Pendennis*] in eagerness to find out what happens on the last page" (Sutherland, 1976, p. 114)—*Esmond*'s careful and complicated plot produces true suspense. Sutherland also notes that holding back the last payment until publication meant that this was the best edited and proofread of Thackeray's books. He concludes that George Smith, the publisher, "deserves some credit for the glories of *Esmond*" (Sutherland, 1976, p. 116).

The effects of the publication system varied with circumstances, for the system produced a variety of arrangements between publishers and authors with differential amounts of power and different degrees of mutual trust, which in turn produced different pressures on the author. Bulwer Lytton's *The Last Days of Pompeii* had redundant chapters and extraneous songs and lyrics because the original manuscript was some fifty pages short of what was needed to fill up the three volumes in which it was being sold (Sutherland, 1976, p. 57); Trollope's language was bowdlerized to satisfy the religious scruples of C. E. Mudie, who ran the great circulating library of the period, sales to which constituted a large part of a successful novel's profits (Sutherland, 1976, p. 27).

Barbara Rosenblum's (1978) somewhat different picture of contemporary art photography reminds us that art, compared with other kinds of work, is not totally constrained by distribution channels. Comparing the work of art photographers to that of photojournalists and fashion photographers, she demonstrates that in the latter two cases the content of the photograph is determined by the channels through which it moves. News photographs reflect the typical choices of editors in their content and imagery, and the mechanism of newspaper reproduction in the technical details of how they are shot and printed, while fashion photographs subordinate everything to the immediately expressed desires and criticisms of the client, who is often present while the pictures are being made. In contrast, art photographers deal with a much looser system, which accepts a wider variety of possible works, and contemporary art photography in fact contains a greater variety of styles and subject matters.

The requirements of culture-industry distribution systems produce more or less standardized products, the standardization resulting from what the system finds convenient to handle rather than from any independent choice made by the maker of an art work. The standard features of the works so produced may become a kind of aesthetic criterion people use in assessing works, so that a work which does not exhibit them seems crude or amateurish. Network television programs have a technical polish which becomes the standard for judging independent television work, even though the polish produces constraints which cruder independent work wants to fight clear of. A book whose pages are not justified on the right looks cheap, and no one can avoid noticing the "cheapness" of a film which does not spend the money necessary to produce the sumptuous and realistic look Hollywood labels "production values."

ART AND DISTRIBUTION

Artists produce what the distribution system can and will carry. It is not that nothing else can be produced. Other artists, willing to forego the possibilities of support and exposure characteristic of a particular art world, do produce other kinds of work. But the system will ordinarily not distribute those works, and such artists will be failures, unknowns, or the nuclei of new art worlds that grow up around what the more conventional system does not handle. The development of new art worlds frequently focuses on the creation of new organizations and methods for distributing work.

Some work is right for any system, and any work could be right for some system, though perhaps not for any system at the moment in existence. Charles Newman has taken issue with theories that the novel, as a form, is dead or worn-out, arguing instead that:

> the cost of producing and marketing what we *make* [serious fiction] has simply exceeded the industry's profit margin, and this particular disease has been masked long enough by theories of dying form and metaphors of terminal illness. (Newman, 1973, p. 7)

So the point is not that work cannot be distributed, but that contemporary institutions cannot or will not distribute it, and that they thus exert, like every other established part of an art world, a conservative effect, leading artists to produce what they handle and thus get the associated rewards.

Change takes place, as succeeding chapters show, both because artists whose work does not fit and who thus stand outside the existing systems attempt to start new ones and because established artists exploit their attractiveness to the existing system to force it to handle work they do which does not fit.

5 • Aesthetics, Aestheticians, and Critics

AESTHETICS AS ACTIVITY

Aestheticians study the premises and arguments people use to justify classifying things and activities as "beautiful," "artistic," "art," "not art," "good art," "bad art," and so on. They construct systems with which to make and justify both the classifications and specific instances of their application. Critics apply aesthetic systems to specific art works and arrive at judgments of their worth and explications of what gives them that worth. Those judgments produce reputations for works and artists. Distributors and audience members take reputations into account when they decide what to support emotionally and financially, and that affects the resources available to artists to continue their work.

To talk this way describes aesthetics as an activity rather than a body of doctrine. Aestheticians are not the only people who engage in this activity. Most participants in art worlds make aesthetic judgments frequently. Aesthetic principles, arguments, and judgments make up an important part of the body of conventions by means of which members of art worlds act together. Creating an explicit aesthetic may precede, follow, or be simultaneous with developing the techniques, forms, and works which make up the art world's output, and it may be done by any of the participants. Sometimes artists themselves formulate the aesthetic explicitly. More often they create an unformalized aesthetic through workaday choices of materials and forms.

In complex and highly developed art worlds, specialized professionals—critics and philosophers—create logically organized and philosophically defensible aesthetic systems, and the creation of aesthetic systems can become a major industry in its own right. An aesthetician whose language foreshadows a sociologically based system I will examine later describes aesthetics and aestheticians this way:

> Aesthetics is . . . the philosophical discipline that deals with the concepts we use when we talk about, think about or in other ways "handle" works of art. On the basis of their own understanding of the Institution of Art as a whole, it is the task of aestheticians to analyze the ways all the different persons and groups talk and act as members of the Institution, and through this to see which are the actual rules that make up the logical framework of the Institution and according to which procedures within the Institution take place. . . .
>
> Within the Institution of Art specific statements of fact— results of a correctly performed elucidation and interpretation of a work of art, say—entail specific evaluations. Constitutive rules lay down specific criteria of evaluation that are binding for members of the Institution. (Kjørup, 1976, pp. 47–48)

We need not believe that it works so neatly to see that art world participants understand the role of aestheticians and aesthetics this way.

An art world has many uses for an explicit aesthetic system. It ties participants' activities to the tradition of the art, justifying their demands for the resources and advantages ordinarily available to people who produce that kind of art. To be specific, if I can argue cogently that jazz merits as serious consideration on aesthetic grounds as other forms of art music, then I can compete, as a jazz player, for grants and fellowships from the National Endowment for the Arts and faculty positions in music schools, perform in the same halls as symphony orchestras, and require the same attention to the nuances of my work as the most serious classical composer or performer. An aesthetic shows that, on general grounds successfully argued to be valid, what art world members do belongs to the same class as other activities already enjoying the advantages of being "art."

As a result, the title "art" is a resource that is at once indispensable and unnecessary to the producers of the works in question. It is indispensable because, if you believe art is better, more beautiful, and more expressive than nonart, if you therefore intend to make art and want what you make recognized as art so that you can demand the resources and advantages available to art—then you cannot fulfill your plan if the current aesthetic system and those who explicate and apply it deny you the title. It is unnecessary because even if these people do tell you that what you are doing is not art, you can usually do the same work under a different name and with the support of a different cooperative world.

Much work in all media is carried on as something other than art. As we will see later, people draw and photograph as a part of enterprises devoted to the production and sale of industrial products, make quilts and clothing as a part of domestic household enterprises, and even produce work entirely on their own, with a minimum of cooperation from others and with no socially communicable justification at all, let alone a philosophically defensible aesthetic.

To return to the uses of an aesthetic for an art world, we can note that a well-argued and successfully defended aesthetic guides working participants in the production of specific art works. Among the things they keep in mind in making the innumerable small decisions that cumulatively shape the work is whether and how those decisions might be defended. Of course, working artists do not refer every small problem to its most general philosophical grounding to decide how to deal with it, but they know when their decisions run afoul of such theories, if only through a vague sense of something wrong. A general aesthetic comes into play more explicitly when someone suggests a major change in conventional practice. If, as a jazz player, I want to give up the conventional twelve- and thirty-two-bar formats in which improvising has traditionally gone on for those in which the length of phrases and sections are among the elements to be improvised, I need a defensible explanation of why such a change should be made.

Furthermore, a coherent and defensible aesthetic helps to stabilize values and thus to regularize practice. Stabilizing values is not just a philosophical exercise. Art world participants who agree on a work's value can act toward it in roughly similar ways. An aesthetic, providing a basis on which people can evaluate things in a reliable and dependable way, makes regular patterns of cooperation possible. When values are stable, and can be depended on to be stable, other things stabilize as well—the monetary value of works and thus the business arrangements on which the art world runs, the reputations of artists and collectors, and the worth of institutional and personal collections (see Moulin, 1967). The aesthetic created by aestheticians provides a theoretical rationale for the selections of collectors.

From this point of view, aesthetic value arises from the consensus of the participants in an art world. To the degree that such a consensus does not exist, value in this sense does not exist: judgments of value not held jointly by members of an art world do not provide a basis for collective activity premised on those judgments, and thus do not affect activities very much. Work becomes good, therefore valuable, through the achievement of consensus about the basis on which it is to be judged and through the application of the agreed-on aesthetic principles to particular cases.

But many styles and schools compete for attention within an organized art world, demanding that their works be shown, published, or performed in place of those produced by adherents of other styles and schools. Since the art world's distribution system has a finite capacity, all works and schools cannot be presented by it and thus be eligible for the rewards and advantages of presentation. Groups compete for access to those rewards, among other ways, by logical argument as to why they deserve presentation. Logical analysis seldom settles arguments over the allocation of resources, but participants in art worlds, especially the people who control access to distribution channels, often feel that what they do must be logically defensible. The heat in discussions of aesthetics usually exists because what is being decided is not only an abstract philosophical question but also some allocation of valuable resources. Whether jazz is really music or photography is really art, whether free-form jazz is really jazz and therefore music, whether fashion photographs are really photography and therefore art, are discussions, among other things, about whether people who play free-form jazz can perform in jazz clubs for the already existing jazz audience and whether fashion photographs can be exhibited and sold in important galleries and museums.

Aestheticians, then, provide that element of the battle for recognition of particular styles and schools which consists of making the arguments which convince other participants in an art world that the work deserves, logically, to be included within whatever categories concern that world. The conservatism of art worlds, arising out of the way conventional practices cluster in neatly meshed packages of mutually adjusted activities, materials, and places, means that changes will not find an easy reception. Most changes proposed to art world participants are minor, leaving untouched most of the ways things are done. The world of symphonic music, for instance, has not changed the length of concert programs very much in recent years, for the very good reason that, because of union agreements, it would increase their costs to lengthen the programs and, because audiences expect eighty or ninety minutes of music for the price of a ticket, they dare not shorten them very much. (That was not always the case. Probably as a result of the unionization of musicians, among other things concert programs have shortened appreciably since, say, Beethoven's time, as figure 13 shows [Forbes, 1967, p. 255].) The basic instrumentation of the orchestra has not changed, nor have the tonal materials used (i.e., the conventional tempered chromatic scale) or the places in which the music is presented. Because of all these conservative pressures, innovators must make a strong argument in defense of any substantially new practice.

TODAY, WEDNESDAY, APRIL 2nd, 1800, Herr Ludwig van Beethoven *will have the honor to give a grand concert for his benefit in the Royal Imperial Court Theatre beside the Burg. The pieces which will be performed are the following:*

1. A grand symphony by the late Kapellmeister Mozart.
2. An aria from "The Creation" by the Princely Kapellmeister Herr Haydn, sung by Mlle. Saal.
3. A grand Concerto for the pianoforte, played and composed by Herr Ludwig van Beethoven.
4. A Septet, most humbly and obediently dedicated to Her Majesty the Empress, and composed by Herr Ludwig van Beethoven *for four stringed and three wind instruments, played by Herren Schuppanzigh, Scheiber, Schindlecker, Bar, Nickel, Matauschek and Dietzel.*
5. A Duet from Haydn's "Creation," sung by Herr and Mlle. Saal.
6. Herr Ludwig van Beethoven *will improvise on the pianoforte.*
7. A new grand symphony with complete orchestra, composed by Herr Ludwig van Beethoven.

Tickets for boxes and stalls are to be had of Herr van Beethoven at his lodgings in the Tiefen Graben, no. 241, third story, and of the box keeper.

PRICES OF ADMISSION ARE AS USUAL.

THE BEGINNING IS AT HALF-PAST 6 O'CLOCK.

FIGURE 13. Program of a concert given by Ludwig von Beethoven, April 2, 1800. Concert programs were longer in Beethoven's time than they are today. This program for a concert in Vienna is taken from Forbes, 1967, p. 255.

Writers on aesthetics strike a moralistic tone. They take for granted that their job is to find a foolproof formula which will distinguish things which do not *deserve* to be called art from works which have *earned* that honorific title. I emphasize "deserve" and "earn" because aesthetic writing insists on a real moral difference between art and nonart. Aestheticians do not simply intend to classify things into useful categories, as we might classify species of plants, but rather to separate the deserving from the undeserving, and to do it definitively. They do not want to take an inclusive approach to art, counting in everything that conceivably might have some interest or value. They look, instead, for a defensible way to leave some things out. The logic of the enterprise—the bestowing of honorific titles—requires them to rule some things out, for there is no special honor in a title every conceivable object or activity is entitled to. The practical consequences of their work require the same exclusionary approach, for distributors, audiences, and all the other participants in an art world look to aestheticians for a way of making hard decisions about resources in a clearcut and defensible, rather than fuzzy and arguable, way.

Aestheticians might well argue that they do not intend to make evaluative judgments at all, but simply to arrive at a clearcut delineation of the categories of art and nonart. Since all the societies in which aestheticians engage in this activity use *art* as an honorific term, the very making of the distinction will inevitably assist in the evaluation of potential candidates for the status of art work. Aestheticians need not be cynical participants in art world conspiracies for their work to have this utility.

That aesthetic positions frequently arise in the course of fighting for the acceptance of something new does not alter the situation. Such positions, too, need to show that some things are not art in order to justify the claim that something else is. Aesthetics which declare that everything is art do not satisfy people who create or use them in the life of an art world.

AESTHETICS AND ORGANIZATION

The rest of what aestheticians and critics do is to provide a running revision of the value-creating theory which, in the form of criticism, continuously adapts the premises of the theory to the works artists actually produce. Artists produce new work in response not only to the considerations of formal aesthetics but also in response to the traditions of the art worlds in which they participate, traditions which can profitably be viewed (Kubler, 1962) as sequences of problem definitions and solutions; in response to suggestions implicit in other traditions, as in the influence of African art on Western painting; in response to the possibilities contained in new technical developments; and so on. An existing aesthetic needs to be kept up to date so that it continues to validate logically what audiences experience as important art work and thus to keep alive and consistent the connection between what has already been validated and what is now being proposed.

Aesthetic principles and systems, being part of the package of interdependent practices that make up an art world, will both influence and be influenced by such aspects of it as the training of potential artists and viewers, financial and other modes of support, and the modes of distribution and presentation of works. They will especially be influenced by a pressure for consistency implicit in the idea of art.

Art is too crude a concept to capture what is at work in these situations. Like other complex concepts, it disguises a generalization about the nature of reality. When we try to define it, we find many anomalous cases, cases which meet some, but not all, of the criteria implied or expressed by the concept. When we say "art," we usually mean something like this: a work which has aesthetic value, however that is defined; a work justified by a coherent and defensible aesthetic; a work recognized by appropriate people as having aesthetic value; a work displayed in the appropriate places (hung in museums, played at concerts). In many instances, however, works have some, but not all, of these attributes. They are exhibited and valued, but do not have aesthetic value, or have aesthetic value but are not exhibited and valued by the right people. The generalization contained in the concept of art suggests that these all co-occur in the real world; when they do not co-occur we have the definitional troubles which have always plagued the concept.

Some participants in art worlds try to minimize these in-consistencies by bringing theory and practice into line so that there are fewer anomalous cases. Others, who wish to upset the status quo, insist on the anomalies. To illustrate the point, consider this question: How many great (or excellent, or good) works of art are there? I am not concerned with fixing a number myself, nor do I think the number (however we might calculate it) is important. But looking at that question will make clear the interaction of aesthetic theories and art world organizations.

In 1975, Bill Arnold organized The Bus Show, an exhibition of photographs to be displayed on five hundred New York City buses (Arnold and Carlson, 1978). He intended by this means "to present excellent photographs in a public space" and thus to bring good art photography to a much larger audience than it ordinarily reaches and to allow many more photographers' work to be seen than ordinarily would be (see figure 14). The photographs were to be displayed in the space ordinarily used for advertising; to fill the advertising space on one bus required 17 photographs of varying sizes from nine to sixteen inches in height. To fill five hundred buses thus required 8,500 photographs, all of them to be current work by contemporary photographers.

Are there actually 8,500 excellent contemporary photo-graphs which merit that kind of public display? To ask the question presupposes an aesthetic and a critical position from which we could evaluate photographs, deciding which ones were or weren't of sufficiently high quality. Without attempting to specify the content of such an aesthetic, imag-ine a simplified case. Suppose quality is a unidimensional attribute such that we can rank all photographs as having more or less of it. (In fact, competent members of the art photography world, even those who belong to one of its many competing segments, use a large and varied assort-ment of dimensions in judging photographs.) We can then easily tell whether any photograph is better than, worse than, or equal to any other. But we would still not know how many were worthy of public display, how many merited being called "great" or "excellent" or "beautiful," how many de-

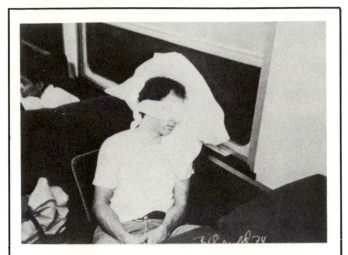

The Bus Show

There will be an exhibition of photographs in 500 New York City public buses in May of 1975. The purpose of the show is to present excellent photographs in a public space. All prints will appear with the photographer's name and the picture's title.

Photographs accepted for the exhibition will become part of the permanent collection of the Library of Congress. Send duplicate prints of each photograph you wish to submit; one print will go on a bus, the other to the Library of Congress. You must state what rights you grant to the Library of Congress with each photograph: loan, reproduction, or neither without your specific approval.

You may submit photographs to be considered for one person shows or as part of the group exhibit. Since the photographs will be placed in the interior advertising space of the buses there are certain size requirements, and in the case of one person shows, a specific number of photographs are needed to fill the available spaces. If you are submitting for group exhibition, send us any number of photographs in any of the size categories. For one person shows, you must submit the exact number of photographs needed to fill a bus, in each of the size categories. The size requirements and number of photographs for each bus is as follows: 14 photographs with an image height of 9 inches; one horizontal photograph with an image height of 13 inches; two verticals with an image height of 16 inches. Photographs not accepted for one person shows will automatically be juried as part of the group exhibition.

All work must be unmounted and untrimmed. Remember to submit duplicate prints of each photograph. Work not accepted will be returned if postage is included. On the back of each print write your name, the picture's title, and the rights you grant to the Library of Congress. Enclose a 3" x 5" file card with your name, address, and phone number. Mail prints to: Bus Show, Photography Department, Pratt Institute, Brooklyn, New York 11205. For information call (212) 636-3573. The deadline for submission is March 1, 1975.

This exhibition is made possible with support from the New York State Council on the Arts. Poster © 1975 by Pratt Institute. Photograph by Bill Arnold.

FIGURE 14. Poster advertising The Bus Show. The Bus Show, organized by Bill Arnold in 1975, proposed to exhibit 8,500 contemporary photographs of high artistic quality in the advertising spaces on New York City buses. Arnold gathered material for the show by advertising to art photographers. (Courtesy Bill Arnold.)

served inclusion in a museum collection or mention in a comprehensive history of art photography.

To make those judgments requires establishing a necessarily arbitrary cutoff point. Even if a substantial break at some point in an otherwise smooth distribution makes it easy to see a major difference on either side of it, using such a break as the cutoff point would be practically justifiable but logically arbitrary. But aesthetic systems propose and justify such judgments and divisions of existing art works all the time. In fact, The Bus Show shocked the photography world by implying that the line could justifiably be drawn where it would have to be drawn in order to fill all five hundred buses, and not where it would more conventionally be drawn (if we wanted to have a show of the best in contemporary photography we might include, if we followed current museum practice, one to two hundred prints).

If aesthetic systems justify dividing art works into those worthy of display or performance and those not, that will influence and be influenced by the institutions and organizations in which such displays and performances occur. Institutions have some leeway in the amount of work they can present to the public, but not much. Existing facilities (concert halls, art galleries and museums, and libraries) have finite amounts of space, existing canons of taste limit the use to which that space can be put (we no longer feel it appropriate to hang paintings floor to ceiling in the manner of the Paris Salon), and audience expectations and conventionalized attention spans impose further limits (more music could be performed if audiences would sit through six-hour instead of two-hour concerts, although the financial problems, given current union wage scales, would make that impossible anyway). Existing facilities can always be expanded by building and organizing more, but at any particular time there is only so much space or time and only so many works can be displayed.

The aesthetic of the world which has such facilities at its disposal can fix the point on our hypothetical one dimension of quality so as to produce just the number of works for which there is exhibition space. It can fix the standard so that there are fewer works to be displayed or rewarded than there is room for (as when an award committee decides that no work is worthy of a prize this year). Or it can fix the standard so that many more works are judged adequate than there is room for. Either of the latter two situations throws into doubt the adequacy of the art world's institutional apparatus, the validity of its aesthetic, or both. There is, thus, some pressure for an aesthetic standard flexible enough to produce approximately the amount of work for which the organizations have room and, conversely, for the institutions to generate the amount of exhibition opportunity required by the works the aesthetic certifies as being of the appropriate quality.

The distribution system itself requires materials to distribute, generating a further pressure for changes in aesthetic judgments in the form of rediscoveries of works and artists hitherto not rated very highly. Moulin points out that Old Masters and other "consecrated" paintings of unquestioned value increasingly move into private and museum collections and disappear from the market made by dealers and galleries. She quotes a French dealer:

> It is impossible to make money selling Renoir if you do not belong to the great dynasty of dealers. Since they can only be found with difficulty, the paintings still in circulation reach such prices that it is impossible to build up a stock of them. Dealers then become the intermediaries between two collectors or between a collector and a museum. Rediscoveries are due to the fact that what has already been discovered can no longer be found. (Moulin, 1967, p. 435, my translation)

A rediscovery consists of a campaign to call to the attention of potential buyers artists whose work is still relatively available and thus sells at a reasonable price.

Moulin points out the role of specialists in aesthetic judgments in this process:

> The revaluation of certain styles and certain genres is not independent of the efforts of specialists, historians or museum curators. . . . [There is an] involuntary collaboration between intellectual research and commercial initiatives in the rediscovery and launching of artistic values of the past.

The judgments of connoisseurs give authority, but successive generations of specialists do not illuminate the same sectors of the past. Many factors can contribute to changing the direction of their curiosity. ... The mercantile aspects are situated at the level of consequences, not causes. Historians turn away from fields already well swept by erudition where, in the present state of research, attempts to overturn chronology and appreciation are condemned to defeat. They are attracted to the zones of shadow. (Moulin, 1967, p. 430, my translation)

So art historians discover value in previously unstudied painters just as dealers look for such works to sell. Moulin mentions exhibits devoted to the friends of already famous artists and quotes the following:

Kikoïne, born on May 31, 1892 in Gomel, was part of the famous group of the Zborowski Gallery, of whom he and Kremegne were, at the time, the most expensive. Since then, the other members of the group—Modigliani, Pascin, Soutine— have died and their works can only be found at very high prices. The Gallery Romanet will devote large exhibits to the two survivors: the first to Kikoïne, at the beginning of June, the second to Kremegne, during the 1957–58 season. (Moulin, 1967, p. 438, quoting from *Connaissance des Arts*, no. 64, June 15, 1957, p. 32, my translation)

A further rough agreement between the amount of work judged interesting or worthwhile and the amount of room in the distribution system comes about when artists devote themselves to work for which there is room, withdrawing their efforts from media and formats which are "filled up." Insofar as aesthetic systems change their criteria to produce the number of certified works an art world's distributive mechanisms can accommodate, even the most absolute of them, those which most resolutely draw a strict line between art and nonart, in fact practice a relativism which defeats that aim.

When new styles of art emerge they compete for available space, in part by proposing new aesthetic standards according to which their work merits display in existing facilities. They also create new facilities, as in the case of The Bus

FIGURE 15. The Bus Show, installed. Because no one could know where any particular photograph was at any particular time, The Bus Show could not really be reviewed, and no artist could gain much in reputation from participating in it. (Courtesy of Afterimage, Visual Studies Workshop.)

Show (see figure 15). (New facilities do not do all the jobs people want them to do. The Bus Show had the great disadvantage that it could hardly help build anyone's reputation. Since no one knew where the bus carrying the work of specific photographers was at any particular time, critics could not review them, unless they happened on the work by accident, and friends and fellow artists could not see it either.) Art worlds differ in their flexibility, in the ease with which they can increase the number of works easily available for public inspection in conventional facilities. Modern societies have relatively little trouble accommodating vast amounts of printed material in libraries (although not in easily accessible bookstores [Newman, 1973]). Music can similarly be distributed in recorded performances in large amounts. But live performances of musical works of various kinds have so few outlets that it becomes reasonable for people to compose music solely for recordings, even to the extent of relying on effects which cannot be produced live, but require the mechanisms of an elaborately outfitted studio.

THE INSTITUTIONAL THEORY OF AESTHETICS: AN EXAMPLE

This book, focusing as it does on questions of social organization, does not attempt to develop a sociologically based theory of aesthetics. In fact, from the perspective just sketched, it is clear that developing an aesthetic in the world of sociology would be an idle exercise, since only aesthetics developed in connection with the operations of art worlds are likely to have much influence in them. (Gans, 1974, is an interesting attempt by a sociologist to develop an aesthetic, especially in relation to the question of the aesthetic value of mass-media works.)

Ironically enough, a number of philosophers have produced a theory that, if it is not sociological, is sufficiently based on sociological considerations to let us see what such a theory might look like. This institutional theory of aesthetics, as it has come to be called, can serve as an example of the process just analyzed—the development of a new aesthetic to take account of work the art world has already accepted. Perhaps equally ironically, a more sociological conception of an art world than that theory contains provides solutions to some of its problems, and I have detoured from the main line of my argument long enough to suggest those solutions. (For a more abstract sociological explication of the theory, see Donow, 1979.)

The preceding analysis suggests that new theories, rivaling, extending, or amending previous ones, arise when older theories fail to give an adequate account of the virtues of work widely accepted by knowledgeable members of the relevant art world. When an existing aesthetic does not legitimate logically what is already legitimate in other ways, someone will construct a theory that does. (What I say here should be understood as pseudohistory, indicating in a narrative form some relationships which may or may not have arisen exactly as I say they did.)

Thus, putting it crudely, for a long time works of visual art could be judged on the basis of an imitative theory, according to which the object of visual art was to imitate nature. At some point that theory no longer explained well-regarded new works of art—Monét's haystacks and cathedrals, for instance, even when rationalized as experiments in capturing the relationship between light and color. An expressive theory of art then found the virtues of works in their ability to communicate and express the emotions, ideas, and personalities of the artists who made them. That theory in turn had to be repaired or replaced so that it could deal with geometric abstraction, action painting, and other works that did not make sense in its terms (similarly, neither these theories nor their analogues would be able to say anything useful about aleatory music).

The institutional theory aims to solve the problems raised by works that outrage both commonsense and finer sensibilities by showing no trace of the artist at all, either in skill or intention. Institutional theorists concern themselves with works like the urinal or the snowshovel exhibited by Marcel Duchamp (see figure 16), whose only claim to being art apparently lay in Duchamp's signature on them, or the Brillo boxes exhibited by Andy Warhol (see figure 17). The commonsense critique of these works is that anyone could have done them, that they require no skill or insight, that they do not imitate anything in nature because they are nature, that they do not express anything interesting because they are no more than commonplace objects. The critique of those with finer sensibilities is much the same.

Nevertheless, those works gained great renown in the world of contemporary visual art, inspiring many more works like them. Confronted by this fait accompli, aestheticians developed a theory that placed the artistic character and quality of the work outside the physical object itself. They found those qualities, instead, in the relation of the objects to an existing art world, to the organizations in which art was produced, distributed, appreciated, and discussed.

FIGURE 16. *Marcel Duchamp,* In Advance of the Broken Arm. *Duchamp's "readymades," created when he signed some already-existing artifact, outraged both commonsense and critical sensibilities. (Yale University Art Gallery, Gift of Katherine S. Dreier for the Collection Société Anonyme.)*

FIGURE 17. Andy Warhol, Brillo. *Pop Art works provoked the criticism that anyone could have done them, that they did not require or embody the special gifts of the artist. (Photograph courtesy of the Castelli Archives.)*

Arthur Danto and George Dickie have presented the most important statements of the institutional theory. Danto dealt with the essence of art, with what in the relation between object and art world made that object art. In a famous statement of the problem, he said:

> To see something as art requires something the eye cannot descry—an atmosphere of artistic theory, a knowledge of the history of art: an artworld. (Danto, 1964, p. 580)

The theory out of which the idea of making the Brillo box came, the relation of that idea to other ideas about what makes art works art and to the other objects those works inspired—all of these make a context in which the making of the Brillo box and the box itself become art because that context gives them that sort of meaning. In another version:

> The moment something is considered an artwork, it becomes subject to an *interpretation*. It owes its existence as an artwork to this, and when its claim to art is defeated, it loses its interpretation and becomes a mere thing. The interpretation is in some measure a function of the artistic context of the work: it means something different depending on its art-historical location, its antecedents, and the like. As an artwork, finally, it acquires a structure which an object photographically similar to it is simply disqualified from sustaining if it is a real thing. Art exists in an atmosphere of interpretation and an artwork is thus a vehicle of interpretation. (Danto, 1973, p. 15)

Dickie deals with organizational forms and mechanisms. According to his definition:

> A work of art in the classificatory sense is 1) an artifact 2) a set of the aspects of which has had conferred upon it the status of candidate for appreciation by some person or persons acting on behalf of a certain social institution (the artworld). (Dickie, 1975, p. 34)

A sizable and interesting secondary literature has grown up around this point of view, criticizing and amplifying it (Cohen, 1973; Sclafani, 1973a and 1973b; Blizek, 1974; Danto, 1974; Mitias, 1975; Silvers, 1976). (Sociologists will see a family resemblance between the institutional theory of art and the various sociological theories which make their subject matter the way social definitions create reality (e.g., the so-called labeling theory of deviance [see Becker, 1963]), for both see the character of their subject matter as depending on the way people acting collectively define it.)

Philosophers tend to argue from hypothetical examples, and the "artworld" Dickie and Danto refer to does not have much meat on its bones, only what is minimally necessary to make the points they want to make. Nor do the criticisms made of their positions often refer to the character of existing art worlds or ones which have existed, emphasizing instead logical inconsistencies in the constructs used in the theory. None of the participants in these discussions develops as organizationally complicated a conception of what an art world is as does this book, although my description is not incompatible with their arguments. If we use a more complicated and empirically based notion of an art world, however, we can make headway on some problems in which the philosophical discussion has bogged down, thus perhaps being helpful to aetheticians and simultaneously deepening the analysis of the role of aesthetics in an art world.

Who?

Who can confer on something the status of candidate for appreciation, and thus ratify it as art? Who can act on behalf of that social institution, the art world? Dickie settles this question boldly. He describes the art world as having core personnel who can act on its behalf:

> A loosely organized, but nevertheless related, set of persons including artists . . . , producers, museum directors, museum-goers, theater-goers, reporters for newspapers, critics for publications of all sorts, art historians, art theorists, philosophers of art, and others. These are the people who keep the machinery of the artworld working and thereby provide for its continuing existence. (Dickie, 1975, pp. 35–36)

But he also insists that:

> In addition, every person who sees himself as a member of the artworld is thereby a member. (Dickie, 1975, p. 36)

That last sentence, of course, warns aestheticians that Dickie's approach will probably not help them distinguish the deserving from the undeserving; this definition is going to be too broad. They cannot accept the implications of Dickie's remark, that the representatives of the art world who will be conferring the honorific status of art on objects are self-appointed, and express their discontent in a rash of humorous examples. What if a zookeeper decides that he is a member of the art world and, in that capacity, confers the status of candidate for appreciation, and thus of art work, on the elephant he tends? That couldn't really make the elephant a work of art, could it? Because, after all, the zookeeper really couldn't act on behalf of the art world, could he? We all know the answers: the elephant just isn't an art work (Dickie, 1971; Blizek, 1974).

But how do we know that? We know it because we have a commonsense understanding of the organization of art worlds. A relevant feature of organized art worlds is that, however their position is justified, some people are commonly seen by many or most interested parties as more entitled to speak on behalf of the art world than others; the entitlement stems from their being recognized by the other participants in the cooperative activities through which that world's works are produced and consumed as the people entitled to do that. Whether other art world members accept them as capable of deciding what art is because they have more experience, because they have an innate gift for recognizing art, or simply because they are, after all, the people in charge of such things and therefore ought to know— whatever the reason, what lets them make the distinction and make it stick is that the other participants agree that they should be allowed to do it.

Sociological analysts need not decide who is entitled to label things art (or, to use Dickie's language, to confer the status of candidate for appreciation). We need only observe who members of the art world treat as capable of doing that, who they allow to do it in the sense that once those people have decided something is art others act as though it is.

Some common features of art worlds show that the philosophical desire to be able to decide definitively between art and nonart cannot be satisfied by the institutional theory. For one thing, participants seldom agree completely on who is entitled to speak on behalf of the art world as a whole. Some people occupy institutional positions which allow them, de facto, to decide what will be acceptable. Museum directors, for instance, could decide whether photography was an art because they could decide whether or not to exhibit photographs in their museums. They could even decide what kind of art (e.g., "minor" or whatever the opposite of that is) photography was by deciding whether photographs would be exhibited in the main galleries in which paintings were ordinarily exhibited or confined to a special place with less prestige in which only photographs were shown. But other participants argue that museum directors are incompetent to make the judgments they do make, that in a better world they would not be allowed to make such judgments, because they are ignorant, prejudiced, or influenced by extraneous considerations. Some think they are too avant-garde and do not give proper attention to established styles and genres, others just the opposite (see Haacke, 1976). Many participants find institutional officials unacceptable arbiters because of substantial evidence which shows that they represent the rich and powerful of the communities they serve (see Catalog Committee, 1977; Haacke, 1976; Becker and Walton, 1976), their decisions thus representing class bias as much as aesthetic logic.

Art world members also disagree over whether the decisions of occupants of certain positions really make any difference. This disagreement reflects the ambiguous position of those people in the art world. It is frequently just not clear whether a particular critic's decision has any consequence, whether others base their own activities on that decision, and very often that depends on a variety of contingencies that arise from political shifts and struggles within the art world. Insofar as art world members find the status of whatever pronouncements they make ambiguous, the status of such people as critics, dealers, and prize and fellowship committees is equally ambiguous. The ambiguity, not remediable by philosophic or social analysis, is there because the people whose deference would ratify the status defer sporadically and erratically.

Thus, the institutional theory cannot produce the all-or-nothing judgments aestheticians would like to make about whether works are or are not art. Since the degree of consensus about who can decide what art is varies greatly from one situation to another, a realistic view reflects that by allowing art-ness, whether or not an object is art, to be a continuous variable rather than an all-or-nothing dichotomy.

Likewise, art worlds vary in the kinds of activities by their members which embody and ratify the assigning of the status of art to an object or event. On the one hand, such material benefits as the award of fellowships, prizes, commissions, display space, and other exhibition opportunities (publications, productions, etc.) have the immediate consequence of helping the artist to continue producing work. On the other hand, more intangible benefits, such as being taken seriously by the more knowledgeable members of the art world, have indirect but important consequences for artistic careers, placing the recipient in the flow of ideas in which change and development take place and providing day-to-day validation of work concerns and help with daily problems, things denied those who are merely successful in more conventional career terms.

What?

What characteristics must an object have to be a work of art? The institutional theory suggests that anything may be capable of being appreciated. In fact, in response to a critic who says that some objects—"ordinary thumbtacks, cheap white envelopes, the plastic forks given at some drive-in restaurants"—just cannot be appreciated (Cohen, 1973, p. 78), Dickie says:

> But why cannot the ordinary qualities of *Fountain* [the urinal Duchamp exhibited as a work of art; see figure 18]—its gleaming white surface, the depth revealed when it reflects images of surrounding objects, its pleasing oval shape—be appreciated. It has qualities similar to those of works by Brancusi and Moore which many do not balk at saying they appreciate. Similarly, thumbtacks, envelopes, and plastic forks have qualities that can be appreciated if one makes the effort to focus attention on them. One of the values of photography is its ability to focus on and bring out the qualities of quite ordinary objects. And the same sort of thing can be done

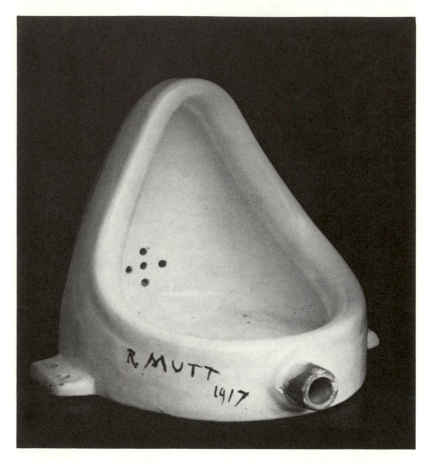

FIGURE 18. Marcel Duchamp, Fountain. *Aestheticians disagree about what qualities a work of visual art must have to be art. Can the physical properties of a work like* Fountain *be appreciated? (Photograph courtesy of the Sidney Janis Gallery, New York.)*

without the benefit of photography just by looking. (Dickie, 1975, p. 42)

Can anything at all be turned into art, just by someone's saying so?

it cannot be this simple: even if in the end it is successful christening which makes an object art, not every attempt at christening is successful. There are bound to be conditions to be met both by the namer and the thing being named, and if

they are completely unsatisfied, then saying "I christen . . ."
will not be to christen. (Cohen, 1973, p. 80)

Cohen is right: not every attempt to label something art is successful. But it does not follow that there are therefore some constraints on the nature of the object or event itself which make certain objects ipso facto not art and incapable of being redefined in that way.

The constraints on what can be defined as art which un-doubtedly exist in any specific art world arise from a prior consensus on what kinds of standards will be applied, and by whom, in making those judgments. Art world members characteristically, despite doctrinal and other differences, produce reliable judgments about which artists and works are serious and therefore worthy of attention. Thus, jazz players who disagree over stylistic preferences can neverthe-less agree on whether a given performer or performance "swings," and theater people make similarly reliable judg-ments of whether a particular scene "works" or not. Artists may disagree violently over which works and their makers should receive support, and marginal cases (especially those in styles just being incorporated into the conventional prac-tice of the art world or those on the verge of being thrown out as no longer worthy of serious consideration) will provoke less reliable judgments. But most judgments are reliable, and that reliability reflects not the mouthing of already agreed-on judgments, but the systematic application of similar stan-dards by trained and experienced members of the art world; it is what Hume described in his essay on taste, and resem-bles the way most doctors, confronted with a set of clinical findings, will arrive at a similar diagnosis (analogies can be found in every area of specialized work).

In that sense, not everything can be made into a work of art just by definition or the creation of consensus, for not everything will pass muster under currently accepted art world standards. But this does not mean that there is any more to making something art than christening it. The entire art world's agreeing on standards some works meet so clearly that their classification as art is as self-evident as the way others fail to meet them is also a matter of christening;

the consensus arises because reasonable members of the world have no difficulty classifying works under those circumstances. Constraints on what can be defined as art exist, but they constrain because of the conjunction of the characteristics of objects and the rules of classification current in the world in which they are proposed as art works.

Furthermore, those standards, being matters of consensus, change. Much of the running dialogue of artists and other participants in art worlds has to do with making day-to-day adjustments in the content and application of standards of judgment. In the early 1930s jazz players, critics, and aficionados all agreed that electrical instruments could not produce real music. Charlie Christian's performances on the electric guitar convinced so many people that his playing produced the same sort of experience as music played on nonelectrical instruments that the canon was quickly revised.

How Much?

Aestheticians, both the institutionalists and their critics, worry about the effect of aesthetic theorizing on artists and art worlds. They fear, for instance, that a too-restrictive aesthetic theory would unnecessarily depress artists and might unduly constrict their creativity. This overestimates the degree to which art worlds take their direction from aesthetic theorizing; the influence usually runs in the other direction. But the institutionalists draw one important implication from their analysis: if practicing artists want their work accepted as art, they will have to persuade the appropriate people to certify it as art. (While the basic institutional analysis suggests that anyone can do that, in practice these theorists accept the existing art world as the one which has to be persuaded to do the job.) But if art is what an art world ratifies as art, an alternative exists, one analyzed in more detail in a later chapter, the strategy of organizing de novo an art world which will ratify as art what one produces. In fact, the strategy has been used often and with considerable success. Many more people have tried it and failed, but that doesn't mean it is not a reasonable possibility.

Several difficulties arise in creating a new art world to ratify work which finds no home in existing art worlds. Resources (especially financial support) will already have been allocated to existing artistic activities, so that one needs to develop new sources of support, pools of personnel, sources of materials, and other facilities (including space in which to perform and display works). Since existing aesthetic theories have not ratified the work, a new aesthetic must be developed, and new modes of criticism and standards of judgment enunciated. To say that these things must be done, however, raises an interesting definitional question of the kind philosophical analysis provokes. How much of the apparatus of an organized art world must be created before the work in question will be treated seriously by a larger audience than the original group who wanted to create the new world? What it takes to convince people will vary a great deal. Some require an elaborate ideological explanation. Others—theater managers, operators of recording studios, and printers—only ask that their bills be paid.

The question of how much institutional apparatus is required to satisfy the definition need not, indeed should not, be answered by setting some specific criterion or precise point on a continuum. The activities involved can be carried on by varying numbers of people, and without the full-blown institutional apparatus of such well-equipped worlds as surround contemporary sculpture and painting or symphonic music and grand opera. When we speak of art worlds, we usually have in mind these well-equipped ones, but in fact paintings, books, music, and all sorts of other artistic objects and performances can be produced without all the support personnel these worlds depend on: critics, impresarios, furnishers of materials and equipment, providers of space, and audiences. At an extreme, remember, any artistic activity can be done by one person, who performs all the necessary activities; this is not common and not a condition many artists aspire to (though one they sometimes yearn for when they have trouble with their fellow participants). As the number of people involved grows, the activity reaches a point where some stable nucleus of people cooperates regularly to produce the same sort of work; as the number grows larger, it may reach a point at which individual artists can produce work for a large audience of people they don't know personally and still have a reasonable expectation of being taken seriously. Call the first point of organization an esoteric world and the latter one exoteric. The names and the cutoff points matter less than the recognition that they are arbitrary, the reality being a variety of points that vary along several continua.

How Many?

Neither Dickie nor Danto is very clear as to how many art worlds there are. Dickie says:

> The artworld consists of a bundle of systems: theater, painting, literature, music, and so on, each of which furnishes an institutional background for the conferring of status on objects within its domain. No limit can be placed on the number of systems that can be brought under the generic conception of art, and each of the major subsystems contains further subsystems. These features of the artworld provide the elasticity whereby creativity of even the most radical sort can be accommodated. A whole new system comparable to the theater, for example, could be added in one fell swoop. What is more likely is that a new subsystem would be added within a system. For example, junk sculpture added within sculpture, happenings added within theater. Such additions might in time develop into full-blown systems. (Dickie, 1975, p. 33)

Blizek (1974) sees that this is an empirical question, but also sees that the definition of "art world" is so loose that it is not clear whether there is one art world, of which these are subparts, or a number of them possibly unrelated and, furthermore, that if there are a number of art worlds they might conflict. Several remarks are relevant here.

Empirically, the subworlds of the various art media may be subdivided into separate and almost noncommunicating segments. I have spoken of schools and styles as though they competed for the same rewards and audiences (and will again, in discussing processes of change in art worlds), but often they do not. Instead, members of one group develop audiences and sources of support from sectors of the society that would not have supported the other art world segments with which they might compete. Many painting worlds rely on the same suppliers as recognized contemporary artists for materials, but have separate, and often very successful, arrangements for exhibiting, distributing, and supporting their work. The Cowboy Artists of America, for instance, produce paintings for people who would like to buy the work of Charles Russell and Frederick Remington, genre painters of the American cowboy West who are exhibited in "real" museums, but can't afford them or can't find any to buy.

> Despite determined inattention by Eastern art critics, cowboy painting and sculpture are so popular that their prices are inflating faster than intrastate natural gas. Cowboy art has its own heroes, its own galleries and even its own publishing house. (Lichtenstein, 1977, p. 41)

At an extreme, much of the apparatus of an art world can develop around the work of a single artist, in relative isolation from the larger, recognized world of that medium. All that is needed is someone to provide the resources. Consider the case of Edna Hibel. Although her work has been exhibited in a number of reputable places over the years, she does not have a major reputation among contemporary artists or collectors. Nevertheless, an entire museum is devoted to her work:

> The Hibel Museum of Art, Palm Beach, is the inspiration of Ethelbelle and Clayton B. Craig. Long Edna Hibel's foremost collectors, the Craigs conceived the Hibel Museum to be the permanent repository for their world famous collection of Hibel art.... On their first visit [in 1961] to the then newly opened Hibel Gallery in Rockport, Massachusetts, Ethelbelle and Clayton Craig fell in love with Edna's art, and bought five Hibel paintings for their already extensive collection of art.... As the Craig collection grew, and their understanding and appreciation of the artist and her work deepened with the passing years of friendship and mutual respect, the Craigs' home became a virtual museum of Edna Hibel's art.... The

Craigs determined not to allow Edna Hibel's work to become so scattered that students, scholars and admirers would be deprived of the opportunity to view a significant cross section of her work in one location. From that moment on, they increased the tempo of their collecting, and broadened the scope of their acquisitions of the Hibel masterworks.... At long last, the Craigs' dream has been realized and the Hibel Museum of Art is a reality. The Craig Collection is the nucleus of an already growing body of Edna Hibel's work contributed by her enthusiastic admirers. Located in Palm Beach, the Hibel Museum stands as a living tribute to the Craigs' generosity, foresight, and dedication. (Hibel Museum of Art, 1977)

Regional segments, not so isolated as this, are usually oriented to the metropolitan centers of the "big" art world (McCall, 1977). Their participants suffer from a lack of exhibition opportunities, and even more from the sense that successes in their region will do them little or no good in the larger world they aspire to, a world almost totally unaware of them.

If we define art worlds by the activities their participants carry on collectively, we can ask what activities a general art world—one which encompasses all the conventional arts—might carry on collectively so that we might want to refer to it as one art world. I can think of two.

First, the various media-oriented subcommunities suffer from many of the same external constraints, which pose the same or similar problems for them. Thus, a depression might make it harder for all art forms to secure financial support (although this was not the experience of the Great Depression in the United States). A government might censor all the arts in a similar way, so that the experience of people in one area could be read as a sign of what could be expected in another. Thus a theatrical designer might decide what projects to undertake on the basis of whether he thought the censors would allow them to be staged, arriving at that assessment by hearing what they had done to a recording by a popular singer, a recent novel, or a new film. Insofar as the participants in all these worlds share experiences, interpretations, and predictions vis-à-vis the censors, they engage in a form of collective activity and thus constitute an art world. Should they combine to combat or protest censorship, or cooperate to circumvent it, they would in that way as well be engaging in the collective action that constitutes an art world.

Second, artists in various media-oriented worlds may try to achieve similar kinds of things in their work and may share ideas and perspectives on how to accomplish them. During periods of intense nationalism, artists may try to symbolize the character and aspirations of their country or people in their work. To do that, they have to find imagery and techniques which will convey the ideas and feelings they have in mind as well as finding the ideas and feelings themselves. Insofar as participants in various worlds debate these questions across media lines, they might be said to participate in one general art world.

Organizations for one medium often use people from other fields as support personnel for the work that is central in their own field. Visual artists create settings for theatrical and dance performances, writers produce librettos for operas, musicians compose and play backgrounds for films, and so on. When artists cooperate in that way across subworld lines, they might be said to be participating in a general art world. Furthermore, because of the possibility of such collaboration, people from worlds not already so connected may find it interesting to contemplate new forms of collaboration, thus creating further links in a general art world. Finally, participants in specific art worlds often come from a limited sector of the surrounding society, for instance the educated upper middle class or the petty aristocracy. They may have attended school together or come from families connected by kinship or friendship, and these connections will serve to create a general art world or, at least, to provide the regular interaction which might enable them to collaborate in the kinds of activities already mentioned.

The analysis of this problem makes it clear that speaking of art worlds means using shorthand. The term *art world*, remember, is just a way of talking about people who routinely participate in the making of art works. The routine interaction is what constitutes the art world's existence, so questions of definition can generally be resolved by looking at who actually does what with whom. In that way, the logical and definitional problems of the institutional aesthetic theory (which has a strong empirical component) can be resolved by knowledge of the facts of any particular case.

AESTHETICS AND ART WORLDS

The institutional theory of aesthetics, then, illustrates the process analyzed in the first part of this chapter. When an established aesthetic theory does not provide a logical and defensible legitimation of what artists are doing and, more important, what the other institutions of the art world —especially distribution organizations and audiences—accept as art, and as excellent art, professional aestheticians will provide the required new rationale. If they don't, someone else probably will, although the rest of the participants might just go ahead without a defensible rationale for their actions. (Whether one is required or not depends on the amount of argument over what they are doing they are confronted with.) Imitative and expressive theories of art and beauty failed to explain or give a rationale for the enjoyment and celebration of contemporary works of visual art widely regarded as excellent. Given the amount of argument and competition for resources and honors in the world of contemporary art, and the number of professional philosophers who might find the problem intriguing, it was almost certain that something like the institutional theory would be produced.

By shifting the locus of the definitional problem from something inherent in the object to a relation between the object and an entity called an art world, the institutional theory provided a new justification for the activities of contemporary artists, and an answer to the philosophically distressing questions leveled at their work, which asked for a demonstration of skill or beauty, thought or emotion, in the works regarded as excellent, and which wanted to know if the same works could not have been produced by a chimpanzee, child, insane person, or any ordinary member of the society without particular artistic talent. The latter suggestion—that anyone could do it—was perhaps most damaging. It implied that artists have no special gift or talent, and thus that the rationale for regarding them as special members of the art world (or the society), entitled by virtue of the display of that talent to special rewards, was fallacious. The institutional theory allows art world participants to define that special talent in a new way, as (for instance) the ability to invent imaginative new concepts, and thus gives legitimacy to the artist's special role and rewards.

Our analysis of the institutional theory adds some nuances to the description of art worlds. We see that art world officials have the power to legitimate work as art, but that power is often disputed. As a result, the aesthetician's desire for definitive criteria by which to distinguish art from nonart, criteria congruent with the actions of art world officials, cannot be satisfied. That is of some interest because aestheticians are not the only ones with such a desire. In fact, sociologists often insist that fields like the sociology of art or religion or science settle on some definitive criterion for their subject matter. If that criterion is expected to be congruent with either popular or official conceptions of art, the sociological wish for a definitive criterion is likewise unsatisfiable.

We see, too, that in principle any object or action can be legitimated as art, but that in practice every art world has procedures and rules governing legitimation which, while not clear-cut or foolproof, nevertheless make the success of some candidates for the status of art very unlikely. Those procedures and rules are contained in the conventions and patterns of cooperation by which art worlds carry on their routine activities.

We see how one might speak of all the arts as comprising one big art world. Insofar as members of specialized subworlds cooperate in some activities related to their work, that cooperative activity—be it vis-à-vis government censorship, the development of nationalist art, or multimedia collaboration—can be seen as the operation of one big art world. Such cooperation may be relatively uncommon, and probably is most of the time in any society, so that we might want to say that the operative art worlds are those of the particular media. However, this, like others, is an empirical question, whose answer will be found by research.

We see, finally, that aestheticians (or whoever does the job) provide the rationale by which art works justify their existence and distinctiveness, and thus their claim to support. Art and artists can exist without such a rationale, but have more trouble when others dispute their right to do so. Art worlds, as they develop, therefore usually produce that rationale, whose most specialized form is aesthetics and whose most specialized producer, the philosopher.

6 • Art and the State

States, and the governmental apparatus through which they operate, participate in the production and distribution of art within their borders. Legislatures and executives make laws, courts interpret them, and bureaucrats administer them. Artists, audiences, suppliers, distributors—all the varied personnel who cooperate in the production and consumption of works of art—act within the framework provided by those laws. Because states have a monopoly over making laws within their own borders (although not over the making of rules privately agreed to in smaller groups, so long as those rules do not violate any laws), the state always plays some role in the making of art works. Failing to exercise forms of control available to it through that monopoly, of course, constitutes an important form of state action.

Like other participants in the making of art works, the state and its agents act in pursuit of their own interests, which may or may not coincide with those of the artists making the works. Many states regard art as more or less a good thing—at the very least, as a sign of cultural development and national sophistication, along with modern highways and a national airline—and make laws and regulations

165

which favor the arts in various ways. When artists support their activities by turning their work into property of some kind, which they then exchange for money, the laws the state makes and enforces concerning property rights affect them directly. The state may even find it expedient to make special laws regarding the disposition of artistic property to protect artists' rights and reputations.

Other citizens may find artists' activities distasteful, alarming, or genuinely harmful. Other state laws—governing noise and pollution, or blasphemy and bad taste—may protect them against these artistic nuisances, and constrain the production of some kinds of art works.

Finally, the state always has an interest in the propensity of its citizens to mobilize or be mobilized for collective action. Political leaders usually believe that the symbolic representations embodied in both high and popular art affect whether citizens can be mobilized and for what ends. Revolutionary songs may provide the basis for revolutionary action; patriotic songs and films may reinforce existing beliefs and systems of stratification. Some art makes people discontented, destroys their moral fiber, and makes them unfit to play the roles and do the work the state wants done. Other art works implant and support habits and attitudes the state finds congenial or thinks necessary to its own goals.

Political and administrative leaders may be just as calculating as the above suggests. Just as frequently, their own aesthetic beliefs lead them to view what supports their political interests as great art or beautiful, and to see what might undermine their interests as bad art, or not even art, mere trash. The merging of politics and aesthetics thus affects what can be counted as art at all, the reputations of whole genres and media as well as those of individual artists. The interests of states vary, and their interests in art vary accordingly. An industrialized society's government may prize order and harmony over discord and "anarchy," while a developing society's leaders may be concerned that art will divert people from the hard work and steady habits thought essential to economic growth. One state may forbid art works which show racial mixture, while another encourages or even demands them.

The state pursues these interests both by supporting what it approves and by discouraging or forbidding what it disapproves—by intervening in the production of art it considers inimical to its interests, by censoring it partially or completely, even by imprisoning or killing those who produce or consume it.

PROPERTY

Many, but not all, societies treat art as a commodity which can be bought and sold like any other commodity. Artists and business people collaborate—as we have seen, often unwillingly and with great mutual mistrust—to produce objects and events which can be marketed, sold, and distributed under the laws the state provides for the regulation of such activities. In making and enforcing these laws, the state displays no particular interest in works of art as such. Its concern, rather, lies in creating the conditions for routine economic activity, art simply being one of the commodities traded.

The law conceives and treats property as a bundle of rights. The rights of the owner of a piece of property vary depending on the kind of property it is. Art works similarly vary in the way the law distributes rights in them to the several categories of people involved in their production.

The basic property right is a monopoly over the physical possession of the object. Artists who produce objects, like visual artists, typically sell the right to physical possession of a unique or semiunique object: a painting, sculpture, or one of a limited number of prints or photographs. The purchaser (or recipient of a gift) retains possession and may sell or give the right of possession to another person or to an institution. Some objects do not have that kind of unique value. A printed copy of a book has limited value (unless it is a scarce copy of an originally small edition); the work's value resides in the words, not the physical object they happen to be embodied in. (A literary work in the author's own hand, such that the calligraphy is an intrinsic part of it, would be unique; but even such works can be and are reproduced, so that many people can own copies of them.) When you buy a book you get the right to your copy, to read where and when you want. What the writer and publisher own is the right to print and sell copies for others to read.

Performing artists sell the right to be present at an event which consists of the artist doing something artistic: dancing, playing music, or acting. Their property rights consist in being able to prevent others from seeing or hearing what they do without paying for it (this was the basis of a suit by a circus performer to prevent a television station from broadcasting film clips of him being shot out of a cannon). Performing artists often perform works created by others (composers, playwrights, or choreographers), in which case the creator of the performed work can sell or license the right to perform it, in public or private, for profit or not.

When objects or performances are made into property to be sold, the legal system created by the state defines who has what to sell, and the conditions and terms under which the sale may occur.

Unique and semiunique objects pose problems of property rights, for both producers and consumers, different from those posed by works considered reproducible. The laws made and enforced by the state both create and solve (or fail to solve) these problems. For instance, the question of fakes arises in a different way in the two cases. A literary document may not be what it purports to be—may not, for instance, really be the autobiography of Howard Hughes—but the book you purchase will be a copy of the purported autobiography of Howard Hughes. On the other hand, unique objects, by definition scarce, acquire a value beyond that of objects of appreciation pure and simple. It then becomes worthwhile to create works which can be passed off as something other, more valuable, than what they really are. Fakers of paintings may add or change signatures, complete unfinished canvases, misrepresent the work of pupils or assistants as that of a more well-known master, copy an existing valuable painting, or fabricate a pastiche in the style of someone whose work has high value (Bauman, 1972, pp. 932–34). A legal scholar contends that existing laws do not protect buyers against being sold faked paintings:

Even though all states have enacted penal statutes that prohibit forgery, such statutes do not deal specifically with the creation or marketing of false paintings. The California statute is typical: anyone who signs the name of another with fraudulent intent or attempts to pass as genuine any forged writings is guilty of forgery. The statute deals primarily with forgery of writings or instruments such as checks or bank notes, while forged paintings are not mentioned. Even if the statute were amended to include paintings, numerous alternatives for faking paintings are left uncovered. (Bauman, 1972, p. 940)

The state, that is, has not enacted laws sufficiently oriented to art works, and the laws it has enacted, devoted mainly to protecting the integrity of commercial paper, do not do the job.

In comparison, art works produced in numerous copies—books, records, and films—create no problems of fakery, because no one has an incentive to produce fakes. The number of copies already available makes the value due to authenticity too little to make it worthwhile to expend the energy necessary to make a credible fake. Because there are so many, you can tell by simple comparison if you have what you want. But people do copy the original, not to defraud consumers, who get what they pay for, but rather to steal royalties from the owner of the rights of reproduction: the author, publisher, recording artist, or record company. These works create worries for the producer rather than the consumer.

The state creates legal protection in the form of copyright laws for artists whose work appears in multiple copies. Copyright is usually rationalized as the law of patents is, as a way of promoting invention or artistic creation by assuring the profits from the work to the worker by giving him a monopoly for a limited period. The laws assume that without such protection no one would expend the effort necessary to produce the works, whose production the state finds desirable and wishes to encourage. (That is not necessarily true; folk artists, as we will see later, do not participate in the market in such a way as to need or want such protection.)

The effect of copyright law on the content of works can be seen by examining the effects of its absence. As Wendy Griswold (1981) has shown, American novelists of the nineteenth century specialized in stories of adventure and the Wild West because publishers could get fiction of other popular kinds (e.g., novels of manners) more cheaply by pirating British novels, to whose authors they paid no royalties because there was at the time no effective international agreement on copyright.

Artists take advantage of these rights by contracting with business people—gallery owners, impresarios, and managers of culture industries—who, as we have seen, know how to turn aesthetic value into economic value and have the organizational means to do so. Financially ignorant, artists frequently discover that their contracts do not give them the benefits they expected; R. Serge Denisoff explains the situation of rock musicians:

> Most contracts include advances for signing as well as a percentage of the profits from record sales. . . . Many advances are against royalties, meaning that the $20,000 given an artist by Warner Brothers or Capitol Records will have to be repaid to the company before the act receives any income from a successful record. Other expenses such as studio, production and promotion costs, are frequently included in contracts as an advance against royalties. Advances vary from company to company and from artist to artist. MC5 received a $50,000 advance followed by $20,000; like the [Grateful] Dead, they found themselves $128,000 in debt to Atlantic Records. It is quite possible that an act with a poorly negotiated contract can have a gold record [with net domestic sales of one million dollars] and still not make any money. (Denisoff, 1975, pp. 68–70)

Like all contracts, artists' contracts with distributors rest on a basis of customary practice, which often nullifies the advantages they seem to provide. Moulin points out that French art dealers:

> have a tendency to deny . . . any legal value to the contract. They insist on the secondary character of the legal obligation in relation to the moral obligation. The contract is, according to them, a gentleman's agreement and what counts is per-

sonal loyalty and the value of one's word, much more than the legal significance of the agreement, which only perverts the close ties between people. . . . Their objective is to dissociate by all means the relations between artists and dealers from their economic and legal context. (Moulin, 1967, p. 322–23, my translation)

Not surprisingly, artists find this works to their disadvantage:

Artists, for their part, refer to the inequality of power existing between the contractors. . . . They estimate that the stocks accumulated by the dealer on the one hand and the solidarity between dealers on the other guarantee the latter against any eventual recourse by the artist, whatever might be the legal protections benefiting the authors of objects which are not simple commercial products, but rather the expression of a creative personality. . . . [Quoting a painter:] "And then, if you start a lawsuit, you would be sunk. It would not be easy to find another dealer to take you on after that. The dealers stick together on that point." (Moulin, 1967, p. 324, my translation)

As in the case of fakes, the law frequently does not specify rights clearly, and legal proceedings are necessary to establish who can do what with the work. The practice of publicizing popular records by having disk jockeys play them on the radio relied on legal interpretation:

The practice of broadcasting records was attractive, especially to smaller stations, considering the minimal investment necessary to fill air time. The opposition of sheet music publishers and a number of performers such as Fred Waring and Bing Crosby at the outset hampered the broadcasting of gramophone records, but did not end it. As Judge Learned Hand was to rule, copyright control ended with the sale of the record. Radio stations, therefore, "could not be restrained from using records in broadcasts." This interpretation of the 1909 copyright law, coupled with the publishers' realization that radio could provide a forum for their songs, uplifted the status of radio as the central avenue for public recognition of a songwriter's product. (Denisoff, 1975, p. 219)

Whether manufacturers could sell machinery with which private citizens could record films and other television programs similarly had to be settled by the courts.

The taxation policies of a country affect the production and distribution of art works. Moulin points out (1967, p. 58, citing Reitlinger, 1961) that English painting of the eighteenth century began to be collected in the United States after the 20 percent duty on classic works of art was repealed in 1909, and that modern French paintings began to be collected after the duty on contemporary works was abolished in 1913. She notes, in addition, that the speculation characteristic of the art markets she studied has been supported by the absence, in France, of a tax on capital gains and, in the United States, by the tax breaks available to collectors who donate works of art to public museums. Every change in such laws immediately affects the markets for art works and thus the professional lives of everyone involved in the relevant art world.

Much of what I have said is, of course, irrelevant to art worlds operating in countries which do not have a capitalist market economy. When economic activity is regulated by, for instance, a state bureaucracy, the rules of that bureaucracy define who has what kinds of rights in works of art and how those rights may be transferred. I am not familiar with any of these systems or their effects on the workings of art worlds. Insofar as artists become state employees, their situation might be similar to that of industrial scientists in the United States, whose inventions typically belong to the firms they work for.

In addition to creating the framework of property rights within which the routine economic activities of art worlds can go on (and thus providing the legal basis for distribution organizations), governments can (although they often do not) make laws which protect artists' reputations by safeguarding the link between the person and the work on which those reputations are based. Suppose I know just what an artist intended in a work—not so easy to know—can I, legally or morally, alter it just because I own it? If I sell you my painting can you paint a mustache on one of the figures in it, as Duchamp did on a reproduction of the Mona Lisa? Or, once you have bought the work, can I come to your home and demand the right to alter it?

Art worlds allow the alteration of art works when the

changes do not affect the artist's reputation, and condemn it when the changes will confuse our judgment and put assessments of the artist in doubt. Art world participants define art works as the product of someone's personal vision, mediated by his skill, taste, and sensibility. Art worlds produce, maintain, and destroy reputations on the basis of the assessments their members make of the works artists present as representing them at their best; your reputation as an artist depends on your work, insofar as that work, given the conditions of its creation, can be viewed as your responsibility. If other people change your work (if, under some circumstances, you change it yourself), it no longer truly reflects your artistry (or lack of it) and cannot be the basis for reputational judgments.

Because works affect reputations, artists usually refuse to release them for public consideration (whatever form that takes in their world) until they are prepared to accept the world's judgment of them. This is one of the few places the law sometimes affects the making of reputations. French law (which, Moulin remarks, gives the artist more precise and extended guarantees than the law of other countries) recognizes the "moral rights of the artist," which include the right not to have one's work altered and the right not to have unfinished work circulated, both rights linked to the act of creation. Moulin cites the suit painter Georges Roualt brought against the heirs of Ambrose Vollard, the well-known art dealer, to recover 819 unsigned paintings he had signed over to the dealer. She quotes court decisions which, despite the agreement Roualt had signed, concluded that:

> the sale of an unfinished canvas does not transfer the property since, until it has achieved the degree of perfection of which the painter is the sole judge, he can repent having painted a work he thinks unworthy of his genius and deny entirely that what he has created is the materialization of his thought. (Quoted in Moulin, 1967, p. 326, my translation)

The link the court found is one that participants in art worlds believe in, especially in the visual arts, where works are so frequently unique objects. That explains the strong emotion aroused when people do in fact change works. Clement

Greenberg created a storm of protest when he repainted a David Smith sculpture; others said Smith had intended the sculpture to weather and that Greenberg was interfering with that intention. In a different kind of case, Robert Rauschenberg created a strong aesthetic effect with very simple means, by manipulating this feeling: he erased, with the artist's consent, a drawing by Willem DeKooning. The result gets its effect less from its appearance than from the action it records.

Because the work forms the basis of the maker's reputation, art world participants believe that artists themselves ought not to change a work once released to the world. It is as though artists who did that were trying to cheat in the reputational game they are playing with history, withdrawing or altering what has been judged inferior so that the world's final judgment will rest on a revised, incomplete body of work that shows only their best side.

Art world participants do not ask for legal protection when alterations in the work leave the original version still available for inspection and evaluation. Literary artists frequently do what visual artists are usually not allowed to do: they revise their work and may even do their best to suppress earlier versions of which they no longer approve, buying up editions and refusing permission to print items to which they hold the copyright. Henry James rewrote his novels extensively for the collected edition. Composers do the same; Stravinsky redid many of his works years after they were composed. In these cases, of course, the printings and recordings of earlier versions are still available, so that the artist's reputation simply has a new work added to it. No unique object has been destroyed by the act; a new one has instead been added to what is available.

Similarly, no one requires legal protection for reputations when, as in the performing arts, responsibility can be spread among the participants, some being responsible for the plan of the work, others for its execution. Composers are not responsible for what musicians do to their work any more than we hold playwrights responsible for performances of their plays. Since the work is never a sufficient guide to how it should be performed, every performance varies, the variations possibly being ones the author never intended or thought of and might not now approve. In that sense, every performance changes what the original maker intended, and changes the work. If the original makers retained control over the licensing of performances, they could in principle prevent performances which would "deface" the original. That control can at most be retained for the few years during which a copyright runs, when one could refuse to license performances by people one thought might do the work badly. But once permission to perform has been given, the composer or author cannot prevent a bad performance or one which (while not necessarily bad) will produce a result completely different from, perhaps antithetical to, what he envisioned. Had Shakespeare been present to see the Mercury Theater production of *Julius Caesar* in contemporary dress (see figure 19), he could not have prevented Orson Welles' innovations if he disapproved, since his work was by then in the public domain.

Probably Shakespeare would not have cared, since the work was well enough known that Welles would have been blamed for whatever in the production did not work. Contemporary playwrights worry more about this, since they may get the blame for performances that do not represent their intentions. In general, all the parties to the cooperation that creates a work of art who are defined as "artists" and awarded the prestige that goes with the title receive their share of the responsibility for the result. Participants may then worry only about what they can be held responsible for. Actors will thus perform in plays they think inferior but which provide a vehicle for their talents, and playwrights may prefer a bad performance to none at all, trusting the audience to distinguish their merits from the company's incompetence. Artists generally have no legal recourse in matters that affect their reputations, although the French laws on painting show what protection the state could provide if it wished.

In short, the state creates a body of law that protects some of the rights people have in artistic works regarded as prop-

FIGURE 19. Orson Welles' modern-dress production of Julius Caesar. *Playwrights have little control over how their plays are presented, especially after they are dead. Orson Welles and the Mercury Theater staged Shakespeare's* Julius Caesar *in modern dress in 1937 to point up parallels with contemporary political events. (Photograph courtesy of the New York Public Library.)*

erty. When the cooperation that produces art works takes place in a market economy, general mercantile law and specific laws relating to artistic property govern that cooperation and create the situation in which specific career and commercial strategies may be followed.

NUISANCE

The state also cooperates in the production of works of art when it intervenes on behalf of nonartists who claim that artists' work is interfering with some right of theirs. In this case, as in the creation and enforcement of laws governing property rights, the state has no direct interest in the works of art themselves; its interest is confined to keeping peace among its citizens and, by enforcing the rules of the game, seeing that they may enjoy the rights guaranteed them.

(Keep in mind that the cooperation of any of the participants of which I speak may be seen by the other participants, particularly the artist, as noncooperation. That is, the state may act so as to limit what artists do or prevent them from doing anything at all, in which case that is the state's contribution to the network of collective activity which produces the work in its final form. The point is not that the state helps artists to achieve their purposes, but that it influences the final form of the work, by intervening or not in any of the ways described here.)

Citizens may complain that what an artist does interferes with their peaceful and legitimate enjoyment of their own property and pursuits and may ask the state to prevent the artist from continuing to do those things. Many complaints deal with simple physical discomforts and annoyances. Film crews disrupt a neighborhood with their trucks and equipment when they film on location; musicians practice long hours or play loudly and disturb people in the surrounding area who can hear them through walls that keep out ordinary sounds; visual artists make a mess or create smells that permeate an area outside the studio in which the work is being done (e.g., the plastics used in some contemporary sculpture create annoying and possibly toxic odors).

Under U.S. law, the state does not enter these situations unless someone makes a complaint, so that artists may be able to create such nuisances without interference for long periods of time. In all the relevant respects, they can be thought of (and their offended neighbors usually so think of them) as not very different from industrial or business polluters. They are in fact subject to the same laws and sanctions. The difference between artists and industrial polluters lies not in the laws but in their ability to fight them. A company whose noisy machines bother nearby residents can delay enforcement through legal actions most artists could not afford.

Governments may exempt artists from these constraints,

just as they exempt other industries, when they find it in the public interest to do so. Cities often allow film crews to use streets as sets, closing them off to public use for long periods, and justify the practice by the amount of money these workers spend in local businesses.

Without such exemptions, what aggrieved parties complain of can usually best be dealt with by doing something to minimize the nuisance: soundproofing performance areas, installing ventilation systems adequate to the odors and other contaminants the work produces, or compensating complainers for their discomfort (film companies often make donations to local causes to soften the complaints of inconvenienced residents). Such solutions raise the artist's cost of working (just as pollution controls raise the cost of industrial production). Since most art requires more money than artists have (film companies are an exception), complaints about nuisances may effectively prevent artists from working at all or at least prevent them from producing their work in the way they would like. Thus, the possibility of such trouble constrains most artists to produce work of a kind and in a way that will not provoke claims of nuisance or, alternatively, to find places to work and perform where no neighbors will complain. The rock musicians Bennett (1980) studied rehearsed in isolated mountain cabins to avoid dealing with irate city neighbors.

What can reasonably be considered annoying enough to constitute a legal nuisance? A sign whose revolving light shines in my window while I am trying to sleep is pretty clearly a nuisance. Is a sign containing an abstract design unintelligible to me? Is it if I find the design a symptom of godless atheism? Can I be annoyed in a legally actionable way by a picture of a woman in chains I find sexist, even though it does not meet the legal criteria for obscenity? By a picture of an interracial group giving a clenched hand salute I find politically disturbing? Or will I be told that if I don't like it I don't have to look at it?

People sometimes complain not only in their own behalf, but to protect the general public from what may appear to be offensive art works. They often allege that some material may be permissible if circulated privately but not when it is broadcast in such a way that members of the public cannot prevent themselves from seeing or hearing it. Thus, the word *fuck* might be permitted in a book a reader knew contained it, but not on a billboard, where one could not know it was there without first reading the sign. Some complain about the manner of circulation rather than the content: the commuters who sued to prevent Grand Central Station from broadcasting music and advertisements to them as they walked through it were not complaining about the particular songs or ads they heard, but rather about being required to hear anything without having personally decided to do so.

Legal systems vary considerably in their willingness to intervene to protect the public against objectionable art works. Denisoff (1975, pp. 402–18) describes how the Federal Communications Commission, under heavy right-wing pressure, required radio stations to screen popular records for possible prodrug messages, implicitly threatening the suspension or removal of licenses. He quotes the commission's public notice:

> [whether] a particular record depicts the dangers of drug abuse, or, to the contrary, promotes such illegal drug usage is a question for the judgment of the licensee. The thrust of this *Notice* is simply that the licensee must make that judgment and cannot properly follow a policy of playing records without someone in a responsible position . . . knowing the content of the lyrics. (Denisoff, 1975, p. 407)

Since radio stations are the chief medium through which records are sold and stations refused to risk their licenses by playing songs which the FCC might construe as prodrug, recording artists and companies faced one more hurdle in their attempt to construct popular hits.

Where a legal system guarantees what are called in the United States First Amendment rights—freedom of speech and expression—artists may defend themselves against such complaints by claiming constitutional protection. (In the case of the FCC order against drug lyrics, stations made such a claim and lost.) The problems here overlap with those involved in state censorship, and I will treat them under that heading.

In short, the state can affect the production of art works by acting, through its legal system, to protect the rights of non-artists who claim to have been annoyed or inconvenienced by what the artist does, either by the result or the process. Artists, aware of this possibility, shape their works to avoid such problems (undoubtedly the vast majority of art follows this course) or plan for the troubles they are likely to have.

INTERVENTION

The state, finally, affects what artists do and produce by directly intervening in their activities. Intervention takes various forms: open support, censorship, and suppression. In this case, the state acts in behalf of its own interests, taking actions designed to further those causes and activities its agents think crucial or important for its and their survival and well-being. To be sure, these activities are often legitimated by reference to the general welfare, as are all government activities, but they are not undertaken, as are the activities just discussed, on behalf of some citizen who invokes the power of the state to enforce the rules of the game in his interest. The state acts because it has interests of its own.

The interests the state pursues through its intervention in the arts have to do with the preservation of public order—the arts being seen as capable both of strengthening and of subverting order—and with the development of a national culture, seen as a good in itself and as something which promotes national unity ("our heritage") and the nation's reputation among other nations.

The state pursues its interests by giving or withholding the forms of support artists need and depend on which the state can influence. Since artists can buy much of what they need if they have the money, the state can influence the work they do by making funds available for some kinds of work but not for others. The state can also influence other things artists need. Access to distribution channels may be controlled by private persons or organizations—by art dealers, magazine editors, or television network executives—but the state may intervene in the selection process by forbidding those people to distribute works, kinds of work, or the work of particular artists. The state may forbid artists access to the means of producing artistic work, an especially potent form of control in media whose machinery and materials are so expensive that individuals cannot afford them (e.g., filmmaking). Finally, to make art artists need to stay alive and free to carry on their work. The state exercises ultimate coercion by depriving them of freedom or life. Every artist, however apolitical, thus depends on the state not exercising those powers in order to continue work. Artists remember, as they work, that the state can support their work or use police power to suppress it. Their work shows the result, either in conventionally staying within allowable bounds or in the chances it takes and the way it takes them.

Support

Governments may regard the arts, some or all of them, as integral parts of the nation's identity, things it is known for as Italy is known for opera, and subsidize them as they would any important feature of the national culture that could not support itself. They may regard the arts as a positive force in national life, a force which supports social order, mobilizes the population for desirable national goals, and diverts people from socially undesirable activities (many governments clearly believe in the circus part of the bread-and-circuses theory of government). Government support of the arts often means preserving in museums what has already been done; that impulse leads new nations to demand that works of art former colonial powers have removed be returned to be incorporated into the national heritage. But it also often includes support for working artists, training institutions, performing groups, exhibition spaces, publication, and expenses of production, as well as fellowships and other grants which free artists' time for work.

Jane Fulcher has described the "Orphéon," a working-class mass choral society supported by the government of Second Empire France to "ameliorate" the condition of workers and thus to "pacify" them:

> The proletariat was a pariah class, "without morals," the "classe Dangereuse": the workers' cabarets were called "dens of debauchery" and of clandestine political agitation. They had to be replaced by "moral amusements," "safe" entertainments like the Orphéon. . . . With the recent revolutionary insurrection of workers still vividly imprinted in their memories, conservatives and officials, obsessed with suspicion, desired above all "harmonious" art. The Orphéon stood for the ideals they cherished. . . . The Orphéon was a means to "cultivate" the workers, . . . to imbue them with "taste," to assuage and "soften," to help form "judgment"—to "moralize." . . . The Orphéon was given tremendous support, in both practical and ideological terms. (Fulcher, 1979, pp. 51–52)

When the government sees artistic activities as supporting national interests, it provides financial support which otherwise would have to come from elsewhere or would not be available at all. It may give a direct financial subsidy, to be spent as the individual artist or the organizers of the art group see fit; or access to government-owned exhibition or performance spaces which otherwise would have to be paid for; or materials or salaries for specific personnel or categories of personnel.

Whatever form support takes, government agencies can change their minds about how much they will give, what they will give it for, and who they will give it to. Both what artists and organizations actually produce and the responses to it influence these decisions. More precisely, the responses a work evokes in the constituencies to which the government and its agencies are responsive influence future allocations. In parliamentary democracies, legislators fear that opponents will tell the voters who elect them that they have voted to spend money on works which are foolish, obscene, unintelligible, or unpatriotic. Members of the U.S. Congress have periodically complained, on behalf of constituents, about art works the State Department has circulated in overseas exhibitions, books placed in U.S. Information Service libraries, or projects funded by the National Endowment for the Arts. State art agencies have frequently been attacked for supporting obscene or unpatriotic work.

On the other hand, when a small dictatorial group not immediately responsible to the citizenry runs the government—as in a military dictatorship or some other form of one-party state—the constituency influencing the choices of those who allocate support for the arts may be limited to that small group of power wielders. As long as they approve, or at least do not complain, art bureaucrats can pursue whatever course they want. Brazilian intellectuals, for instance, usually explain the films Embrafilm (the government film organization) chooses to finance by referring to the current policies of the ruling military group, explaining an emphasis on historical romances celebrating great moments in Brazilian history by the government's desire to build a greater sense of national purpose and mission. Ruling cliques gauge the effect of the arts on their larger purposes and instruct art bureaucrats to allocate support accordingly. (When power is tightly held, disproportionate weight may be given to the random opinions of people connected to the powerful—a general's wife may complain that a film was too risque, and the people who made it may have trouble financing their pictures from then on.)

Art bureaucrats have, in addition to their political constituency, a constituency in the art worlds they work with. In a totally authoritarian state, the art world constituency is ineffectual, but in other situations it constitutes an autonomous source of power. Some influential people personally interested in the arts use their power and influence on behalf of increased or continued government support. Artists, their friends, and their families constitute a block of votes which might be cast for those who further their artistic interests. Some legislators develop a specialty in legislation pertaining to the arts and use all the devices of parliamentary activity in support of their topic, getting financial and other forms of support from their art constituency in return. If the state undertakes to help art, the superiors of art bureaucrats will want audiences and artists to believe that the help is real;

the bureaucrats must therefore cultivate those constituents. Thus, the people who give fellowships to photographers devote considerable time to explaining those awards, and the rationale behind them, to the art photography world.

Government support takes on importance as it becomes a larger proportion of the available support for the arts. Where art activity takes place in the marketplace, artists can always seek (and perhaps find) financial support by trying to attract an audience or clientele there. If the government does not subsidize the publication of my book, some publisher may take a chance on it without subsidy, or I can put the money up myself (thus the continued existence of vanity presses). If, on the other hand, all books are published by a state-controlled publishing house, I don't have those alternatives. Government policy on support becomes de facto censorship.

But alternatives to government support are seldom totally unavailable. Thus, even where most theater is state-subsidized, some subgroup may use its resources to finance an elaborate theatrical life which is not restricted by what the government will pay for; Polish student groups have for years supported a professional student theater, which does plays the state theater will not do (Goldfarb, 1978). At one extreme, the Russian institution of *samizhdat* provides a primitive kind of publication in which private individuals reproduce the work, typing and retyping manuscripts the Soviet government will not publish and which, in fact, have been forbidden publication. It is easier to find other means when the medium requires less; literature costs less than theater. When government support dominates the arts budget, artists must take into account as a constraint what the government will and won't support. If other forms of support are available—other patrons or the open market—the government will simply be one among many sources, and artists will get what they can from it to support what it will support and find other support elsewhere.

Since anyone who gives support can also withhold it, government agencies also influence what artists do by not supporting what they find offensive, useless, or inappropriate. They cannot prevent art works from being done when other modes of support are available, but if the easiest way to find support is through the government, the inertia of established ways will cause artists to look for projects they can do within the limits of what the government will support. The manipulation of support is thus the least coercive method of government control of the arts and, consequently, the least effective. What the government will use it for depends on what results it is trying to achieve. By becoming an integral part of the cooperative network that creates art, the government achieves the same kind of influence other cooperators in that network have, but is one of the few such parties with overt political goals and the only one with such massive resources (see Clark, 1976, 1977).

Censorship

At the other extreme of coercion, governments act overtly to prevent some art from being done, destroy the results once they are done, or imprison or destroy the artists. In such cases, a less drastic mode of government action—suppression by benign neglect—turns into active intervention. These cases show that the government, however little it does, is inescapably an important part of the cooperative art-producing network: since it *might* intervene to prevent the production or distribution of art works, even if it seldom or never does, failure to act is a crucial form of cooperation in artistic activities. Artists count on that failure in states which seldom or never act as censors. Because the state might act at any time, because it can even if it doesn't, all works of art have a political meaning—by acting or failing to act, the government indicates that it does or does not think a particular work politically important or dangerous. Even work whose maker had no political intent acquires political meaning in the light of government actions.

The state may attack the artist or the work, or attack the artist by attacking the work. In totalitarian societies, artists run a considerable risk. Because their work might mobilize mass uprising or defections, the regime may deal with them as it deals with other politically dangerous types. Irving Louis Horowitz has classified governments on the basis of the way they deal with dissident elements, the types ranging from "genocidal societies in which the state arbitrarily takes the lives of citizens for deviant or dissident behavior" to "permissive societies in which norms are questioned and community definitions rather than state definition of what constitutes normative behavior emerge in the decision-making process" (Horowitz, 1980, pp. 44–45). The artist, only one of the potential dissidents or deviants governments treat in this range of ways, is subject in some societies to the most extreme sanctions.

In states which do not act against the artist directly, the most complete form of censorship is the total destruction of the works the government finds offensive. The modern archetype of such action is book burning, even though that actually destroys, not the work itself, but only some copies of it; the work will continue to exist in areas the government has no jurisdiction over, notably other countries with different political systems and aims. (Ray Bradbury's *Fahrenheit 451* considers the more extreme case in which every physical copy has been destroyed by an implacable and efficient regime; even there the work continues to exist by being recorded in people's memories.)

Visual art works which exist in unique copies can be completely destroyed. That often occurs as a side effect of such political upheavals as foreign conquests or civil war. The destruction of so many great works of religious art in England after it broke with Roman Catholicism exemplifies the process, as does the destruction of Aztec and Inca art by Spanish conquerors. In the first case, the king wanted to destroy symbols of religious authority and power to which the common people might continue to respond; in the second, the conquerors simply wanted the precious metals the works were made out of. (Conceptual art works resemble literature in this respect—any particular copy can be destroyed, but the idea exists as long as anyone knows it.)

Most censorship is not so ruthless and complete. It interferes with the distribution, rather than the creation or continued existence, of the works. The state forbids their sale, exhibition, or performance in the places where and to the people whom, in the ordinary workings of the art world, they would be sold, exhibited, and performed. That is, since art worlds have standard ways of distributing works to audiences (whether through a network of middlemen or directly), censorship consists of forbidding the artist access to those institutional arrangements, so that the work can be done but cannot be appreciated or supported in the usual way. Thus, the state may forbid an author to send a literary work through the mail, when that is the ordinary method of distributing poetry magazines, or to sell a book or magazine on public newsstands. It may forbid visual artists to display their paintings in galleries and museums, or forbid musicians and dramatists to perform in concert halls and theaters. Determined artists find other places where it is not (or not yet) illegal to continue their activities. They may organize "clubs," whose members may, in the privacy of their "private club," enjoy films or plays which cannot be shown publicly. Government censors often accept this kind of open sham, since it achieves their chief purpose, to prevent mass circulation of work which might mobilize undesirable public activities. Even very repressive governments can be quite indifferent to the art a small, cultured elite consumes. They only worry when the same material becomes available to larger audiences. (The *samizhdat* system of reproducing typescripts of banned literary works in Russia effectively achieves this end.) This reminds us that the state is primarily interested in the way art affects mass mobilization—it supports art so that the population can be mobilized for the right things, and bans art because it fears people will be mobilized for the wrong things.

Almost all governments have the idea, enforced through censorship, that some topics and treatments of them are offensive to public morals. Censors usually regard the depiction or discussion of some activities as obscene or sacrilegious and thus morally repugnant. They think these depictions would offend many people and therefore stir up public conflict. They would, in addition, corrupt, tempting citizens to engage in the depicted activities themselves, and that would destroy the moral fiber of the nation and its ability to act together in pursuit of common goals. This danger is often thought most threatening to children who, their moral constitutions not yet fully formed, are most likely to be led astray. Furthermore, societies can sometimes create a convergence of national goals and the aspirations of families so that the family desires its children to grow up to be the kind of citizens—ambitious and hardworking, or passive and obedient—political leaders want to ensure stability and progress. When individual, family, and national projects converge (Velho, 1976, 1979), censorship designed to protect children from being led astray seems reasonable and normal to everyone. It embodies the conventionally acceptable account of the proper role of government. (Denisoff quotes a right-wing critic of the Beatles: "Let's make sure four mop-headed anti-Christ beatniks don't destroy our children's emotional and mental stability and ultimately our nation" [Denisoff, 1975, p. 385].) More extreme kinds of censorship extend that acceptable logic to areas where the need is not as universally taken for granted as is the need to protect children.

The potential for government intervention, as suggested earlier, gives every work of art a political dimension. If the state refuses to censor a work, people may decide that after all it does not contain any dangerous political content, no matter how much the artist may have intended just that. Conversely, if the state suppresses an art work, people will try to find some dangerous or radical political message in it, and will usually succeed, no matter how innocent of such intent the artist was.

Here is an example. I spent the fall of 1976 in Brazil, living in Ipanema, a fashionable section of Rio de Janeiro. As was customary for inhabitants of the area, we spent a good part of every Sunday at the beach, meeting friends and acquaintances in the *carioca* version of a Parisian cafe. One Sunday, on the way to the beach with a number of people, we saw that the fences surrounding the many construction sites in the area had been spraypainted with poetry. We all assumed that the poem was political. Even though it appeared on the surface to be an innocent love poem, we knew that the lan-

guage of love has often served as an open disguise for political thought in authoritarian societies. Brazilian intellectuals,
particularly, are accustomed to read political meanings into
popular songs and verse, thinking with good reason that the
authors intended them to do so (Sant'Anna, 1978). The
country was on the verge of an election as well. Although the
outcome was not in doubt—everyone took for granted that
the government would not let the opposition win—the election had aroused enough interest that the poem might well
refer to it. Furthermore, if it was not political, why was it
spraypainted on public walls instead of using more conventional channels of distribution? All these being good reasons
for suspecting political content, we read the interminable
stanzas, which went on for blocks. Finally, however, even the
most politically minded interpreters among our friends decided that they could not discover a hidden content, con-
cluding reluctantly that it was simply a case of a poet who
had not been able to get his work published. Using the means
of distribution suited to an underground political message in
a country in which censorship was then a daily fact gave the
poem a political potential. (Indeed, it is possible that government officials might have seen the political message
which even our politically sensitive friends could not find.)

Artists plan their work having in mind how potential state
action will affect them. Here is another example from Brazil.
The Censura was pervasive. Records, films, and plays had to
be approved before release and distribution. Even though
preliminary versions had been approved, the final ready-to-
sell version might be held up indefinitely by the censor's
refusal to approve. Plays were refused approval on opening
night. One day at the beach, someone asked one of our
acquaintances what he, a theatrical designer, was working
on. He mentioned a number of projects including an interesting one he thought he would nevertheless turn down.
Why? Because it was very political and he had heard rumors
that, in the end, the censors would not allow it to be done.
Why waste his time on something that would never be produced? People began discussing recent events to see whether
censors were in fact becoming less restrictive. Someone

mentioned that a new recording by Chico Buarque, a popular singer, held up by the Censura for several months because of the political nature of some of the lyrics, had finally been released. Someone else said it had been, but that since its release the police had been picking up copies from local record stores. I said that that couldn't be true because I had just bought two copies locally the day before. Someone speculated that perhaps they were picking them up only in certain neighborhoods. The set designer listened interestedly, since all of this could indicate more or less lenience on the part of the censors, which would affect his decision on which jobs to accept.

Censorship affects the calculus with which participants in making art assess the likely consequences of taking part in any particular project. The likelihood of one consequence or another varies from time to time and place to place, so that up-to-date news of what the authorities have done can influence decisions. Censors can thus divert people from antigovernment art by small gestures which affect that calculation.

Whatever form of censorship a society practices—whether it is openly political or exercised in the name of good taste and the protection of children—it becomes, like all the other regular activities conventionalized in an art world, an enormous constraint internalized by most participants, who thus do not even experience it as a constraint. Chico Buarque, the Brazilian singer just mentioned, himself a victim of considerable censorship, described these effects graphically in an interview:

> [The censors] mutilate all the characteristics of an epoch. These kids who are beginning to make music today. Can you imagine? If, in their first attempts . . . everything is already prohibited, that produces a monstrosity of self-censorship, fatal to any kind of creative activity. They are a generation born within the system of censorship, to whom the certificate of liberation [the censor's OK] is as normal and necessary as their identity card. To me, to a generation that created itself almost without censorship, it's shocking to have to send texts . . . for a government official to examine, to say whether

it can be released or not. For the kid who comes up now, it's not like that. That's why so many people compose in English [instead of Portuguese], because it's easier to get through. "The next time I'm going to get it right, since it seems that I did something wrong." That can be the thinking of a kid who starts out and finds himself censored. (Chrysôstomo, 1976, p. 4, my translation)

To summarize, the state participates in the network of cooperation, the art world, which produces the works characteristic of a particular medium at a particular time. It creates the framework of property rights within which artists get economic support and make reputations. It limits what artists can do when it protects people whose rights may have been infringed by artists intent on producing their work. It gives open support to some forms of art, and to some practitioners of those forms, when they appear to further national purposes. It uses state power to suppress work which seems likely to mobilize citizens for disapproved activities or prevent them from being mobilized for appropriate purposes.

The state thus acts like other art world participants, providing opportunities to get art work done by giving support both directly and indirectly for what it approves of, and acting as a constraint on other activities by preventing access, for works deemed unsatisfactory, to some of the facilities ordinarily available to all participants. Thus, the state may prevent works from being distributed (the most usual form of intervention) or from continuing to exist, or may punish those people guilty of creating undesirable work by death, imprisonment, or other kinds of sanctions. In this sense, all artists depend on the state and their work embodies that dependence.

7 · Editing

When T.S. Eliot's widow published a photographic reproduction of the manuscript of her husband's famous poem
The Waste Land after his death, the literary world learned
how much the final version of the work owed to two other
people: Eliot's first wife, Vivian, and his friend Ezra Pound.
In their various ways, the two had radically altered the poem,
and their alterations contributed considerably to its distinc-
tively modern look, to some of the features for which Eliot
was especially praised.

Part 4 of the poem, "Death by Water," consisted in Eliot's
original of more than ninety lines of a quite conventional
character. Pound didn't like it and crossed most of it out in
the manuscript, leaving only the last ten lines, which began
"Phlebas the Phoenician, a fortnight dead...." Much less
prepared for, the section explains itself less and, in modern
style, requires more work of the reader. Valerie Eliot explains
what happened, relying on correspondence between the two
men:

> Depressed by Pound's reaction to the main passage, Eliot
> wrote: "Perhaps better omit Phlebas also???" "I DO advise
> keeping Phlebas" replied Pound. "In fact, I more'n advise ...
> he is needed ABSOlootly where he is. Must stay in." (Eliot,
> 1971, p. 129)

And he did stay in.

The editorial work went beyond cutting and minor alterations. Part 2, "A Game of Chess," includes a conversation with someone identified as a thirty-one year old woman who has had more children than she wants because "Albert won't leave her alone." Eliot originally wrote a line for Albert's wife's conversational partner which explained all the unwanted children: "You wanted to keep him at home, I suppose." Vivian Eliot crossed this out and substituted "What you get married for if you don't want to have children?" Eliot deleted "to have," but Mrs. Eliot's line appeared otherwise unchanged as line 164 of the poem, marking an important change in the tone of the passage (Eliot, 1971, pp. 14–15, 20, 21, and 139).

Saxe Commins, a longtime editor for Random House, worked closely with the poet Robinson Jeffers over a period of many years, and his changes (made as suggestions rather than changes) affected the tone and content of much of Jeffers' work. Jeffers' long poem *The Double Axe* contained a number of bitterly anti-Roosevelt and anti-Truman lines Commins found offensive and thought others would find so offensive as to hurt the book's reception. He suggested that Jeffers change these vindictive lines. When the final version arrived, he wrote Jeffers unhappily:

> I noticed, of course, all the changes you have made and in almost every instance they are immense improvements. There are two, however, which give rise to misgivings on my part. I refer to page 25, where you changed the line
>
> > To feed the vanity of a paralytic and make
> > > trick fortunes
> >
> > to
> > To feed the power-hunger of a paralyzed man and
> > > make trick fortunes.
>
> This is hardly a change at all. Would you consent to a further revision to make it read
>
> > To feed the power-hunger and make trick fortunes.
>
> (Commins to Jeffers, 12 February 1948)

Jeffers replied:

If you insist, let the verse read "To feed the power-hunger of a politician"—instead of "paralyzed man." And I hope you will always protest when Caesar's epilepsy is mentioned. Or Dostoevski's—though it influenced his genius, just as Roosevelt's paralysis influenced, and to some extent excuses, his character. This is my reason for speaking of it.
(Jeffers to Commins, 19 February 1948)

Jeffers similarly agreed to alter a passage referring to "little Truman" to read "Harry Truman" (Commins, 1978, pp. 125–29).

Maxwell Perkins, editor for Scribners, constructed the novels for which Thomas Wolfe became famous. Wolfe gave him boxes of raw first draft and Perkins cut and rearranged the material into the form in which it was published.

All of these cases exemplify the process of editing in its most obvious form, in which a professional editor, or friends, relatives, and colleagues acting in that capacity, make (or help the artist to make) the choices which give the work its final shape. They take this out, put that in, change wording and style, rearrange sections—all those changes make the work what it finally is. But editors are not the only ones who do things and make choices that affect the character of the resulting work. Every participant in the cooperative network that creates the work—whose members we have been describing in earlier chapters—has some such effect. If we generalize the analysis, and make what editors do stand for the multiple choices made throughout the life of a work by the many different people who cooperate in its making, we can see how art worlds affect the character of the works made by their members. We can see how, in fact, it is not unreasonable to say that it is the art world, rather than the individual artist, which makes the work.

CHOICES

I find it useful to think of an art work taking the form it does at a particular moment because of the choices, small and large, made by artists and others up to that point. Shall I press the shutter-release button on my camera now or wait a minute? Shall I play the next note louder or softer? With what kind of attack? Longer or shorter than the similarly marked notes that surround it? Shall I put a spot of blue here, or perhaps green, or maybe nothing at all? As these choices are made, from moment to moment, they shape the work. Suppose I undertake, as a photographic project, to investigate the life and culture of the Italian community of San Francisco's North Beach district. Following the typical practice of contemporary photographers, whether they are interested in that kind of documentary project or in the exploration of some more formal and abstract artistic problem, I will make a very large number of photographs. Each exposure will be a choice from a large number of possibilities. I might decide to concentrate on portraits of older people, believing that close-ups of their faces will contain the essence of the culture. I might, conversely, decide to photograph such neighborhood events as the Columbus Day Parade or the blessing of the local fishing fleet (see Becker, 1974, and figure 20), or such neighborhood institutions as taverns, restaurants, grocery stores, and churches. In either case, I then choose lenses, films, times of day, and particular people and places. Having done that, I make many exposures of each portrait subject and even more of the people and places I select as characteristic of the area. I vary distances and angles, and shoot essentially the same subject repeatedly, expecting that momentary variations in expressions, moods, postures, and groupings will make important differences in the result.

I might thus expose as much as ten to twenty rolls of thirty-six exposure film during a day of serious work, and might devote anywhere from one to one hundred days (or more) to the project. But I would not, when I presented the results of my work in a book or exhibit or photo essay, use all those images. After all, on the above schedule I might produce as many as twenty or thirty thousand separate frames of film, most of which would be technically usable. But the average exhibit would contain thirty or forty images, and a book might use as many as one hundred. I would make contact sheets which showed every frame, review them

FIGURE 20. Howard S. Becker, The Blessing of the Fishing
Fleet in San Francisco, *print and contact sheet. Editing consists of
choosing, from among the available possibilities, what you will present to the audience. Having decided to include these altar boys (a) in
my photographic representation of a neighborhood religious ritual, I
still had to choose this frame in preference to (b) several other frames
I had made, those in turn representing a choice of ways to photograph them from a larger selection of possibilities (see Becker, 1974).*

carefully, make preliminary selections into rough work prints, and experiment with various selections and arrangements, putting some in, taking some out. When an invitation to publish or exhibit arrived, I would make a final selection, but that selection might be changed on later occasions. (W. Eugene Smith's photographic investigation of a Japanese fishing village poisoned by industrial wastes, *Minamata*, appeared in several versions of varying lengths which permit comparison of the varying selections, a magazine version in 1974 and the book in 1975.)

That description gives only a rough idea of the number of choices made in the course of such a project. Nevertheless, it is sufficient to show how a final work—in this case, a photographic exhibit or book—arises out of a much larger body of possibilities. Some of those possibilities never take physical form because the photographer rejects them before shooting them. Others get onto the film and the contact sheet but are never printed; of those printed, most do not survive the later weedings-out. But the possibilities were there to choose from and remain there in the negatives, to be chosen, perhaps, at some later time.

A similar process occurs in every art form. Artists consider themes, materials, sequences and combinations, and lengths and sizes, and choose among them. They may choose one possibility in this work and an alternative in a later version, perform a work one way one time and choose a variation the next. Some choices become habitual. Some get embodied in physical objects and thus become permanent. Others are ephemeral, the works disappearing when they are finished, to be replaced on another occasion by another version.

My description of the choices that constitute a work of art is deceptively oversimplified. I described the artist making the work, as though only one person were involved. In fact, as I demonstrated earlier, a great many people are involved in the organized division of labor I have called an art world. Their choices, made throughout the life of a work, and the artist's knowledge of what their standards and choices will probably be, constitute the mechanism by which participation in an art world affects what artists do and the character of the work.

My description is oversimplified in another way. I described the choices made in a restricted range of time, beginning with the genesis of the artist's idea and ending with the artist delivering the finished product—the one the artist is prepared to accept as truly representing his or her "spirit," to use the words of the French court in the Roualt-Vollard case—to the agents of the distribution system. In fact, as earlier chapters hinted and this one will document, consequential choices occur over a much longer period. Art worlds, through the activities of participants other than the artists, affect art works beyond the life of the work's original maker.

All these choices, made by all these participants over the work's life, are what give meaning to the assertion that art worlds, rather than artists, make works of art. The literary editor, the prototypical nonartist participant in these fateful choices, exemplifies what I have in mind sufficiently to warrant calling the entire process of choosing, by whomever and whenever, editing.

THE EDITORIAL MOMENT

I noted in chapter 1 that, while many people participate in the making of any art work, art worlds (and the societies in which they operate) ordinarily award only a few the honorific title of artist, treating them as the ones whose choices really matter, whose actions reveal the rare gifts only artists have, whose reputations will be made or broken by the works' reception. That makes sense because those people ordinarily make many of the choices and, knowing that they will be praised or blamed for the results, choose more carefully than more anonymous, less responsible actors. So we can begin our analysis of the way art worlds shape the choices of their participants (and thus the character of their typical works) with the actions of artists, seeing how these result from artists' acceptance of art world constraints and their internalized dialogue with the art world's other members. We can focus, in a necessarily speculative account, on the actual moments of choice. Call them editorial moments.

Imagine what is clearly not true, that every last detail of the work as it ultimately occurs results from someone's, presumably the artist's, conscious choice, ignoring for now the many choices made by others besides the officially designated artist. Ignore, as well, the fact that the people who create art works do not deliberate over every choice. If musicians had consciously to devise scales and build instruments before they could make a new work, for instance, they would have neither time nor energy to produce work, at least not in the quantities possible if they do not make all the choices consciously.

When we make a detailed analysis, which critics and historians sometimes make, of an art work's development through successive sketches or drafts, we explore the areas of choice the artist was aware of, the alternatives more or less consciously chosen between. Such developments contain an infinity of choices we might investigate; the sum of those choices is the work. Artists make the choices with reference to the organization they work in; that, at least, is the assumption of the analysis that follows. It is not easy to find out about these matters and thus prove the assumption, because artists find it difficult to verbalize the general principles on which they make their choices, or even to give any reasons at all. They often resort to such noncommunicative statements as "it sounds better that way," "it looked good to me," or "it works."

That inarticulateness frustrates the researcher. But every art's practitioners use words whose meanings they cannot define exactly which are nevertheless intelligible to all knowledgeable members of their world. Jazz musicians say that something does or does not "swing"; theater people say that a scene "works" or does not "work." In neither case can even the most knowledgeable participant explain to someone not already familiar with the terms' uses what they mean. Yet everyone who uses them understands them and can apply them with great reliability, agreeing about what swings or works, even though they cannot say what they mean.

Consider the possibility that most of the choices made by artists during editorial moments are made with reference to some such undefinable but perfectly reliable standard like "it swings" or "it works." That artists can cooperate on the basis of such undefinable standards and aesthetic principles suggests that they do not work by consulting a set of rules or criteria. Rather, they respond as they imagine others might respond, and construct those imaginings from their repeated experiences of hearing people apply the undefinable terms to concrete works in concrete situations. A musician plays; others tell him that he has or has not swung. He listens to something, ventures an opinion as to whether it swings, and finds out whether others agree with him or not. From a multitude of similar experiences he learns what the standard means, how to use it as others do.

We can refer, to understand how artists cooperate on the basis of such reliable vagueness, to George Herbert Mead's analysis of "taking the role of the other" (Mead, 1934; Blumer, 1966). Mead opposed a simple-minded stimulus-response psychology, in which people simply do, in the presence of the appropriate stimulus, whatever they have been conditioned to do.

He suggested that, instead, people move actively through their environments, searching for objects to direct their activity toward. When they meet such an object (and he included among objects other people), they immediately interpret its meaning by imputing to it various tendencies to respond to the actions they might undertake. Thus, people gradually shape a line of action by taking into account not only their own impulses but also the imagined responses of others to various actions they might undertake. It is not crucial that their assessments be correct; people are often wrong about such things. But it is crucial that, by and large, people act with the anticipated reactions of others in mind.

This implies that artists create their work, at least in part, by anticipating how other people will respond, emotionally and cognitively, to what they do. That gives them the means with which to shape it further, by catering to already existing dispositions in the audience, or by trying to train the audience to something new. Photographers have to learn, for instance, to respond to their own photographs in the same way others will, to recognize consciously what others will respond to more or less unwittingly. Doing that makes it possible to construct photographs deliberately to produce particular emotional effects.

During the editorial moment, then, all the elements of an art world come to bear on the mind of the person making the choice, who imagines the potential responses to what is being done and makes the next choices accordingly. Multitudes of small decisions get made, in a continuous dialogue with the cooperative network that makes up the art world in which the work is being made. Artists ask themselves, "If I do it this way, how will it feel? To me? To others?" They also ask themselves whether, if they do it that way, resources will be forthcoming, whether other people they depend upon for cooperation will in fact cooperate, whether the state will intervene, and so on. In short, they take the point of view of any or all of the other people involved in the network of cooperative links through which the work will be realized, and modify what they are doing so as to fit in more or less easily with what others have in mind to do. Or they may not modify it, understanding the price they will probably have to pay.

This process takes place very clearly when artists choose the materials they will work with. Suppose I am a composer. What instruments shall I write for? In principle, I can choose any combination of instruments I can think of: four Jew's harps and a washtub bass or a conventional string quartet, a duo, or an orchestra of one hundred players and several choruses. I can write a sonata for unaccompanied anything; sonatas, accompanied and unaccompanied, have been written for every conceivable instrument. If you compose an instrumental sonata, you know it will probably get played, especially if it is for instruments not ordinarily used for solo performance. Trombone players and double bassists hunger for additions to the limited solo repertoire for their instruments, and virtuosi of these instruments frequently commission new works. Composers, when they decide what instruments to score their ideas for, know that works written for two violins, viola, and cello—the conventional string quartet—have a substantial chance of being played because string quartets already exist, ready to play works written for them. If, on the other hand, they write for bassoon and harmonica or for organ, snare drum, and bass saxophone, they know that those players will have to assemble themselves specially for the occasion and that friction itself will prevent the work being played often (and when it is played, it will likely be in a music school, where it is easiest to assemble such odd groupings). You might say that the world of organized music needs string quartets in a way that it does not need works for more unorthodox combinations of instruments—except, of course, when someone commissions a work for an unorthodox combination, in which case the prearranged sale of the work to some already mobilized customer solves the problem.

Artists similarly take the imagined responses of others, learned through their experience in an art world, into account when they complete a work. How do artists know when they are through, when to stop painting or writing? Their decisions on these matters often take into account the way other members of the art world will react to what they decide. If you interview artists about this, they often cannot tell you how they know when they are done. What they can tell you is not so much when a work *is* done as when it *must be* done. When artists tell you when something must be done, they are not talking about anything inherent in the nature of the medium or form they work in, but rather something about the obligations generated by the art world.

Thus, if the opening of a play is announced for January 3, it will have to be performed on that date—or we will have to refund money, tell critics not to bother to show up, lose audiences, lose the chance to do other plays, and damage the confidence of actors and theater owners severely. The production and distribution systems of many arts produce such deadlines. I know that I must produce fifteen lithographs by a certain date, because my gallery has announced the show for that date, the critics will be there, and the work must be available to be seen and written about. Most arts either provide such dates for their practitioners or give them means with which to generate them. As the artist stands over the stone drawing, he knows the date by which his fifteen prints must be ready. Suppose our movie is to open at Radio City Music Hall on Christmas Day. Not only do we know when we must be finished, but we can also construct a time table, working backward from that date, specifying when the various elements of the work must be done. If it is to open on Christmas, we know when the music must have already been recorded; if we know that, we know when it must have already been written; if we know that, we know when the finished scene must be ready so that the music can be synchronized with it; and so on.

Saxe Commins actually wrote a book for an author who failed to produce a biography of Lillian Russell whose publication was planned to coincide with the opening of a movie about her. When, a few weeks before the announced publication date, the author had not produced a page of finished manuscript, Commins moved in with him and turned stacks of raw data into a book (Commins, 1978, pp. 153–69).

Few people respond to works of art as self-consciously as trained artists do. Most people know that a musical piece makes them feel sad, but do not know the melodic and harmonic devices by which that effect has been achieved. Being self-conscious about the process, artists guess wrong less often than non-artists do. They predict the likely response of others correctly and create, more or less, the effect they want.

Artists can predict accurately because the artistic process is so conventionalized. Since we conventionally experience minor keys as sad or mournful, composers can consult their own reactions for a guide: "If I write this in a minor key, it will affect people as sad, since it makes me sad, and will produce the emotion I am after." Such formulas enable artists to anticipate others' responses with great accuracy.

Conventions become embodied in physical routines, so that artists literally feel what is right for them to do. Sudnow's (1978) analysis of how he learned to play jazz piano shows how conventions of the craft get embodied in the tiniest details of the artist's physical experience and makes clear the inseparable connection between the physical act and the conceptual work that go into making art; in fact, to speak of them as two different things that need connecting misstates the case. As a result, while much of what artists do is conventional, it is not therefore easily changed. They experience conventional knowledge as a resource at a very primitive level, so deeply ingrained that they can think and act in conventional terms without hesitation or forethought. They experience editorial choices as acts rather than choices. Sudnow demonstrates graphically that what he learned was as much a way of reaching for a handful of notes on the piano as it was a way of thinking about how those notes would combine to make a melody. He does not say, but it is also true, that in those moments of simultaneous feeling and thinking what is being thought consists of a continual dialogue with the world relevant to the choices being made. The editorial and creative moment fuse in a dialogue with an art world.

Being creative as well as reflective, innovative as well as repetitive and routine, editorial moments embody an interesting and difficult dilemma for artists. To produce unique works of art that will be interesting to audiences, artists must unlearn a little of the conventionally right way of doing things they have learned. Totally conventional pieces bore everyone and bring the artist few rewards. So artists, to be successful in producing art, must violate standards more or less deeply internalized.

Thus, although artists ordinarily take into account the imagined responses of other members of the art world during the artistic moment, they learn to ignore them at times. They also learn to ignore the responses of people who do not belong to the art world. That is equally hard, since most members of art worlds (other than the few who are born into them) were once nonmembers and learned all the things nonmembers still know and believe. But artists have to do many things normal people don't do: many exercises for actors, for instance, consist in behaving in public in ways ordinary people behave only in private. They may have to touch people who are relative strangers to them, engage in emotional outbursts, take off their clothes—things nonactors would be too shy to do before others. Other arts require people to get their hands dirty with paint, clay, or other materials. Since children are usually trained not to get dirty, it takes some doing to overcome that training. My wife once taught a ceramics class at a downtown night school. The first night two rather well-dressed women came into the ceramics room and, when they saw piles of wet clay around, asked with horror, "You mean you have to do it with your hands?" When they were told that, yes, they did have to do it with their hands, they left and got their money back.

Still another lay reaction artists have to master is a dislike of waste. The Tactile Art Group, the seminar referred to in chapter 3, attempted to invent a new art form as a simulation exercise in the sociology of the arts. We chose the tactile mode, an area of experience we thought had not been used to its full artistic potential, and week after week attempted to create works based on the sense of touch. One of the best-liked works produced during our investigation, "Cookie," was a performance piece, during which the artist poured various foodstuffs, including a freshly broken egg, over the hands of an audience member (see figure 21). Wasting that egg upset our group: we could hear our mothers asking with horror how many eggs we proposed to waste in this foolishness, did we know that eggs were food, and what about the starving people in wherever-it-is. The example is trivial, but in fact many in our group at first found it distasteful to waste food. We continued to use foodstuffs as one of the main tactile materials in our works, soon over-coming that qualm. Sometimes it is not the waste of food or other emotionally laden substances, but simply the waste of money or time that bothers novices. Fledgling photographers learn that most of the film they expose, contrary to the lay expectation that every picture should come out, will be wasted and not worth printing. Teachers of photography spend considerable time teaching students not to expect every attempt to be perfect, that a lot of film and paper must be wasted to get what might, with luck, be one good photographic print.

FIGURE 21. *A performance of* Cookie *by members of the Tactile Art Group. Like many artists working in new genres, the group had no special materials or instruments available to it and relied on ordinarily available foodstuffs and household items.*

Writers often find, as do photographers, that the subjects they feel most at home with and can exploit most thoroughly violate the confidence and privacy of their friends, associates, lovers, and neighbors. Any well-socialized person knows better than to violate those elemental relations of trust, yet artists often feel compelled to do it. Being artists may not protect them from the anger of those they exploit, but audiences who know none of the people involved are more forgiving, the more so the longer ago the violation. Truman Capote's stories of Eastern society figures gave the general public intimate, gossipy details of a number of more or less well-known scandals he had learned about by becoming friendly with the people involved. Larry Clark's photographic book *Tulsa* (1971) contained photographs of drug users, his friends since adolescence, who had no notion that they would one day find themselves in a book (the book was withdrawn after someone sued). Capote and Clark had learned, as many writers and photographers do, to produce innovative work by shutting some potential participants out of the interior dialogue informing the many editorial choices that constitute the work.

Sometimes artists cannot think of a way around the complaints they envision lay audiences making, and suppress work that nevertheless interests them enough to complete. Thus, when artists die they often leave behind a body of secret work, which they let only a few trusted friends see during their lifetimes, lest it create embarrassments for themselves or others. Mark Twain suppressed his pornographic writings in deference to his wife's wishes, E. M. Forster withheld a homosexual novel for publication after his death, and Toulouse-Lautrec kept his more explicitly sexual brothel pictures locked up. It would be interesting to compare, for a variety of artists during different periods, the work they made and threw away, the work they made and kept but did not feel it safe, politic, or wise to show to anyone else (each choice reflecting the social constraints they operated under), and the work they actually displayed to the public as characteristic, the work they were willing to let decide their reputations and professional fates.

The importance of learning to incorporate other members of the cooperative network into the interior dialogue through which the artist makes the work can be seen by considering two marginal cases. Art students frequently have trouble working because, not incorporating relevant others, they do not know how to solve common problems with maximum efficiency and minimum trouble. It is easiest to uncover the dialogue with the art world which underlies the semiautomatic operations of experienced practitioners by watching those for whom none of it is automatic because they are still learning.

Chandra Mukerji (1977) describes film students' learning to incorporate the imagined reactions of others into their decisions as games they play to practice thinking in filmic conventions. Students play games as a form of practice because no film school gives students sufficient equipment to try out all their ideas in actual film production. Instead, students play at filmmaking by describing what they would like to do; other students foreshadow the likely responses of other film world participants in their comments on the feasibility and probable effect of an idea. As Mukerji explains:

> Since the rules film students use in their games are filmmaking conventions, when they play these games they are practicing the use of these conventions. Students start with an idea from their own imaginings, explaining how it could be made into an element of a film. (Mukerji, 1977, p. 25)

She quotes a student:

> Well, basically, I got the idea when I was there (at an auction) and thought it would be easy. I wanted to show the three types of people at house sales and how they react. I wanted to have visuals of the people standing in line outside (the house), the family inside, looking empty and examining their possessions, and the professionals running the house sale. The sound would be interviews with all three types of people, alternating with the picture. I thought you could just go to one, photograph those elements that occur in every house sale: the line, the professionals and how they do their work, the family looking stunned and the house left a com-

plete mess. Now I don't know why he thinks that would be so hard. . . . (Mukerji, 1977, pp. 25–26)

She goes on:

> He said it would take two or three cameras to shoot. The student who had introduced the idea [into a playful gathering of film students] was told that the idea was not even good enough to play with. [An advanced student who had dismissed the idea as technically too difficult] argued that a film about an auction would require a large number of cameras that no student could hope to find while in school. (Mukerji, 1977, pp. 26 and 28)

(See the account of the professional version of these activities in Rosenblum and Karen, 1979.)

The importance of the interior dialogue with an art world for the artist's decisions shows up in another marginal case, when someone is trying to construct a new art form. Such an enterprise is difficult precisely because the questions that can ordinarily be answered by referring to the imagined responses of others in the cooperative network cannot be answered that way. No cooperative network exists yet, or not much of one. No standard ways of doing business can be used to predict the likely responses of those recruited to such positions as audience member. The lack of conventions manifests itself as a gross inability to make editorial choices or to judge the results of choices made. If you do not know whether a particular choice was good or "worked," you cannot decide whether to change it the next time. Contrast the ease with which people who work in more established forms, which have conventions and canons to be consulted, can advise one another. One of the great difficulties of the Tactile Art Group was that its members could not tell whether they were doing anything worthwhile or were just wasting time and making fools of themselves. When disaffected members denounced the others because the art works they were making were not art, the victims of the denunciations, however much they liked their work, had no critical or aesthetic language or arguments with which to counter the accusation.

EDITING BY OTHERS

Artists, the people who get the credit or blame for art works, typically make many of the choices which shape a work's character. The art world's other participants affect the result by entering into the internal dialogue which precedes and accompanies those choices. But other participants affect art works more directly as well, making choices of their own which, independent of the artist's wish or intention, also shape the work. Sometimes artists recognize the possibility and think of it as they work; often they do not know, and perhaps could not know, what others will do to affect their work, and thus cannot accommodate to it. These fateful actions of others occur during the work's entire life, often after the artists themselves have died; the effects may be temporary or permanent.

Manufacturers and distributors perform an editorial function by failing to make some materials and equipment available. They thus effectively prevent artists from making certain choices or make them prohibitively expensive in time and effort for all but people determined to have just that item as part of their work. When the major suppliers reduce the variety of photographic film and paper available, they force me to edit out of the possible corpus of my work what I might have made with the unavailable materials. Artists notice these constraints when some favorite material disappears from the market—when they can no longer, for instance, get Agfa's Record Rapid paper. But artists are always constrained by the unavailability of materials, especially those that never were made at all, because suppliers didn't know how to make them or had rejected the possibility as impractical or unprofitable. Conversely, when suppliers make new materials available, they add to the possibilities from which artists can choose. The Polaroid system of instant color photography created new artistic possibilities.

Many art works exist in the form of directions to others telling them what to do to actualize the work on a particular occasion. The directions may consist of a musical score, the script of a play, a manuscript to be printed, or plans for a building. Since no directions can fully specify an action to be undertaken, the interpreters of those directions necessarily make choices that are independent of the artist's intentions (no matter how hard the interpreters try to be "authentic"). Fearing that the interpreters will betray them, some artists give minutely detailed directions designed to restrict interpretive choices. A contemporary score might indicate just how many inches from the rim of the snare drum the percussionist shall hit the head with his stick; Renaissance composers, on the other hand, trusted more to the influence of contemporary performance standards and often left even the choice of notes to performers (Dart, 1967). The contemporary composer, John Cage, overcomes the desire of performers to play what they know how to play well and feel comfortable with by using randomizing procedures to create scores that will be unfamiliar to the musicians who play them. Innovative architects try to supervise the details of construction to prevent workmen from sabotaging, by conventionalizing, their designs.

Musical works and plays whose authors are long dead are especially vulnerable to extensive reinterpretation by performers. Shakespeare's plays have been cut, rearranged, and performed in anachronistic costumes to point up contemporary relevances. Directors have emphasized political and psychological themes growing out of theories less than one hundred years old in plays almost five hundred years old. Conductors and musicians habitually edit baroque works, playing them on instruments that did not exist when they were composed, excising repetitions, reinterpreting ornaments.

Many people make similar interpretive choices when executing what seem to be simple craft operations, producing an appreciable effect on the final work. Barbara Hardy notes that:

> George Eliot's punctuation is very light, informal and "modern." In the manuscript all the semicolons here [she is referring to the epigraph to chapter 70 of *Daniel Deronda*], for instance, are commas. The printer formalized her punctua-

tion and it is rash to speak about her "heavy" style without knowing that the heaviness is in part, at least, the result of an imposed style of punctuation. (Eliot, 1967, p. 903)

(The sentence in question reads "In the chequered area of human experience the seasons are all mingled as in the golden age: fruit and blossom hang together; in the same moment the sickle is reaping and the seed is sprinkled; one tends the green cluster and the other treads the wine-press.") Emily Dickinson, after a similar experience with a local printer, simply gave up publishing her work.

Artists do not make everything they do available for public display. They withhold much material as unfinished: drafts, sketches, or projects which did not meet their expectations and which they do not want to affect their reputations. Although artists frequently decide which of their works to make public and which to withhold, during an artist's lifetime friends or professional editors also make those choices, and executors do it after his death. Editors' and executors' choices may not coincide with the artist's, and dead artists cannot prevent their work being shown in a form they may not have wanted. Max Brod ignored his friend Kafka's orders to burn his unpublished manuscripts after his death. Critics and readers appreciate the choice, but it was Brod's and not Kafka's.

Brod made all of Kafka's work available. Other executors choose more selectively and have a correspondingly greater effect on the body of work which thenceforth represents an artist to the public. Consider Eugene Atget, a French actor who decided in his forties, around the turn of the century, that he should spend his life documenting the city of Paris photographically. He acquired a large view camera and went every day to some part of Paris, photographing buildings, store windows, characteristic types of people, parks, markets, and so on. Over a period of thirty years he made thousands of photographs. Few people knew his work. Shortly before his death in 1927, a young American photographer named Berenice Abbott met the old man and decided that he was a photographic genius whose work needed to be preserved and presented to the public. She persuaded him to sit for her camera. When she brought some prints of the portrait for him to see, she found that he had just died. She got control of his negatives, thereby preserving them from probable destruction, and chose from them the work by which he first became known to a larger public than the few artists who had been buying pictures from him. That work might best have been described as Eugene Atget's as selected by Berenice Abbott (1964). In later years, others have made quite different selections from the same body of raw material. In the same way, John Szarkowski and Richard Avedon chose images from the large corpus created as a hobby by the French painter Jacques Henri Lartigue to create a major exhibition and a book, and Nancy Newhall created the image of Ansel Adams as a photographer who specialized in Yosemite and the West by picking the photographs which made up the first books on which his reputation rested. Although Lartigue and Adams were alive, the editors did much the same kind of selective choosing as Abbott, with the same result: the artist was represented by a body of work that reflected someone else's sensibility and standards.

The people and organizations who distribute art works make editorial choices when they refuse to distribute some works, require changes in others before distribution, or (most subtly) create a network of facilities and a body of practice which lead artists in the world whose works they distribute to make works which fit easily into that scheme. When the recording industry chose to standardize the ten- and twelve-inch seventy-eight-rpm disc, jazzmen chose work for recording that fit into the associated time constraints. Longer works could not be properly or profitably distributed. Live performances often ran longer than recorded versions, because musicians included more improvised choruses, but the actual composition fit the standard formats. When introduction of the long-playing record eventually eased this distributional constraint, most LPs continued to consist of a number of tracks of approximately the length once dictated by what fit on a ten-inch seventy-eight-rpm disc. It took years for jazz composers to take advantage of what the LP had made possible (e.g., Eddie Sauter's forty-eight minute "Focus," composed for saxophonist Stan Getz and a string orchestra). Curators, publishers, conductors, and theatrical and movie producers all perform editorial functions by creating and maintaining channels of distribution more adequate for some kinds of work than for others, and totally inadequate for still others. They thus select, or lead makers of art works to select, choices which fit easily into the available system.

Though audiences are among the most fleeting participants in art worlds, devoting less time to any particular work or to works of a kind than more professionalized participants, they probably contribute most to the reconstitution of the work on a daily basis. Audiences select what will occur as an art work by giving or withholding their participation in an event or their attention to an object, and by attending selectively to what they do attend to.

Remember that the object of our analysis is not the art work as isolated object or event but the entire process through which it is made and remade whenever someone experiences or appreciates it. That gives a special importance to the audience's contribution. From this viewpoint, any work has only those characteristics its observers notice and respond to on any particular occasion. Whatever its physical properties, they do not exist in the experience of people who do not know or care about them. They appear and disappear, depending on what the audience knows how to perceive (Bourdieu, 1968). What audiences know thus makes the work, if only temporarily. For that reason, what audiences choose to respond to affects the work as much as do the choices of artists and support personnel.

Malraux, Eliot, and other critics have noted that the appearance of a new art work changes the character of those that preceded it. Danto's analysis (1964, pp. 582–84) suggests that that happens because the new work calls attention to a property all works had which went unnoticed because it did not vary from work to work. Thus, we might say that conceptual art pieces made some audiences realize that a physical object was not a crucial component of visual art; for some works (see the works of Haacke [1976], for instance) the physical object is only a way of embodying an idea, and other embodiments of it would serve just as well. The idea is the artist's contribution, not the object. Audiences who accept that premise then look at earlier works as embodiments of ideas as well as beautiful objects, adding to them a characteristic that they may not have had before. Audiences make new choices of what to attend to, and the work changes accordingly.

Smith (1979) has described the variety of possibilities she has paid attention to in one of Shakespeare's sonnets (Sonnet 116) over a period of years. She prefaces her account by noting the varied reception the sonnets have received since they were written:

> [T]he sonnets have been characterized, by men of education and discrimination, as inept, obscure, affected, filled with "labored perplexities and studied deformities," written in a verse-form "incompatible with the English language," a form given to "drivelling incoherencies and puling, petrifying ravings." We might recall especially Henry Hallam's remarking of the sonnets that "it is impossible not to wish that Shakespeare had not written them," and that his assessment or distress was shared, at some point in their lives, with some variations, by Coleridge, Wordsworth and Hazlitt.
>
> *Wish Shakespeare had not written them?* Lord, man, we may wish to shout back into that abysm of time, did you really *read* them? Well, presumably Hallam did read them, as did Dr. Johnson, Coleridge, Wordsworth, Hazlitt and Byron (from each of whom I have been quoting here): but whether any of them read the same poems we are reading is another question. Value alters when it alteration finds. The texts were the same, but it seems clear that, in some sense, the *poems* weren't. (Smith, 1979, p. 10)

I will sample just a few of the varied qualities she found in Sonnet 116, thereby doing an injustice to a subtle analysis:

> As a discriminating young snob, I was pre-disposed to find the value of any poem inversely proportional to the frequency of its appearance in anthologies. Moreover, I had heard this one read too often at the wedding ceremonies of friends. It be-

came an embarrassment just to glance at its opening lines, an agony to recall the couplet. And, to cap it, a professor whose *opinions* I valued very highly had once demonstrated in class, with great wit and dash, that the sentiments of 116 were as inane as its logic was feeble and its imagery vague. . . . [Ten years ago] I discovered an altogether different 116. It was not, as I had previously thought, the expression of the poet as Polonius, intoning sentimental *sententiae* on the virtue of remote virtues, but rather the poet as Troilus or Hamlet or Lear, in a fury of despair, attempting to sustain the existence, by sheer assertion, of something which everything in his own experience denied. *So,* I might have said then, to be sure the arguments are frail and the sentiments false and strained: but this is nonetheless a powerful sonnet because, among other things, that very frailty and strain and falseness are expressive of what is strong and true, namely the impulse *not* to know, *not* to acknowledge, not to "admit" what one does know and would wish to be otherwise.

A lovely reading of the poem, I think . . . when I believe it. And it does have the virtue of rescuing, for me, the value of one sonnet: which is to say, of letting me have, as something good, what would otherwise be something bad—which, in the total economy of the universe, must be reckoned as a profit. But, as for evaluating the sonnet: that I cannot do. Not only does its value, for me, depend upon which of two mutually incompatible interpretations I give it (and I still can give it either) but I'm also aware of the fact that I sometimes enjoy it even when I'm giving it the weak interpretation, and sometimes enjoy elements of it when I'm barely giving it any interpretation at all. For example, it's sometimes nice just to experience again the semi-abstract symmetries of its syntax and sound-patterns, those boldly balanced mouth-filling clauses: *Love is not love/ Which alters when it alteration finds/ Or bends with the remover to remove.* . . . a pleasure to say. Or again, like Professor B., I sometimes enjoy "bombast," and can take pleasure in the sheer excesses of the poem, as such. Experienced against a daily background of scrupulously qualified professional precision, in which one has heard one's colleagues or oneself saying, often enough, things like: "Well, it seems to me that, in a sense, it might be possible, under certain circumstances, for some forms of what is commonly referred to as 'love' to have a relatively lengthy duration"—it's really *nice* to hear a good, strong, unqualified absolute or two:

>Oh, no, it is an *ever*-fixèd mark
>That looks on tempests and is *never* shaken. . . .
>Love *alters* not. . . .
>But bears it out even to the edge of *doom*.

It's just an element of the poem, but it's there among the others; and sometimes it just hits the spot. But, of course, nothing hits the spot *all* the time, because the spot is always different. (Smith, 1979, pp. 12–14)

Audiences vary from time to time and place to place in what they attend to. Since audience responses are typically as conventionalized as those of other participants in art worlds, even though stratified by nearness to the professional core, audience members respond in general as do other members of their segment, and choose much the same things out of the work's possibilities as others do. As we saw in chapter 2, audiences can both learn to experience new elements and forget how to experience old elements of a work, as we have lost the ability to respond directly to the religious and geometric elements of fifteenth-century Italian painting without special training (Baxandall, 1972).

If the choices of audiences and support personnel can remake works so drastically, we can reasonably think of art works as not having a stable character. Even when they are physically stable, retaining those characteristics the artist chose, they differ in the way they appear in people's experience. It is not just that they are differentially evaluated. Different qualities actually come and go as people attend to them differently. Bodies of work by a particular artist change their character even more, as editors add to or subtract from the corpus.

DEATH AND CONSERVATION

Some editorial choices have more profound effects, changing the physical object itself. Those effects last, while the effects of Smith's varying interest in this or that quality of Sonnet 116 leave the object intact for others to make something else of. Art works, we might say, are maimed or die.

Just as works are created anew each time someone experiences them, they die when no one ever again experiences them directly, or even secondhand, by hearing the descriptions of those with firsthand experience. Since art works can die, some artists, sensitive to that possibility and wanting a reputation that will survive them, take into account in making the choices which create the work that some choices have a lower mortality rate than others.

Art works die either because someone executes them, as in the politically motivated destruction considered earlier, or of neglect, because no one cares enough to save them. John Phillips (1973), discussing the destruction of religious sculpture and buildings in England in the sixteenth and seventeenth centuries, notes the important part "picturesque ruins" played in later English romantic painting and poetry, pointing out that those ruins, once functioning religious buildings, were "the destroyed fabric of the medieval church in England" (Phillips, 1973, p. x). His description of the combination of motivated depredation and neglect that produced those ruins exemplifies the way art works die:

> The proud abbey at Glastonbury was suppressed in 1539 and given over to pillage and destruction in the name of reform. When it came into the possession of the Lord Protector Somerset, he stripped the roofs of lead and arranged for a group of about two hundred Flemish weavers to take over the deserted buildings. Six houses were refurbished, but most of the buildings remained in great need of repair. Under Queen Mary the weavers left the country, and though there were hopes of restoring the abbey, little was done.
>
> In the early seventeenth century, Glastonbury was quarried. Frequently, gunpowder was employed to hasten its demolition; the abbey's squared freestone, rubble core in the walls, and heavy stones of the foundation were tempting prizes for neighboring builders. It is possible that the solid foundation across the marshland which acted as support for the causeway to Wells was formed from the stones of Glastonbury.
>
> Early in the eighteenth century, it seems that the abbey was tenanted by a Presbyterian who committed much havoc; every week, he sold a pillar, a buttress, a window joint or an

angle of fine hewn stone to the highest bidder. Continued depredation throughout the eighteenth century and into the nineteenth reduced most of the remaining fabric. Today, Glaston-
bury's foundations have almost completely disappeared.

Yet these strange, desolate piles are still capable of moving
us deeply. . . . (Phillips, 1973, p. ix)

Executioners have a hard time killing art works so thoroughly that they never appear again, especially when the
work exists in multiple copies (books as opposed to
paintings) or when a work's uniqueness does not define it
(performances as opposed to objects). As long as the ideas
contained in it persist, the work continues to exist. So poetry
that has been banned and is no longer printed by government printers will exist if people have memorized it. Even
objects that have been destroyed may continue to exist, in
reproductions, photographs, drawings, or other aids to memory. Conceptual art works can never be destroyed physically, since only the idea need survive. At the extreme, works
exist in title only. Scholars attribute one hundred and eleven
titles to Sophocles, but seven tragedies and part of a satyr
play are all whose texts survive; Aeschylus wrote a trilogy
about Prometheus, but only *Prometheus Bound* still exists,
while *Prometheus the Fire-Bearer* and *Prometheus Unbound*
have disappeared (Hooper, 1967, pp. 267 and 190).

Nevertheless, works die. As a matter of logic, works which
have truly been killed, for whatever reasons, cannot be
known to us; if their memory survives so that we know of
them, they still live. In fact, the political effort to kill art
works and, on occasion, their creators may fail precisely
because the only objects and ideas worth killing are those
which have already interested a large audience or are likely
to do so. When a government tries to kill them it stimulates
further interest and multiplies the number of copies in existence, both physically and in people's heads.

Art works may be killed as a more or less unintended
consequence of some other destructive activity. Wars frequently destroy art works in areas subject to bombing or
other attacks, as occurred during World War II in Europe
and during the war in Vietnam. Art works more often die of

neglect than from deliberate destruction. Social and physical entropy inevitably lead to the scattering and loss of art objects. To persist, works of art must be stored so that they are not physically destroyed. To persist in the life of an art world, they must not only remain available by continuing to exist, they must also be easily accessible to potential audiences. Museums, libraries, archives of all kinds, and other common institutions protect art works and prevent their disappearance. Museums and libraries usually separate their active collections, items easily available to the public, from inactive collections, stored where they can only be gotten to with special effort. Some objects are thus very alive, displayed on walls or available in library stacks, while others are in storage, where only scholars and others who know they are there and request special access can get at them. In either case, the works exist in an art world's life in a way that is not true of works which, continuing to exist physically, can only be found in scattered attics, secondhand stores, or little-known churches. These lost works cannot be found by the conventional methods by which interested parties search for material that interests them, not being listed in library catalogues, in *catalogues raisonées* of the work of well-known artists, or in lists of museum holdings. People who want to experience these works for scholarly or other reasons will not know they are there to experience.

How do museums and other storage institutions decide what goes into their collections and what does not merit such care? They usually explain that their job is to conserve the cultural heritage of the country or of all humanity. But that does not explain much. You would be hard put to construct on the basis of such statements a formula whose application would produce the collections those institutions contain. The museums contain works selected by a network of curators, museum trustees, patrons, dealers, critics, and aestheticians. They contain work that meets the aesthetic standards of some or all of those people, and those standards develop in response to the requirements of such institutions as museums.

Because the prevailing aesthetic does not make them

officially art, works not defined as art remain in such unofficial collection and storage places as attics and secondhand stores. Only when someone's aesthetic, backed by the resources necessary for storage, labels work as art does the work get into the easily accessible museum system. But many eccentric and individualistic people have command of such resources: rich people, kings, commissars. Rich people have frequently founded small museums to preserve materials they found interesting but which had not previously been thought worth such preservation. The Museum of American Folk Art in New York preserves items that were not always kept in museums, although now they commonly are: merry-go-round horses, quilts, weather vanes, and tavern signs. Only recently have such collections, originally limited to folk art of the original thirteen American colonies, included work by later immigrants to the United States. This probably reflects an ideological shift from a celebration of the essentially British past of the United States to a democratic inclusion of the art of groups whose culture had formerly been thought primitive, lacking in artistic merit, and un-American, such as American blacks and Hispanics.

Similarly, the work of naive artists—who work in no established medium and belong to no organized art world—often fails to survive, as we will see when we consider them in the next chapter. Not being integrated into any conventional system of creating and distributing art, the works suffer from natural decay, the offended sensibilities of neighbors, the resulting actions of municipal and county building departments and zoning commissions, and the vandalism of neighborhood children. Few works can withstand such a combination of assaults, unless (as sometimes happens) artists, dealers, and collectors become interested, finding in the work hitherto unnoticed virtues. Acting together, they may succeed in incorporating the work into an art world's storage system and thus save it.

Self-conscious art worlds, then, organize to preserve some of the work done in them. Whatever that world's aesthetic ratifies as sufficiently important artistically or historically will be placed in the appropriate repositories and kept alive (or, at least, in suspended animation). Aesthetic decisions decide the life or death of works. Even more, they decide the life and death of genres. Works in a medium or style defined as not art have a much shorter life expectancy than those defined as art. No organizational imperatives make it worth anyone's while to save them.

No one knows what proportion of the art works created at any particular time survive more than a very short time, in any of the senses of survival we have spoken of, let alone what kinds of work survive through the operation of available collection-storage systems. Most amateur work (I don't use the word pejoratively, merely to refer to work done by people who are not professionals as the particular art world defines it) probably survives, if at all, by becoming embedded in a family system as a memento of the person who made it, and goes out of existence when and if that family breaks up and its belongings are dispersed. Family collections of photographs are an obvious example (although the growth of a professionalized interest in just such collections for scholarly and aesthetic purposes has made them more collectable and thus preserved work which would otherwise have disappeared [see, for instance, Talbot, 1976, and Seiberling, n.d.]). Work contained in scientific archives or the collections of commercial photographers similarly may survive, to be discovered as aesthetically interesting by later generations (as in Lesy's [1976] use of the files of Caulfield and Shook, a firm of Louisville commercial photographers).

What kinds of professional work survive is a more researchable question. One could in principle monitor all the professional work being done in a given medium at some particular time (as White and White [1965] attempted for nineteenth-century French painting). We could then follow a sample, to discover the life span and crucial periods of a work's life.

Work that survives physically can be rediscovered and incorporated into a medium's history (see the analysis of revivals of Renaissance English plays in Griswold, 1980), becoming part of the corpus artists have in mind as they work and audiences have in mind as they experience the results. We have already seen how historians remake the history of a field by rediscovering forgotten masters of painting, literature, or music. The process is especially visible in fields newly discovered to have artistic value. Thus, photographic historians have been reconstituting the history of the medium by discovering bodies of work, describing them, publishing their findings (in the new *Journal of the History of Photography*), and thus moving unknown survivors to the "known and catalogued" category of the photographic world. In so doing, of course, they follow the dictates of an aesthetic that is being created collectively as the work proceeds, an aesthetic which creates the medium's ancestry.

Because art works can die, some artists do what they can to preserve their work; sometimes substantial portions of art worlds join in the effort. Consider the problem of physical deterioration. Works of visual art, by virtue of the nature of their materials and the effects of weather, temperature, and chemical pollution, can deteriorate badly. Paintings crack, sculptures break. Photographs, chemically made, suffer from chemical deterioration. Photographers and museums which collect photographs have jointly developed a standard of archival processing, designed to guard against this hazard by prescribing procedures for removing the most dangerous chemicals from the print. Similarly, many photographers are reluctant to make, and museums are reluctant to collect, color photographs, which are chemically less stable and are shorter-lived than black-and-white. Individual painters and, more importantly, museums and even such cities as Venice and Florence, attempt to do something about the increasing danger to visual art works from industrial and automobile pollution, which have severely damaged in a relatively few years works that had lasted for centuries without visible harm.

Artists can also take precautions to save their work from social and political execution, hiding dangerous meanings, avoiding dangerous topics. Phillips describes how the makers of English tomb sculpture avoided the destruction of images that followed the break with the Roman Church:

> Religious feelings of the wealthy could no longer be expressed in the adorning and erecting of churches, nor could even their

tombs reflect their devotion through images of the Blessed Virgin or of the saints. The new tombs erected during the late sixteenth century were magnificent and sumptuous revelations of the deceased's rank and station and were adorned with the personified, abstract virtues of the departed: faith, wisdom, charity, hope. All sorts of symbolic ornaments came to be carved on tombs: Indians, skulls and crossbones, scythes, urns, weeping cherubs holding doused torches were substituted in place of the traditional Christian symbols that were every day being destroyed. These changes of a conceptual nature suggest not a progress from religious to secular representation: rather, the character of the traditional Catholic imagery gave way to a new religious imagery devoid of traditional identifications and hence safe. (Phillips, 1973, pp. 118–19)

Some of the most important choices that affect an art work, then, are those which destroy or preserve it. The people who make those choices range from librarians and museum curators to neighborhood vandals and political censors. What survives those choices constitutes the corpus of work by which an artist, or a genre or medium, is known. What is lost contributes to no reputation. Though I have concentrated on the visual arts, because works in them usually exist as unique physical objects, the analysis could easily be extended to arts which take the form of multiple objects (e.g., books) or performances.

Let these choices which so immediately affect the existence of a work stand for the multitude of choices affecting the work's character which are made by people other than the artist. Artists, as I have said, make many of the important decisions, but not all of them. Others affect the work as well, by participating in the artist's internal dialogue or by doing something themselves, independent of the artist (perhaps even after his death). When we speak of the work of Titian or Mozart or Rabelais, we conventionally take the works attributed to them to constitute all the work those artists did and assume they did it all themselves. Ordinarily, neither assumption is true. For that reason, the assigning and evaluating of artistic reputations has an ironic character. We praise and blame people for what they did not completely do, leaving out of account much that they did do. Likewise, we assess the reputations of whole genres, styles, periods, and countries on the basis of choices made by all sorts of people about whom we know little or nothing, leaving out of account all the work about which we know nothing because it has been purposely destroyed or because it was not saved, as most works are not. I will return to this problem in the last chapter.

8 • Integrated Professionals, Mavericks, Folk Artists, and Naive Artists

Igor Stravinsky had little trouble finding people to play his innovative works, but Charles Ives, the American composer whose career partially overlapped Stravinsky's, never heard some of his own works performed. American parks are filled with statues of famous men (usually by less-than-famous sculptors) but, as Calvin Trillin (1965, p. 75) remarked in explaining why Los Angeles building inspectors wanted to tear down Simon Rodia's Watts Towers, "City building officials who might treat most works of art with deference, if not always with sympathy, tend to treat a large, unlabelled one the same way they would treat an office building, a house, or, most damaging, a structure that fits into no category at all." Contemporary art museums award prizes to works in fabric by specialists in soft sculpture, but country women who make quilts get their prizes at county fairs.

Wherever an art world exists, it defines the boundaries of acceptable art, recognizing those who produce the work it can assimilate as artists entitled to full membership, and denying membership and its benefits to those whose work it cannot assimilate. If we look at things from a commonsense point of view, we can see that such large-scale editorial choices made by the organizations of an art world exclude many people whose work closely resembles work accepted as art. We can see, too, that art worlds frequently incorporate at a later date works they originally rejected, so that the distinction must lie not in the work but in the ability of an art world to accept it and its maker.

If we consider all the people who work in a particular medium, however the art world defines and judges them, we see that they range from people totally involved in and completely dependent on the paraphernalia of an art world to those who are only marginally related to it because their work does not fit in to the way things are done. Some make work that looks like art, or is sometimes seen to do so, but do it in the context of worlds completely separate from an art world, perhaps in a world of craft or domestic life. Still others carry on their activities quite alone, supported neither by an organized art world or any other organized area of social activity.

If we compare these ways of working, the peculiarities of the nonstandard versions of the activity show us how things work when they are done in the standard way. Analytically, that is, we take making art in the context of an art world as the standard way to make art. It need not be, of course, but it is convenient to treat it as standard, because common usage does and thereby hides the ordinary workings of art worlds from us, as what anyone knows and therefore is not worth knowing. The comparison shows us how things that seem ordinary in the making of professional art need not be that way at all, how art could be made differently, and what the results of doing it differently would be. We will see how being connected with art worlds shapes what people do by seeing how differently people do things when they experience neither the advantages nor the constraints of art world participation.

The work people do varies with the nature of their participation in an art world. But that does not mean that the character of their participation can be seen directly in the work itself. I will talk about integrated professionals, mavericks, folk artists, and naive artists. These relational terms do not describe people, but rather how people stand in relation to an organized art world. Likewise, the work shows the signs of their relation to an art world only in relation to the work done by members of contemporaneous art worlds, for the same piece may at some other time show substantial similarities to work being done in an art world and thus not be so different after all.

It is important to keep in mind that these are relational terms, because people often speak of the artists whose work we will discuss as eccentric or crazy or simple country folk. They may indeed be, but that is not what gives their work its interesting features, since plenty of professional artists are just as eccentric or crazy, though few of them are simple country folk. It is hard to ignore the more flamboyant aspects of some of these personalities, but they are not what is crucial.

INTEGRATED PROFESSIONALS

Imagine, for any particular organized art world, a canonical art work, a work done exactly as the conventions current in that world dictate. A canonical art work would be one for whose doing all the materials, instruments, and facilities have been prepared, a work for whose doing every cooperating person—performers, providers of supplies, support personnel of all kinds, and especially audiences—has been trained. Since everyone involved would know exactly what to do, such a work could be created with a minimum of difficulty. Suppliers would provide the proper materials, performers know just how to interpret the directions given them, museums have exactly the right kind of space and lighting for the work to appear in, and audiences respond with no difficulty to the emotional experiences the art work created. Such a work might bore everyone involved. By definition it would contain nothing novel, unique, or attention getting, nothing that violated anyone's expectations. It would create no tension and arouse no emotion. The paintings on motel walls are just such canonical works.

Imagine, too, a canonical artist, fully prepared to produce, and fully capable of producing, the canonical art work. Such an artist would be fully integrated into the existing art world. He would cause no trouble for anyone who had to cooperate with him, and his work would find large and responsive audiences. Call such artists integrated professionals.

Integrated professionals have the technical abilities, social skills, and conceptual apparatus necessary to make it easy to make art. Because they know, understand, and habitually use the conventions on which their world runs, they fit easily into all its standard activities. If they are composers, they write music performers can read and play on available instruments; if they are painters, they use available materials to produce works which, in size, form, design, color, and content, fit into the available spaces and into people's ability to respond appropriately. They stay within the bounds of what potential audiences and the state consider respectable. By using and conforming to the conventions governing materials, forms, contents, modes of presentation, sizes, shapes, durations, and modes of financing, integrated professionals make it possible for art works to occur efficiently and easily. Large numbers of people can coordinate their activities with a minimum investment of time and energy, simply by identifying the conventions everyone should follow.

In emphasizing the relative ease with which integrated professionals get work done, I do not mean that they never have any trouble. Participants in an art world have a common interest in getting things done, but they also have potentially conflicting private interests. Many conflicts between different kinds of participants are, in fact, chronic and traditional. Playwrights and composers want their works performed as they envision them, but actors and musicians like to perform those works so that they show themselves off to best advantage. Authors would like to revise their novels right through the stage of page proofs, but that costs more than publishers like to spend.

Likewise, the conditions of work may be, for the most integrated professional, demanding and difficult. The star of a Broadway show finds herself condemned to two years of eight strenuous performances a week. The composer of a film score may have to produce eighty or ninety minutes of music, meeting complicated technical specifications as well as creating an intangible but important mood, in six weeks. In fact, the more organized the art world, the more likely it is to generate standards difficult for anyone but a well-trained professional to meet. So being an integrated professional, well-adjusted to an art world, does not guarantee an easy or harmonious life.

Integrated professionals operate within a shared tradition of problems and solutions (Kubler, 1962). They define the problems of their art similarly and agree on the criteria for an acceptable solution. They know the history of previous attempts to solve those problems, or some of it, and the new problems those attempts generated. They know the history of work like theirs, so that they, their support personnel, and their audiences can understand what they have attempted and how and to what degree it works. All this makes the joint action necessary to create art works easier.

Relying on this shared history of problems and solutions, integrated professionals can produce work that is recognizable and understandable to others without being so recognizable and understandable as to be uninteresting. They can generate uncertainty in an informed audience as to exactly how they will proceed because the work need not be the mere repetition of ritual moves. They know many ways to manipulate standard materials to create emotional and artistic effects.

Most people who work in an organized art world are, by definition, integrated professionals, for no art world could continue to exist without a ready supply of people capable of turning out its characteristic products. The network of distributive organizations art worlds develop—galleries, concert halls, theaters, and publishing companies—requires the continuous creation of a body of work to be distributed. These institutions may cease operating, thus requiring less work. But while they exist, they look for work to display, and some of the many people who aspire to be integrated professionals will provide it. Furthermore, the aesthetic current in a world will certify as sufficiently good to be displayed roughly the amount needed to fill the display opportunities.

This suggests that art worlds treat the integrated professionals who participate in them, and their works, as interchangeable, as though their distinctive differences and unique abilities nevertheless allowed them to be substituted for one another without harm. If I cannot have a Picasso exhibition for my museum, perhaps I can have Matisse, and that will be just as good—different, of course, but not worse. If Horowitz cannot appear with our orchestra, Rubenstein will be perfectly acceptable. The same is true at every level of renown; anyone who wants to exhibit "Twenty New American Photographers" or publish "Ten New British Poets" will always be able to fill those slots.

To talk about artists and their work as interchangeable, however, does violence to the art world belief that the differences between artists and their work, especially differences of quality, can never be ignored. In this view, a knowledgeable person can always rank artists and works in a given field, distinguishing those worth bothering about from the others. In practice, however, art world participants think a large number of people, not just the very best, worth bothering about, for the practical reasons that you have to encourage many in order to find the few, and that there is no telling when someone not worth bothering about will suddenly become worth it after all. If we bothered only about the *very* best, we would shut our galleries eleven months out of the year, open Carnegie Hall every now and then, and publish many fewer books. But if we did that we would never have the facilities ready for those worth bothering about when they did appear, for you cannot maintain those organizations with such sporadic use.

Art worlds deal with the contradiction between thinking only a few worth caring about and actually paying attention to many more by distinguishing between great artists, however that is defined and whatever words are used to express it, and those who are competent. Using contemporary standards, people can generally make these distinctions easily. Standards change, and the judgments made in an art world seldom coincide with those made later by others, with what will come to be seen as the judgment of history—that is, with the judgment of later members of the same art world.

A less neutral, and less charitable, way of speaking about the bulk of practitioners in any art world would be to say that most of them seem to their peers to be hacks, competent but uninspired workers who turn out the mass of work essential to keep the world's organizations going. Only an organized art world which produces integrated professionals can have hacks. Without the background of organizational need for work to display and a tradition within which ordinary work can be intelligible and interesting, hacks cannot exist. Only against that background does anyone need to take so much work seriously, and provide the means for its makers to continue to exist as artists.

The integrated professionals who run an art world produce large amounts of work. White and White (1965) estimated that in the 1860s the "art machine" of French painting had mobilized five thousand painters, who turned out an estimated two hundred thousand reputable paintings every ten years. Similar figures, if they were available, would probably characterize the world of the American short story in the years when many commercial magazine outlets existed for it and (with an adjustment for the amount of investment required) the Broadway theater in its heyday. The work of those whom contemporary judgment singles out as exceptionally good—contemporary stars, as distinguished from the journeymen and hacks who make up the bulk of the workers—has a greater chance of lasting and being available for later judgment, since it is sanctioned by consensus as the best the world has produced. They get this greater chance because the libraries, museum collections, and similar repositories which preserve art works naturally select what contemporary opinion thinks best. The mechanisms of preservation are sufficiently unselective that much more survives.

Most of this book, of necessity, has been about integrated professionals; what they do is the bulk of what goes on in the name of art in any society. The remainder of this chapter considers some other ways art gets made, both because that illuminates the situation of integrated professionals and because some work made in these other ways, undergoing a reputational change, eventually joins the tradition of some art world.

MAVERICKS

Every organized art world produces mavericks, artists who have been part of the conventional art world of their time, place, and medium but found it unacceptably constraining. They propose innovations the art world refuses to accept as within the limits of what it ordinarily produces. Other participants in the world—audiences, support personnel, sources of support, or distributors—refuse to cooperate in the production of those innovations. Instead of giving up and returning to more acceptable materials and styles, mavericks continue to pursue the innovation without the support of other art world personnel. Whereas integrated professionals accept almost completely the conventions of their world, mavericks retain some loose connection with it but no longer participate in its activities directly.

Mavericks begin their careers as conventional novices. They learn what other young aspirants in their art world learn. Thus, Charles Ives (see figure 22), an archetypal maverick, studied composition at Yale with Horatio Parker, a conventional composer and teacher in the then fashionable German tradition. He learned conventional harmony and counterpoint, and studied approved musical forms, doing classroom exercises which confirmed his ability to handle these standard tasks. He had received similar training from his father, a professional musician in Danbury, Connecticut. But his father, more adventurous if less successful than Parker, had also taught his son to experiment (with polytonality, for instance) in ways then uncommon. So Ives composed music his teacher found unacceptable, foreshadowing what would happen when he tried his luck in the big world of professional music in New York (Rossiter, 1975, pp. 54–64).

Not surprisingly, mavericks get a hostile reception when they present their innovations to other art world members. Because it violates some of the art world's conventions in a blatant way, the work suggests to others that they will have

FIGURE 22. Charles Ives, an archetypal musical maverick. When professional players told him his music was unplayable, he stopped trying to write music they could play. (Photograph by Frank Gerratana, courtesy of the Yale University Music Library.)

trouble cooperating with its maker; its blatant disregard of established practice suggests that the person who made it either doesn't know what is right or doesn't care to do what is right (the same reasoning leads people to overreact to allegedly deviant activities in other areas of life [cf. Becker, 1963]). The conventional orchestral musicians of New York thought Ives' music willfully ignorant or crude, filled with dissonance, formless, and relying tastelessly on vernacular music of the time, both popular and religious, for raw materials. His private papers tell stories of his playing his work for musical friends and acquaintances, only to have them leave the room in horror or disgust. A biographer summarizes Ives' experience with a well-known violinist of the period; the quotations are from Ives' account in his *Memos* (Ives, 1972):

> In 1914, feeling that "it would be a good plan to get one of the supposedly great players" to try over his music, the Ives invited to West Redding one Franz Milcke, whom Mrs. Ives had known in Hartford. This "typical hard-boiled, narrow-minded, conceited, prima donna solo violinist with a reputation gained because he came to this country with Anton Deidl as his concertmaster" dismissed Ives' compositions summarily. "He came out of the little back music room with his hands over his ears," complaining that "when you get awfully indigestible food in your stomach that distresses you, you can get rid of it," but that he could not "get those horrible sounds out of my ears." (Rossiter, 1975, pp. 150–51)

For more than twenty years, Ives' music was not performed in public or taken seriously by professional musicians or serious audiences.

Mavericks typically have such difficulties realizing their works or, in media where realization is easy but distribution the problem (writing, for instance), getting them to audiences and critics. They succeed, when they do, by circumventing the need for art world institutions. They may, for instance, create their own organizations to replace those which will not work with them. Writers publish and distribute their work themselves. Playwrights and directors set up new theatrical companies, recruiting people (mostly those without previous theatrical experience, for professionals will already have rejected them) from outside the world of professional theater to perform. Visual artists create their own display spaces or, more comprehensively, devise works which cannot be exhibited in museums and galleries—earthworks or conceptual art—thus escaping what they feel to be the stylistic tyranny of museum directors, curators, and financial supporters. Dramatic artists dispense with theaters, using spaces available to the public to do street theater. In general, mavericks recruit followers, disciples, and helpers, often, and for good reason, from the ranks of the untrained and unprofessional, and create their own networks of co-operating personnel, especially new audiences.

The most extreme adaptation to being rejected by the or-ganized art world is to truncate the doing of the work, per-haps only thinking of it and not doing it at all. Ives seems to have decided that his music was never going to be played and to have adjusted totally to that possibility. In fact, he came to regard the playing of music as an interference in composition:

> My God, what has sound got to do with music! . . . Why can't music go out in the same way it comes in to a man, without having to crawl over a fence of sounds, thoraxes, catguts, wire, wood, and brass? . . . That music must be heard, is not essential—what it *sounds* like may not be what it *is*. (Quoted in Rossiter, 1975, p. 58)

Any composer, having suffered from performers who did not play what was written as had been intended, might echo those thoughts. But practical people who make their living in the world of music know it is just a feeling, not something you can act on. Ives acted on it, thus displaying the maver-ick's characteristic independence of the art world.

Mavericks do not, nevertheless, totally lose touch with the world of their medium. They usually keep up with what is being done there, even if they do not participate firsthand, by attending to public media; they listen to recordings, see films, read trade and professional publications. But they lose touch with what those media do not report, particularly the day-to-day revisions of the working conventions that govern routine work. In music, they lose touch with the ongoing revisions of performance practice, the conventions by which performers translate written notation into played notes. So, while they remain attuned to general currents of change in the art world, they can no longer participate fully in it.

Mavericks thereby lose or forego all the advantages the integrated professional more or less automatically enjoys. But they also lose the constraints associated with those advantages. Participation in an art world makes the production of art works possible and relatively easy but substantially constrains what can be created. Ives' complete separation from the world of practical music making is almost a laboratory experiment for the discovery of maverick freedoms. Since he eventually gave up hoping to hear his music played, we can see from his later practice what musical composition might be like divorced from an art world's practical considerations.

Ives, for example, never had to finish his compositions, since they were never going to be played. According to John Kirkpatrick, the pianist who gave the first public performance of the *Concord Sonata*:

> Some pieces, like *Concord*, Ives never did the same way twice, and he almost always resented the thought or the fancied obligation that he should put it down precisely, because he loved to improvise it. (Perlis, 1974, p. 220)

We might say that every art work contains an idea which needs to be worked out; the working out shapes it into a final form dictated by the conventions of the contemporary world for which it is made. In that final form, it is presentable—capable of being presented to people who will otherwise regard it as not done and not yet worthy of attention. Presentable forms signal, in a conventional way, that you want your work taken seriously, counted up in the balance of your reputation (thus differing from a "work in progress"). In music, the presentable form is a finished score (or, at least, that's what it was when Ives wrote). The people who led the later movement for the performance of Ives' music had enormous troubles because Ives did not produce finished scores. Their love of his music barely concealed their irritation with his unprofessional ways. Bernard Herrmann, the composer and conductor who conducted some of the first performances of Ives' orchestral works, said:

> I think he was more interested in just writing his own pieces and that was it. That is why they all exist in such terrible states. He wasn't interested enough to take time to do the proofreading. . . . Because of the parts, it was terrible in the

early days to try to achieve an Ives performance. . . . The parts were not copied and collated and corrected. So it was always very difficult. . . . Ives, after all, was a very impractical man when it came to performances of music. By not being a professional musician in the sense that he did not have to make a living out of music, he entered into an abstraction of music. Because it was an abstraction, it didn't deal with any of the realistic problems. (Perlis, 1974, pp. 159–60)

George Roberts, a copyist who helped him prepare some of his scores for publication, described Ives' indifference to the routines of publication:

I did some of the *Concord Sonata*. Every time I went there it was new. The printers were on his neck all the time. He used to laugh about it. He didn't care; he was in no hurry, and he always had something new to put in. (Perlis, 1974, p. 186)

Conventional composers use notation that makes sense to the ordinary performer. After all, notational devices, a shorthand composers can use to make their wishes known to performers, only work if the players can immediately (or with a little explanation) understand them. Ives' notational devices confused conventional orchestral players. For instance, he often used what seemed to be inexplicable spellings of notes. (This is a technical point. Any note can be notated in more than one way; not only can A-sharp be written as B-flat, A can also on occasion be written as B-double-flat, and so on. Standard rules govern when one or another spelling is used.) A sympathetic interpreter who was one of the early conductors of Ives' music, Nicholas Slonimsky, explained that such devices had a meaning, if you had Ives to explain it to you:

For instance, I remember a very strange situation in the viola part [of *Three Places in New England*]: an A sharp that was immediately changed to B flat, and I could not find any justification for the use of that A sharp, and I wanted to change it to a B flat so as not to confuse the player in his part. But Ives said no. He said that A sharp was important because it was proceeding from A as a sort of an unfinished chromatic, and that it would have gone to B but it just didn't, and so therefore B flat would be wrong. (Perlis, 1974, p. 150)

Conductor Gunther Schuller explains the practical impact of some of Ives' notational devices:

> However, some of those rhythms are literally unreadable, so you have to take the concept and translate it into the practical or pragmatic, and that may take a lot of rewriting. Then, you have to practice it that way to get it accurate, but of course that's not enough. You must then retranslate it back into the concept. That takes time, and sometimes you cannot do it in four rehearsals. Sometimes you can't do it in five concerts. With certain musicians, sometimes you can't do it at all. It becomes an enormous problem. (Hitchcock and Perlis, 1977, p. 121)

Not being part of an organized art world in which he was making a reputation that had value, Ives likewise had little interest in taking care of his materials in the standard way. He wrote over already written scores until they were almost unintelligible. The original score for *Chromatimelodtune*, for instance, contains alternate parts for the players, written over each other in pencil and pen; just copying the parts requires essentially compositional decisions. He did not preserve his scores; many were lost and turned up later in unexpected places. No wonder, from this description by Jerome Moross, who collaborated with Herrmann in preparing the Fourth Symphony for performance:

> He gave us this incredible photostat of a manuscript, and we were just appalled at the start. It took us weeks of calling and going back and checking on notes with him. . . . We couldn't decipher the terrible manuscript, and Ives had to make the final decisions of what he had meant. Then there was one movement [the fourth] that he couldn't find at the time. The manuscripts were just in a mess in the closet. (Perlis, 1974, p. 165)

More conventional composers take better care of their work; they may need it another time. Stravinsky, for instance, often rescored works whose copyright was running out, thus continuing to collect royalties on the new version; that shows a professional orientation Ives lacked. He rewrote things because he had no professionally based need to finish them.

Ives rejoiced in not having to do things with the finality, neatness, and conventional devices other composers accepted as the price of having their work done—accepted, as the comments of Herrmann and others suggest, not as unreasonable constraints, but as the sensible measures musicians would want, in their own interest, to take. Because he didn't need to bother with all these conventional requirements, Ives had more time for what he regarded as the core activity, conceiving the music, and was able to escape the practical realities that prevented other composers from writing, or even thinking, the things he thought of. No sensible composer would, without receiving a commission, write a symphony (his Fourth) which uses three distinct orchestras and requires two subconductors to assist the conductor in leading them. Even composers who could contemplate that would not spend their time composing Ives' *Universe* Symphony, which requires, for one part alone, anywhere from five to fourteen orchestral groups and choruses, scattered around mountains and valleys (Rossiter, 1975, p. 109). (Post-Woodstock, that does not seem so fanciful as it once did.) Freed from the constraints of what was practical in his time, Ives could write anything he could imagine and imagine things professionals could not.

Composer Betsy Jolas suggested the same theory of Ives:

> Why not, in fact, admit it: Ives is unequivocally an amateur. Not, to be sure, in the sense of lacking craft—at Yale he got from the tedious Horatio Parker the most traditional training, with all the requisite harmony, counterpoint, fugue—but rather, in the noblest sense, because he *loved* music. . . . even to the point of refusing . . . to make a profession of it.
>
> . . . he *was* a Sunday musician. . . . a free musician, free to pursue his sonorous vision wherever he wished, apart from any practical or economic considerations.
>
> . . . Working essentially in isolation, without contact—or almost so—with the professional musical world of his time, indifferent to current fashions and not seeking performances, Ives was perhaps able, with fewer risks than a career composer, to indulge in "dangerous" experiments, daring to think sometimes even beyond the limits he could actually achieve. (Hitchcock and Perlis, 1977, p. 251)

Because mavericks can ignore the constraints which impede the work of integrated professionals and because they do not participate in the day-to-day interaction of the art world, they have different motives from integrated professionals. Professionals' reasons for doing things are built into the organization of the art world; a person who does not participate in that world cannot give those reasons for doing anything. To be specific, if Ives no longer cared whether his work was performed (whether out of anger, indifference, or resignation), then he could not want to do anything because it would help him get his works performed. If people do things for reasons which are not standard in a particular world, they look (to active members of that world) unsocialized and more than a little crazy—one of the ways we recognize a reliable, well-socialized person is that we immediately understand the reasons for his behavior (Mills, 1940). Ives typically gave idiosyncratic reasons for his musical work, sometimes political, sometimes nostalgic. He often said that he intended some of his most unusual and dissonant effects to recreate the sound of, for instance, a religious revival meeting during which five hundred people would sing the same hymn, many of them out of tune, a few perhaps singing the wrong song altogether. That is very different from the technical reasons a Stravinsky or Schoenberg, similar innovators, would give (cf. Rossiter, 1975, p. 94 *passim*).

Because mavericks give undecipherable reasons for the work they produce, when organized art worlds take the work up, as they sometimes do (a process considered below), professionals disagree about what has been done. Professionals now disagree about whether Ives really knew what he was doing.

Conductor Lehman Engel suggests (Hitchcock and Perlis, 1977, p. 115) that Ives:

> rarely heard anything he wrote. . . . he had had no real experience with music. . . . everything he wrote seemed to indicate his feeling about something that had nothing really to do with music.

Choral conductor Gregg Smith, on the other hand, thinks

Ives' notation was precise, that what he wrote was what he wanted:

> almost every single notation that was a mystery or seemed strange finally came out to be a darned good solution. . . . In *Psalm 90*, there's a bell figure that is a group of nine eighths in 4/4. Well, the real point of that to me is that although the figure starts one eighth note later in each measure, there's a freedom of playing with that figure. . . . He wasn't an amateur; he was a fantastic genius who knew what he was notating, and it's for us to find out what it is about. (Hitchcock and Perlis, 1977, p. 118)

Some professionals think Ives must have been impelled by the same motives as themselves, even when it seems otherwise. Elliott Carter, the well-known American composer, wondered whether Ives really invented all the innovations he has been credited with, considering his habit of constantly revising his scores; for a serious art world professional, the question of who did something first might have an important effect on one's reputation. Did Ives manipulate his reputation by rewriting?

> He was working on, I think, *Three Places in New England*, getting the score ready for performance. A new score was being derived from the older one to which he was adding and changing, turning octaves into sevenths and ninths, and adding dissonant notes. Since then, I have often wondered at exactly what date a lot of the music written early in his life received its last shot of dissonance and polyrhythm. In this case he showed me quite simply how he was improving the score. I got the impression that he might have frequently jacked up the level of dissonance of many works as his tastes changed. While the question no longer seems important, one could wonder whether he was as early a precursor of "modern" music as is sometimes made out. (Perlis, 1974, p. 138)

Because mavericks have had training in the traditions and practices of the art world to which their work is related, and because they maintain an attenuated connection to it, it can assimilate their work, if a sufficient consensus develops among practitioners. Mavericks violate the conventions of art world practice, but they do so selectively and in fact abide by most of them. If James Joyce ignored the literary and even linguistic forms of his day, he still wrote a finished book. He did not, for instance, write a work like Joe Gould's *History of the World*, which would never be finished and most of which was probably never written down (Mitchell, 1965); nor did he devise a literary form that would be chanted instead of being printed or one in which his own personal calligraphy would be an important element of his composition. He wrote a perfectly recognizable European book. Similarly, creators of earthworks create sculpture, after all; the materials, scale, and setting of their works are unconventional, but they share with more canonical sculptors a concern with form and volume. Mavericks, in other words, have taken a slightly different path through the art world's traditional series of problems and solutions. But integrated professionals can retrace the path to the point where the maverick diverged from what became conventional, and thus incorporate the maverick's innovations into the canon.

Work varies in how difficult it is to assimilate. Ives' work, compared with much that followed it, now seems relatively easy. However unusual his notation, however unfamiliar the sounds, however impractical the orchestral sizes he required, he wrote for conventional instruments, used normal instrumental combinations (the symphony orchestra, quartet, and chorus), and familiar musical forms (the symphony, sonata, and art song). Other contemporary composers have gone much further. John Cage, for instance, has required performers to alter their instruments, "preparing" pianos by inserting tacks or other materials between the hammers and strings, or using the mouthpiece of a wind instrument without the body. Performers of some of his works write their own parts, using randomizing devices to manipulate charts he has prepared, from which the part to be performed can be constructed. No two scores or performances of the same composition, therefore, are alike; performers cannot learn a Cage piece as they can one by Schoenberg or Ives.

Harry Partch's compositions likewise make few concessions to conventional practice. He broke with the convention of the chromatic scale on which Western music is built, and devised a scale containing forty-two tones between the octaves (the conventional scale contains twelve tones in the same interval). As we saw in the first chapter, that required numerous other changes: in the construction of instruments, in the training of players, and in notation.

Nevertheless, both Partch and Cage, for all their innovations, retain many conventions of the music world. Their works are of a duration which can be incorporated into concerts of ordinary length, and both relied on the concert and recording as the methods of presenting their work to audiences. People still buy a ticket, file into a hall at an appointed time, and sit quietly while performers play for them.

Mavericks, then, orient themselves to the world of canonical and conventional art. They change some of its conventions and more or less unwittingly accept the rest. The work of these innovators is often incorporated into the historical corpus of the established art world, whose members find the innovations useful in producing the variation required to rescue art from ritual. Innovations become more acceptable through familiarity and association. Their essential fit with all the other conventions makes it relatively easy to assimilate them. Mavericks deal with the people who manufacture the materials used by more conventional artists, but demand new things of them, as they do of the support personnel others rely on. They want to be supported and appreciated by the same audiences more conventional artists play to, although the new and unfamiliar works require audiences to work harder.

Because maverick work shares so much with conventional work, we can see that maverickness is not inherent in the work, but rather in the relation between it and a conventional art world. Maverick work chooses to be so difficult to assimilate that the art world refuses the challenge. If the contemporary art world does adapt, then artist and work lose their maverick quality, since the conventions of the world now encompass what was once foreign. Because the maverick becomes the conventional, and not just because life offers us so many intermediate cases, we cannot draw a firm line between the innovating integrated professional and the maverick.

FIGURE 23. Conlon Nancarrow and the apparatus for creating player piano compositions. Nancarrow creates music by punching holes directly into a player piano roll, thus achieving effects impossible for human performers. (Photograph courtesy of 1750 Arch Street Records.)

Just as not all the work of integrated professionals is thought to be of high quality, so very few mavericks gain the respect of the art world they are quarreling with. In fact, most art world participants probably never hear of the vast majority of mavericks, and very few of those who are heard of are ever thought well of. Instead, they remain curiosities whose work may be revived from time to time by interested antiquarians or, alternatively, may stimulate the imagination of innovative professionals. An interesting musical example is the work of Conlon Nancarrow (1979), who creates music for player piano by the unconventional method of punching holes directly into the piano roll (see figure 23). He can thus produce such effects as the chromatic glissando, otherwise unobtainable on the piano, and has used these possibilities to create music which connoisseurs find interesting and moving. But Nancarrow's innovation requires substantial rearrangement of the relationships between performers and composers, requires an entirely new order of skill in the composer, and is ill-adapted to the conventional practices by which musicians and composers distribute and support their work. So it has never caught on, and conventional musicians aware of his work regard it as an interesting curiosity with no practical relevance. (Other mavericks find it very important.)

I have relied on musical examples to illustrate the case of the maverick, primarily because the complexity of the cooperative musical enterprise makes the dynamics of the phenomenon more obvious. But the same kind of half-in, half-out relation between maverick artists and conventional art worlds can be discovered in every art. Keep in mind that most mavericks' work is not absorbed into the canon of an art world; they remain unknown, and their work is not preserved and disappears along with their name.

FOLK ART

When we attend someone's birthday party, we customarily sing "Happy Birthday" to him. We do not hire professional performers for such an event. It doesn't matter if the singing is out of tune or tempo, as long as the song gets sung. Any competent participant in the culture can manage an acceptable version, since everyone knows it and the standard of acceptability is very low.

"Happy Birthday" is the kind of thing I mean when I speak of folk art. This may be a somewhat eccentric use of the term (see Glassie's [1972] discussion), but I do not refer specially to work done by country folk or to rural remnants of customs once widespread. Rather, I want to talk about work done totally outside professional art worlds, work done by ordinary people in the course of their ordinary lives, work seldom thought of by those who make or use it as art at all, even though, as often happens, others from outside the community it is produced in find artistic value in it.

Folk art, in this sense, is art done by people who do what they do because it is one of the things members of their community, or at least most members of a particular age and sex, ordinarily do. People know that some do these things better than others, but that is a minor consideration. The main thing is that they be done to some minimum standard, be good enough for the purpose at hand. Housewives cook, and, though the people who eat their cooking would rather that they cooked better than worse, it is more important that the meals appear on the table regularly so that the other members of the family can be nourished sufficiently to go about their other business—at least, that is true of the conventional family. Socially competent high school students learn to do current dances; some dance wonderfully, some are terrible, but the main thing is that they dance well enough to join the other kids in social activities that require dancing as a minimal social skill. (Another kind of work done outside the confines of art worlds is craft work, discussed in the next chapter.)

I will use quilting as my major example for analytic purposes. American women have, at various times and places, made quilted bedding. It served to keep people warm (although at some times and for some women it was more a hobby designed to produce items for domestic display) but, in addition to that utility, it often displayed a sophisticated design and color sense that reminds present-day observers of a number of features of contemporary painting. Jonathan Holstein suggests a series of such comparisons:

—That manipulation of geometric form which has characterized the work of many painters since the advent of Abstractionism.
—The optical effects of such quilts as Baby Blocks and the work of Vasarely and others who have explored the possibilities of various modes of retinal stimulation through color and form relationships, optical illusion, manipulations of linear effects.
—The use of repeated images drawn from the environment, as in the Coffee Cups quilt, and the sequential use of images in the works of such artists as Andy Warhol.

—The repetitive use of highly reduced geometric forms, and the work of the systemic painters.

—The color variations on a single format, as in the Amish quilts, and such paintings as Albers' *Homage to the Square* series.

—The manipulation for visual effect of chromatic possibilities in a geometric framework as in such quilts as the Rainbow quilts, and the work of such painters as Kenneth Noland. (Holstein, 1973, p. 113)

Folk artists resemble canonical art world artists in one respect: they belong to and produce their work as part of a well-organized community. But quilters belong, not to a professional or work community devoted to art, but to the very opposite, a local community made up of household units. Quilters make the art works they make as family members and neighbors. Their work therefore reflects the constraints and opportunities of that community, rather than the constraints and opportunities of the art worlds we have so far considered. In the same way, high school dancing arises in the context of the teenage social world and reflects its opportunities and constraints.

Women made quilts because their families needed them to keep warm. According to Holstein:

in earlier times almost all American homes used some quilts, along with their home-woven blankets, if they were not, by force of circumstance, using skins to cover their beds. It is equally probable that for a very long period almost all American women made quilts.

In many parts of the country there was a custom that a young girl make a baker's dozen of quilt tops before she became engaged, twelve utility quilts, undoubtedly pieced, and one great quilt, pieced or appliqué, for her bridal bed. After her engagement, she would take final steps to turn her tops into finished quilts, and these went with her as an essential part of her trousseau. (Holstein, 1973, p. 81)

If they did not make quilts for themselves, women made them for others in need. (The following quotation, and all others not otherwise attributed in this section, are from Patricia Cooper and Norma Buferd's [1977]* study of quilting in the Southwestern United States; the book is composed almost entirely of interviews with quilters, and these are what I quote.)

> One time we quilted for a widow lady that was under hard circumstances and no man. Or if someone new came to the community and was setting up housekeeping, the women of the community would do a Friendship quilt for them. (P. 105)

People made quilts, then, because they needed them. The responsibility, by custom, was the woman's.

Because quilting is communally based, people learn to do it in the course of their routine participation in the community. An eighty-three year old woman tells how she learned to quilt:

> Mama was a beautiful quilter. She done the best work in the county. Everybody knew it. . . .
>
> I always longed to work with her and I can tell you how plain I recall the day she said, "Sarah, you come with me now if you want to."
>
> I was too short to sit in a chair and reach it, so I got my needle and thread and stood beside her. I put that needle through and pulled it back up again, then down, and my stitches were about three inches long. Papa come in about that time, he stepped back and said, "Florence, that child is ruinin' your quilt."
>
> He said, "Well, you're jest goin' to have to rip it all out tonight."
>
> Mama smiled at me and said, "Them stitches is going to be in that quilt when it wears out."
>
> All the time they was talkin' my stitches was gettin' shorter. (P. 52)

Though most women apparently learned from their mothers in this natural way, some managed to avoid it and learned later in life from their peers, less tolerant of imperfect work:

* Excerpts from *The Quilters: Women and Domestic Art*, by Patricia Cooper and Norma Bradley Buferd. Copyright 1977 by Patricia Cooper Baker and Norma Buferd. Reprinted by permission of Doubleday & Company, Inc.

I remember a girl. She was newly married. She had a baby and she joined our club. She had never quilted before and I don't reckon she'd ever seen anybody quilt. She'd belonged to our club, I don't know how long, two or three weeks or maybe a month, before she found out we was going down from the top and plumb through the lining with each stitch. You know what? She was workin' on all her stitches so hard and they was just goin' through the top . . . jest quiltin' along on the top. Would you ever think anybody could be that dumb? She was a sweet little old girl, but she just didn't know no better. "Well, I didn't know you was goin' all the way through," she said. Why everybody in the room jest died. I laughed and everybody did. It was funny, but I felt sorry for her, she hated it so bad. (Pp. 102–3)

Painful or not, the learning is a natural consequence of belonging to a family or to community organizations. Though quilting is traditionally a woman's occupation in the communities in which it is done, men occasionally learn:

My husband tells about the time he got sick with the measles. His mother set him to piecing a quilt and every other block he set in red polka-dot pattern. Said it was his measles quilt. He wouldn't like me to tell it now I know. But lots of cold nights when I'm at the quiltin' frame on one side of the fire, he pulls his big old chair up on the other side and cuts pieces for me. He's even done a bit of piecin' from time to time.

It's a sight, that big old long-legged man with his boot toes turned in to make a lap to do his piecework on. (P. 39)

Novice quilters learn standards as well as technique. Some standards—craft standards—are public and shared:

Mama had the smallest stitches and the smallest feet in the country. She was particular about everything she done. I got that from her. There was an order to everything, and when one of her quilts was done, it was just like the rest, all of a piece and finished right—the corners turned to a tee, like making the bed, every seam straight as an arrow; you know it wasn't hard to stitch good and it was real satisfying to keep everything up to standards. (P. 97)

Other criteria used in judging quilts may not be widely

shared. Quilters and their families admire some quilts more than others. A husband told Cooper and Buferd:

I'm glad Molly got to show you that quilt, but I won't let her sell it. That's the finest thing we ever had in this house. That's the best one she ever done. We had that one on our bed from the first till I told her to put it away for safekeeping. The gold triangles were beginning to show a little wear. (P. 20)

And a quilter said:

I keep my best quilts put up for special occasions, or just to bring out and look at, put on the bed once in a while. I'll pass them on to the kids of course. (P. 108)

Quilters apparently seldom make explicit the aesthetic underlying these judgments and choices; they are, after all, not professional artists or critics. But if we bring the sensibility of someone familiar with modern paintings (of the kind Holstein mentioned) to bear as we look at pieced quilts, some quilts clearly present developments that are interestingly parallel to those of painters. Quilters did describe their working methods to Cooper and Buferd in a way that suggests that they develop private sequences of problems and solutions (of the kind George Kubler speaks of) within the framework of the traditional quilt designs.

Quilt designs, while traditional, are by no means constraining; they allow plenty of room for variation, choice, and the play of individual skill and taste (see figure 24). Many quilts are made up of a simple square module, which can be assembled in a seemingly endless variety of ways to make quite different overall patterns. The "Drunkard's Path," for instance, combines a quarter circle and the negative space that surrounds it to make such overall patterns as the "Drunkard's Path" itself and the "Millwheel." The "Log Cabin" square, consisting of a number of strips butted against one another around a central square (so arranged that the square is half light and half dark, divided along the diagonal), can be arranged in many ways—to produce a pattern of diagonal light and dark stripes across the entire quilt (called "Straight Furrow"), a pattern of concentric squares,

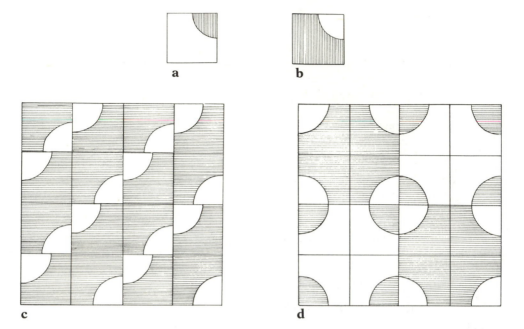

FIGURE 24. Quilt designs. These designs are sometimes made from a simple module, which can be assembled to make a great variety of overall patterns, especially when the tonal values and patterns of the cloth of which the module is made are varied. The "Drunkard's Path" block can be made (a) with a dark quarter circle, the complementary space in the square being light, or (b) with the values reversed. Using block (b), you can create (c) the classic "Drunkard's Path" overall design. Combining (a) and (b) allows you to make the more complicated (d) "Millwheel." (Drawings by Nan Becker.)

alternating light and dark (called "Barn Raising"), or a surprisingly large number of other variations, some of which have traditional names and others not. If you add to these possibilities the endless ways that colors, hues, and print patterns can be built into such arrangements, it is clear that the quiltmaker has a large array of artistic resources to work with. A look at the illustrations in the books I have been citing will confirm that some quiltmakers use them to produce work which, as Holstein claims, resembles that of contemporary painters; but it is a good bet that the quiltmakers would not regard that painting as serious art.

Like artists working within the tradition of an art world, quiltmakers use these resources differently, producing results that, not simply reproductions of traditional patterns, are as different and discriminable as works in traditional artistic media and genres. We can infer how this happens from their descriptions of how they work. We need first to understand the origin of the material that goes into the quilt top. In keeping with the basis of the quilt in family and community life, quilts are, for the most part, made of scraps left over from other utilitarian sewing projects:

> Mother saved pieces from every dress she ever made for me; when I got older she gave them to me to make a quilt. In her day pieced tops were all made from a woman's scrap bag, and at that time, more often than not, the linings were other old worn-out quilts or old blankets. We never wasted a bit of cloth ... used it over and over until it wore out. Waste not, want not. (P. 100)

Quilters sort their scraps by categories:

> Now back here in the back room I got all my materials stored. I put every scrap of material I think I can ever use into them piece bags till I can get to sortin' it. Then I put it into those boxes. Kinda on file. . . . Each box is labeled with the colors of pieces inside, and then some is labeled with plaids and stripes and the kind of pattern if they's already cut. . . .
>
> Now these are for my sunlight and shadows [i.e., light and dark segments] in the Log Cabin. I'm gettin' close to the bottom on my lights. I've got plenty of darks. I have to keep my eyes open for lights. I always know what shade will match what I got in mind. I never buy for my piece bag and I hate to borrow. I like to think I can take care of myself. (P. 100)

Their language scarcely does justice to the complex effects they achieve, and one must suppose, on the visual evidence of the quilts, that they have a more complex understanding of color and design than they can articulate to an interviewer. It seems likely that, while quilters recognize these variations in design and ability, they have no generalized critical or analytic language in which to discuss them. They can speak of ways of sorting materials. They mention optical effects—

"now this one here is like a puzzle"—and how they can be created—"if you just placed dark triangles next to these diamonds, they would stand out." They know and are proud of originality: "Now I like to try to put them colors down in a way no one ever saw before."

But quilters' language does not allow them to discuss their work with one another in the generalized and abstract way that critical and aesthetic formulations help integrated professionals to communicate with one another easily, across space and time, about what they are doing. (Note that mavericks, while denying the standards of the art world, do share its critical and aesthetic vocabularies, and so can communicate with members of that world as well as with each other.)

Without a generalized language of judgment, standards must be local and ephemeral. A set of standards might be applied in the judging at a county or state fair, but that would be as far as it would go, and even that would just be the rendering of a verdict, rather than the reasoned public application of explicit critical criteria. No larger world can grow out of this. How, then, were complicated block designs invented and passed on? Holstein (1973, pp. 55–56) says it was not through women's magazines. He inspected *Godey's Lady's Book*, and found that in the sixty-eight years of its publication it printed only five quilt-block designs, while magazines catering to more rural audiences printed none at all. He speculates that women, "and perhaps their husbands, had a practical knowledge of design which they used in their daily work" (reminding us of Florentine merchants using their practical experience in the appreciation of Renaissance painting [Baxandall, 1972]). The most likely explanation of how designs were passed on, in the absence of encompassing organizations and communications media, is that mother taught daughter and neighbor taught neighbor; people moved around the country and brought their ideas with them for others to observe, imitate, and work with. In other words, communication about this kind of work used existing channels within and between families and communities; that is one of the reasons for calling quilting a community- and family-based art, and it illustrates how the resources art worlds provide for professional artists can be produced for nonprofessionals in other ways. Holstein says that:

> Fairs and other communal gatherings were responsible for the transmission of quilt designs. An unusually interesting new pattern, the invention of a particular woman, or popular in a particular region, would be seen, duly noted, and carried away by women to their homes, and to different regions. It has been said that a new design would be held in memory and the block pieced when the seamstress was back in her house to be stored as a "sketch" for future reproduction. (Holstein, 1973, p. 85)

Quilters' reasons for making quilts arose out of their participation in family and community, and were appropriate and reasonable motives for family members and neighbors to have. They made quilts to keep their families warm, to give as presents to children who were marrying and setting up housekeeping, to help people in adverse circumstances, and to keep themselves busy during dull times or in old age:

> Back in the old days we had to make the quilts so thick. You know in those old dugouts the wind would come through so bad that you really had to be covered to sleep. (P. 45)
>
> Now all the quilts I have are for my five kids and for all the grandchildren. And now their kids are wanting quilts of their own. (P. 140)
>
> I've made several quilts for people who had the misfortune to burn out and lose all their bedding, and other things. Our club makes quilts for folks in times of trouble. (P. 142)
>
> So in the evenin's when he comes in he turns on that little TV and just lays there on the couch watchin' pictures. And I sit right here at my quiltin'. Maybe that don't sound like much, but it's not lonesome. (P. 130)

Quilters usually did some of their work—quilting the finished pieced top to the lining and backing—in cooperation with others, and one motive for quilting was to enjoy the companionship and fun of that sociability:

> In summers we'd put up the [quilting] frame on the screen porch, and when the work was done, Mama would say, "O.K.,

girls, let's go to it." We'd pull up our chairs around the frame and anyone that dropped in would do the same, even if they couldn't stitch straight. Course we'd take out their stitches later if they was really bad. But it was for talking and visiting that we put in quilts in the summer. People would get out after the chores in the summertime and how the word would fly that we had the frame up. Had to have a screened porch 'cause sometimes you'd quilt and visit till midnight by lamplight with the bugs battin' against the screen. (P. 76)

Since everyone involved knows, within limits, as much about what is being done as everyone else, and everyone can do whichever of the several activities involved needs to be done, cooperation occurs easily, with very little friction other than the ordinary friction of human intercourse. To take up a quite different example for a moment, Bruce Jackson (1972) describes how black convicts in Texas prisons coordinate their effort through the use of work songs, the songs providing the rhythm by which such activities as cutting down a tree can be carried out safely (see figure 25). Some men lead the singing better than others, and everybody prefers it when they do the leading. Nevertheless, even a bad leader will serve the purpose as long as he can keep time and be heard over the work noise. Anyone can lead, because everyone knows the song already. The leader's main function is simply to sing out the verses they should use in singing the song. The leader takes the verses from a large pool of verses known to be parts of that song; everyone knows all the parts, and they need not be done in any particular order, nor need any particular number or combination of them be done on any particular occasion.

Because quilts, to return to that example, were the products of a system of families in a community, and not art works produced in an art world, until recently they were preserved, if at all, in those families, passed on from parent to child to grandchild, their value lying partly in their beauty but more in their continuing utility as bedding and their value as sentimental embodiments of family continuity and solidarity. They had no artistic value, were not critically judged works of a named artist, whose reputation would

FIGURE 25. Convicts singing. Folk art occurs as part of the daily activity of members of a community. Texas convicts coordinate potentially dangerous activities like chopping down trees by singing rhythmic songs. (Photograph by Bruce Jackson.)

benefit from the value of the work while it added to it. In fact, quilts were seldom signed and could be attributed to their maker only on the basis of memory and family lore. They were used until they wore out, although some family member might find one especially pleasing and attempt to repair and preserve it. No organization devoted itself to discovering exemplary works, purchasing them, and preserving them for later study and display. Quilts were not art because no one treated them like art. They were the physical embodiment of families and communities, but that was no reason to preserve them; if they were not preserved they could not be admired and eventually seen to have the artistic qualities they might or might not have. Insofar as preservation is necessary for an art work to survive and join the body of a society's recognized, serious art works, quilts could not achieve that status.

That has changed, as it has for many other products of family and community industry, as museums have either devoted themselves to preserving native crafts or recognized artistic merit in such work. Many art museums now have (and some have had for some time) departments of textiles or decorative or minor arts (the name varies), which do all the things for quilts and similar materials that were not done earlier. Not surprisingly, too, some contemporary artists have begun to exploit the aesthetic possibilities of quiltmaking, especially since, as women's art, it now has a special claim to attention.

I have relied almost exclusively on the world of quilting in this analysis of folk art. Many other contemporary American activities fit the model suggested by quilting: woodworking, a men's activity that played a similar functional role in country households; children's games; ballroom dancing among teenagers. Probably more women's and children's activities than men's will take this form, because more of men's activities are developed around work organizations and thus appear, if not as professional art, as the craft of a particular occupation.

NAIVE ARTISTS

A final kind of artist is alternately called primitive, naive, or grass-roots. Grandma Moses is the prototype, although she eventually was discovered by and incorporated into the art world (as sometimes happens to such people). These artists have usually had no connection with any art world at all. They do not know the members of the ordinary art world in which works like theirs (if such exist) are produced. They have not had the training people who ordinarily produce such works have had, and they know very little about the medium they are working in—about its history, conventions, or the kind of work ordinarily produced in it. Unable to explain what they do in conventional terms, naive artists typically work alone, for no one else knows how to furnish the assistance or cooperation they need, and no explanatory language exists. If they do have help, it is because they create their own network of cooperation—recruiting, training, and maintaining a group of people who gradually learn what is needed and how to do it. Most frequently, they at best succeed in recruiting a few people to play the role of appreciators of the work.

That description makes naive art seem more conventional than much of it actually is, by suggesting that it fits into such standard categories as painting. Much does. Grandma Moses is only one of a large number of primitive painters; the most famous is Henri Rousseau. These painters know and abide by the conventions of easel painting, painting on canvases and boards of conventional size with more or less conventional materials. Because they have no professional training, their work characteristically looks literally *naive*, childlike, the way children draw until they learn more sophisticated techniques, if they do, or just stop drawing. Otto Bihalji-Merin (1971) has compiled an illustrated list of more than two hundred naive painters, which obviously is only a tiny fraction of that universe, the fraction that came to the attention of someone looking for work having, by art world standards, aesthetic value. (See also Lipman and Armstrong, 1980.)

Naive work in such conventional media as painting is relatively easy to understand. Naive painters, like any well-socialized member of a Western society, know what paintings look like, and how they are done. The materials for painting are widely available. Anyone with minimal drawing skills can easily begin painting, drawing imagery from conventional stereotypes, traditional subjects, or private obsessions. The work of naive painters varies only a little from the work of amateur painters. Both work without any connection to the world of professional painting, though amateurs may have had classes in painting, belong to clubs of similar amateurs, and participate in a world of Sunday painters. (See the description in McCall, 1977, 1978, and the description of a similar world of china painting in Cincinnati Art Museum, 1976, and California State University, Fullerton, 1977, pp. 113–53.)

Because naive painting resembles conventional painting, the rest of the world assimilates it more easily, and it is therefore not as interesting analytically as another kind of work which is much harder to describe. The difficulty in describing it arises exactly because it has been made without reference to the standards of any world outside its maker's personal life. Its makers work in isolation, free from the constraints of cooperation which inhibit art world participants, free to ignore the conventional categories of art works, to make things which do not fit any standard genre and cannot be described as examples of any class. Their works just *are*, and can be described only by enumerating their features. Once described, they cannot then be assigned to a class; each is its own class, because it was made without reference to anything else, and nothing else has been made with reference to it.

One famous such work is the Watts Towers, constructed in Los Angeles between 1921 and 1954 by Simon Rodia (Trillin, 1965). Too enormous to be called sculpture, the towers are not exactly architecture either, and to call them a monument would be misleading. They consist of several openwork, reinforced concrete towers, the tallest over one hundred feet (see figure 26). Rodia decorated the towers with such easily available materials as pop bottles and dime store crockery. He made impressions in the cement with kitchen utensils and craftsman's tools. He relied on the skills he had learned as a tile setter, and his imagery is quite idiosyncratic. People at first thought it obscurely religious, but when Rodia was rediscovered in Northern California after having disappeared for some years he turned out to be violently anti-religious, though he did not offer any other explanation of the towers' inscriptions and symbols.

James Hampton, a government janitor in Washington,

FIGURE 26. Simon Rodia, the Watts Towers. Naive artists work outside the confines of any art world, accomplishing what they do without the support of others. Rodia explained his work to others, when he bothered to explain it at all, by saying he had done it "all by himself." (Photograph by Seymour Rosen.)

D.C., made a similarly unclassifiable work called *The Throne of the Third Heaven of the National Millenium General Assembly* (see figure 27), which consisted of a garage filled with altars, pulpits, shrines, wall tablets, and other religious articles covered with gold and tin foil (Walker Art Center, 1974, contains descriptions and illustrations of this and several other works I will mention). Clarence Schmidt constructed a number of buildings and decorated the surrounding trees and the land they stood on with silver foil, pink plastic baby

FIGURE 27. *James Hampton,* Throne of the Third Heaven of the National Millenium General Assembly. *Because they work outside organized art worlds, naive artists' work has an idiosyncratic look. Hampton, a government janitor in Washington, D.C., constructed this work in a garage sometime between 1950 and 1964 by covering furniture with tin foil. (Photograph courtesy of the National Collection of Fine Arts, Smithsonian Institution.)*

dolls, and similar materials, all over five acres near Woodstock, New York. Tressa ("Grandma") Prisbrey covered a large lot in Santa Susana, California, with small buildings made of concrete and bottles, filled with dolls, colored pencils, and other common objects, the rest of the area landscaped with planters decorated with auto headlights and other found objects. Jesse "Outlaw" Howard posted his property near Fulton, Missouri, with hand-painted signs carrying religious and political messages; a similar "sign garden" existed for many years on upper Stanyan Street in San Francisco.

The world of contemporary visual art no longer finds these works totally unfamiliar, and they may yet be incorporated under the heading of "environments," or "assemblage," a category which might include the detailed reconstructions of taverns, restaurants, and other peopled places by such sculptors as Ed Kienholtz and George Segal. But that category may have developed in the visual art world partly because art world participants discovered and imitated these unclassifiable works. Some years ago I gave a lecture in a college town in which I mentioned Rodia, Schmidt, and others, and showed slides of their work. A friend who lived there told me that the town had a similar construction going on in it. That didn't surprise me, for such eccentric work is common in small towns. We drove out to see the work, a sort of two-story house covered with doors, windows, and other stuff, much in the style of Clarence Schmidt, and could see the maker, busily attaching some more junk to a wall. My friend waved to him and then remarked casually that the piece would be finished soon, because it was the creator's project for his Master of Fine Arts degree, and he was graduating that spring!

Naive artists typically begin their work accidentally or haphazardly or, I might better say, they do not purposefully start a meaningful activity in a professional world whose organization would make it a real "beginning." Ferdinand Cheval, a rural French postman around the turn of the century, built a *Palais Ideal*, a complex of buildings, reliefs, and sculptures, the work occupying more than thirty years. Describing what he had done in later years, he explained that while delivering the mail he had daydreamed about building a "fairy-tale castle. . . . an edifice filled with gardens, museums, sculptures, and intricate labyrinths. . . . the architecture of ancient times and distant lands . . . combined . . . in a single structure so beautiful and picturesque that it remained uppermost in my mind for ten years." Then:

> One day I stumbled on a stone. And as I looked at it more closely, it turned out to have such a curious shape that I picked it up and took it with me. The following day I returned

> to the same spot and found some even more beautiful stones,
> which I enthusiastically began to collect.
>
> I took this coincidence as an omen. Since nature it-
> self provided sculptures, then I *could* be an architect or
> mason! . . .
>
> And so, for the next 25 years, I moved stones. (Cheval, 1968,
> p. 9)

Herman Rusch, a farmer in Cochrane, Wisconsin, began the *Prairie Moon Museum and Garden*, a two-acre construction of arches, pillars, towers, and other things made of cement, "to dress the place up" (Hoos, 1974, p. 71). Grandma Prisbrey began her work because the trailer she lived in was not big enough for her family or her collection of two thousand pencils. When the work was conceived and executed delib-erately, as some were (e.g., S. P. Dinsmoor's *Garden of Eden*, a half-acre architectural and sculptural politico-religious construction in Lucas, Kansas), the reasons for doing it are personal and not always intelligible, a point I will return to.

These works, not belonging to any tradition of artistically defined problems and solutions, seem to spring out of no-where. No one knows how to respond to them. Audiences (whoever happens to see them) do not know what to make of them, and their makers cannot take advantage of any estab-lished network of cooperation in building them. They work alone. Rodia said:

> I did it all by myself. I never had a single help. One thing, I
> couldn't hire any help, for I no have-a no money. Not a thing.
> If I hire a man, he don't know what to do. A million times, I
> don't know what to do myself. I would wake up all night,
> because this was my own idea. (Trillin, 1965, p. 72)

(There is no technical reason for not using helpers. Antoni Gaudi, the Catalan art nouveau architect, made construc-tions which have many of the same features of the work of Rodia and other naive artists. But, being an established professional architect, though more than a little eccen-tric, Gaudi had rich patrons and clients and could afford to hire and train masons and other craftsmen to work to his designs [Collins, 1960, and Bergós, 1954].)

Naive artists achieve their idiosyncratic style and create unique and peculiar forms and genres because they have never acquired and internalized the habits of vision and thought professional artists necessarily acquire during their training. A maverick has to overcome the habits left by professional training; the naive artist never had them. Many of the artists who make constructions like the Watts Towers got their skills as Rodia did, as members of one of the building trades. Others have been farmers or general handymen. To put it more generally, societies teach many people skills which can be put to artistic use, but teach them in nonartistic settings and for utilitarian purposes. People who have learned these skills can then begin idiosyncratic art enterprises without ever coming in contact with the conventional art world. (This may explain why it is hard to find musical examples to parallel the visual ones: it is relatively unusual for people to acquire musical skills in that casual and unprofessional way, because musical skills are so specialized that they are not useful in nonartistic enterprises.)

Naive artists, unattached to the working organizations of any art world, do not have access to regular supplies of professionally standardized materials. Quite resourceful, they make do with what the environment provides. Rodia used standard materials for reinforced concrete construction, but for ornamentation used tile, pottery, household dishware, sea shells, and soda bottles, as well as impressions of household objects and his own tools. The work reflects the limits of what he had available, as Trillin points out:

> it is apparent that the form the towers took was decided partly by the limitations of his equipment. Since he had no scaffolding, for example, he had to provide his own as he went along. It took the form of horizontal spokes and circles ringing the tallest spires, and the dense spiderweb effect they produce results partly from the fact that no ring is farther from the one below it than a short man can reach. (Trillin, 1965, p. 80)

Louis C. Wippich, whose *Molehill* in Sauk Rapids, Minnesota, is a little like a giant rock garden (the tallest tower is forty-five feet), took advantage of local industries:

> In the 24 years he devoted to construction of the garden, he scavenged the quarries and monument companies for cast-off blocks, damaged grave markers and monument "seconds." From the Great Northern Railroad's car shops he acquired railroad rails, steel cables and wood siding from condemned freight cars. The two homes he built overlooking the gardens were built of freight car wood. The concrete bridges and platforms were reinforced with railroad rails. (Sherarts and Sherarts, 1974, p. 90)

Grandma Prisbrey found everything but concrete, lumber, and tar paper in the city dump, including an estimated one million bottles, automobile headlights, TV picture tubes, discarded dolls, machinery molds and parts, laboratory glassware, pencils, eyeglass frames, beer bottle caps ... (McCoy, 1974, p. 82). James Hampton salvaged materials from the wastebaskets he emptied at work, and "paid neighborhood indigents to collect foil for him, but also scoured the streets himself, carrying a crocus sack that he filled with loot" (Roscoe, 1974, p. 15).

With no professional training and no contact with the conventional art world, naive artists do not learn the conventional vocabulary of motives and explanations for their work. Since they cannot explain what they are doing in conventional art terminology, and since it can seldom be explained as anything other than art, naive artists frequently have trouble with people who demand an explanation. Not fitting into any conventional category, not legitimated by any authentic connection to an established art world, constructions like the Watts Towers, Cheval's *Palais Ideal*, or the hundreds of similar works now being turned up by interested critics require explanation. Many of these artists provide no explanations, apparently believing that what they do is their own business or, since many of the works have some religious intent, between them and God. When they do explain themselves, the idiosyncratic explanations, with no basis in a shared vocabulary of motives, sound extremely eccentric. Here are some examples:

> [Mr. Tracy, of Wellington, Kansas, built a house of bottles. His explanation of it was:] "I saw a bottle house in California and they used only one kind of bottle, so I did them one better and used all kinds." (Blasdell, 1968, p. 32)

> [Herman Rusch explains the work described above thus:] "Like it says, Mister, a man should leave a few tracks and not just canceled welfare checks." (Blasdell, 1968, p. 41)

> [S. P. D. Dinsmoor of Lucas, Kansas, says,] "If the Garden of Eden [the name for the work of art he has constructed] is not right, Moses is to blame. He wrote it up and I built it." (Blasdell, 1968, p. 30)

> [Fred Smith said,] "I'm 166 years old and I'll be better when I'm 175. It has to be in the man. You have to be almost gifted to do what I have done." (Blasdell, 1968, p. 33)

Not surprisingly, people who create such works and give explanations like this are frequently thought by neighbors and others to be crazy. The problem of what the work *is* is central to the reactions of others. Typically having no visible use, the works cannot be explained as utilitarian, as storage or living quarters, for instance. If they have no use, what are they? They might pass as art, except that they do not look like any art the neighbors have ever seen or heard about and the makers have no claim to the status of artist, being simply fellow-residents of the town, often with an independent reputation for crankiness or eccentricity. The maker becomes the object of ridicule, abuse, and unofficial or official harassment. Cheval (1968, p. 11) describes the reaction to his collecting stones preparatory to the construction of the *Palais Ideal*:

> Before long, local tongues began to wag, and soon public opinion had cemented: "Look at the poor idiot, filling up his garden with stones!" People actually thought I was mentally

ill. Some laughed at me; some reproached or criticized me. But since they realized this type of madness was neither dangerous nor contagious, nobody called for a psychiatrist. In time, I ceased to be bothered by their teasing. I realized, you see, that people have always ridiculed and persecuted those whom they cannot understand.

During World War II neighborhood kids, for whom an eccentric like Simon Rodia was fair game, decided that he was using the Watts Towers to send radio messages to Italian submarines lying offshore and began harassing him in earnest, vandalizing the work extensively. In 1954, Rodia, apparently no longer interested in the towers or their future, gave the land to a neighbor and disappeared. In 1959, the City of Los Angeles Building Department decided the construction was unsafe and moved to tear it down.

This raises the question of how such works are preserved, if they are, and how they are protected against such harassment. The conventional defenses and protections afforded conventional art works are lacking. Tressa Prisbrey's son was the local building inspector, which must have saved her from what would surely have been interminable trouble. Wippich's work would probably have been lost if a distant relative had not bought it with the intent of keeping it intact. Local merchants sometimes decide that the work may have some value as a tourist attraction and preserve it for that reason. But many such works—there is no way of knowing how many—have undoubtedly been lost to later audiences.

Perhaps the most important way such works are preserved, no doubt an uncommon way, is that members of some art world develop an interest in them. They see a connection between the solutions naive artists have arrived at and the problems which are now interesting their own professional world. That saved the Watts Towers. Artists and museum people in Los Angeles (organized as The Committee for Simon Rodia's Towers in Watts) discovered the towers (which had been discovered once before, as a tourist attraction that could be seen from the interurban trolleys that once ran in Los Angeles) and moved legally to stop their destruction. Trillin (1965) tells the exciting story of how the City

Building Department attempted to pull one of the towers down, having agreed that if it could withstand a specified stress the entire construction would be spared. In a soap opera ending, the tower proved so strong that the truck attempting to pull it over tore its own axle out. Even so, the towers have been seriously damaged by local vandals. Hampton's *Throne*, more portable, survived by being moved to the National Collection of Fine Arts in Washington, D.C.

Even when they are preserved through the intervention of art world participants, naive artists' works are not easily assimilated by those worlds. They violate many more standards of conventional work than do the works of mavericks, for instance, and do so more comprehensively. They do not fit into available spaces; indeed, they frequently cannot be moved at all. Divorced from the mainstream tradition of any conventional form, it is unlikely that they can be interpreted as having a major place in some form's history. They are, and remain, curiosities.

The primitive quality of naive art, like the maverick quality of maverick art, lies in the relation of its maker to the conventional art world. It is not the character of the work itself that distinguishes naive art, but rather that it has been made without reference to the constraints of contemporary convention. This also solves an otherwise knotty problem: does Grandma Moses' work remain naive once it has been discovered and exhibited in museums and galleries to critical acclaim? To the degree that she, or any discovered primitive, continues to ignore the constraints of the world into which she has been incorporated, it remains what it was. When the artist begins to take account of what her new colleagues expect of her and are prepared to cooperate with, she becomes an integrated professional, even though integrated into a world which has changed itself somewhat to accommodate the variations she created.

CONCLUSION

The difficulties mavericks and naive artists have making their works and getting them distributed, their difficulties with audiences and authorities, indicate the troubles integrated professionals are spared by participating in art worlds recognized as legitimate parts of society. Folk artists show us how artlike works—similar in everything but the label—can be made under different auspices and how the auspices affect the doing.

The difference between the work of integrated professionals, mavericks, folk artists, and naive artists does not lie in its surface appearance or sound, but in the relation between that work and work done by others more or less involved in some art world. The work of naive artists will not always look childlike, but it will look different from work in a similar medium done in a different relation to an art world. Maverick work will be freer of the constraints imposed by cooperative links, as Ives' was, but will also be hampered by the lack of cooperation from others (as Ives might have been hampered by his inability to hear what he wrote played). Folk art, solidly supported by a community, will be limited by the time and materials made available for that sort of work by the communities in which it is made; the available support will probably always be less than would be available to participants in an accepted art world in which the making of the work did not have to take second place to the community's major concerns. Naive art will have the rough edges of idiosyncrasy, unaltered by the opinions or examples of colleagues.

Art worlds, then, help their participants produce work that will earn the material support and serious response of others, help artists connect work to a tradition in which it makes sense, and provide substantial amounts of time and other resources for artistic activity.

Distinctions between these kinds of art are not distinctions of quality; work of every degree of interest can be and has been made in every category. But we always look at non-canonical work—work not done under the legitimate auspices of an art world—from the standpoint of some aesthetic which has its base in some world, probably an art world, in which we participate. That aesthetic is what allows us to select particular works from among the mass of stuff produced by people who are not integrated professionals, to select some works as worth our attention after all, deserving elevation from marginal to central status. Another time, people from some other art world will make still another selection, insofar as the mechanisms of preservation keep work intact so that it can be selected. (See the discussion in Moulin, 1978, pp. 244–47.)

9 · Arts and Crafts

Members of art worlds often distinguish between art and craft. They recognize that making art requires technical skills that might be seen as craft skills, but they also typically insist that artists contribute something beyond craft skill to the product, something due to their creative abilities and gifts that gives each object or performance a unique and expressive character. Other people, also skilled, who support the work of the artist are called "craftsmen," and the work they do is called "craft." The same activity, using the same materials and skills in what appear to be similar ways, may be called by either title, as may the people who engage in it. The histories of various art forms include typical sequences of change in which what has been commonly understood and defined by practitioners and public as a craft becomes redefined as an art or, conversely, an art becomes redefined as a craft. In the first case, participants in an art world borrow from or take over a craft world; in the second, a mature art world begins to exhibit some of the characteristic features of craft worlds. Changes in reputation and changes in organization occur together. The analysis of the complicated relations between art and craft, and of the sequences by

272

which one changes into the other, like the comparative analysis of the previous chapter, helps us to understand how art worlds work.

The last chapter, considering nonstandard ways of making art (ways not connected to an organized art world), treated art worlds as more or less unchanging. This chapter begins to repair that flaw by considering some sequences of change. The chapter to follow goes further, making change in art worlds its central subject.

(As folk terms, *art* and *craft* refer to ambiguous conglomerations of organizational and stylistic traits and thus cannot be used as unequivocally as we would want to use them if they were scientific or critical concepts. Since I will nevertheless speak of art and craft worlds, organizations, and styles of work, it should be understood that in doing so I am referring to one or another aspect of some folk definition. I often refer to particular organizations that come close to realizing the ideal combinations implied by the folk terms, but even these do not live up to the expectations embodied in the ideal, nor does it matter analytically that they do not.)

CRAFT BECOMES ART

As a work ideology, an aesthetic, and a form of work organization, craft can and does exist independent of art worlds, their practitioners, and their definitions. In the pure folk definition, a craft consists of a body of knowledge and skill which can be used to produce useful objects: dishes you can eat from, chairs you can sit in, cloth that makes serviceable clothing, plumbing that works, wiring that carries current. From a slightly different point of view, it consists of the ability to perform in a useful way—to play music that can be danced to, serve a meal to guests efficiently, arrest a criminal with a minimum of fuss, clean a house to the satisfaction of those who live in it.

To speak of usefulness implies the existence of someone whose purposes define the ends for which the objects or activities will be useful. Those purposes arise in some world of collective action in which they are characteristic, part of the definition of what kind of world it is. Serving a meal to guests efficiently might be part of the world of commercial catering, in which the development of a stable clientele who can be fed at a profit is the goal, or it might be part of a domestic world, in which case the object is to satisfy the appetites for food and graceful social intercourse of family, friends, and acquaintances. In both cases, utility is measured by a standard lying outside the world that is or might have been constructed around the activity itself. For there is a world of haute cuisine and etiquette which treats the enjoyment of food and its service as ends in themselves, the measurement of utility referring to standards developed and accepted by knowledgeable participants in that world. (The distinction between utilities which arise in the world constructed around the activity itself and those measured by standards imported from other worlds—call them intrinsic and extrinsic, or practical, utilities—will recur in the analysis.)

Defining craft as the knowledge and skill which produce useful objects and activities implies an aesthetic, standards on which judgments of particular items of work can be based, and an organizational form in which the evaluative standards find their origin and logical justification. The organizational form is one in which the worker does his work for someone else—a client, customer, or employer—who defines what is to be done and what the result should be. Employers understand that the worker possesses special skills and knowledge but regard it as appropriate that they make the final judgment on the result. The worker may know better ways of doing things, not known to someone outside the craft, but recognizes the employer's right to the last word. Both recognize that the object of the activity is to make something employers can use for their purposes, whatever they may be. Although a worker sometimes makes things for his own use, the object is still made to serve someone's need for a useful object.

If you define your work as done to meet someone else's practical needs, then function, defined as external to the work's intrinsic character, is an important ideological and aesthetic consideration. If the piece has no evident or possible practical use, or is totally unsuited to its ostensible use, the craftsman who made it (a craftsman being someone who accepts the craft ideology) will probably receive and feel vulnerable to severe criticism from his colleagues. I will give some examples later.

In addition to function, craftsmen accept a second aesthetic standard—virtuoso skill. Most crafts are difficult, requiring years to master the physical skills and mental disciplines of a first-class practitioner. An expert, having mastered the skills, has great control over the craft's materials, can do anything with them, can work with speed and agility, and can do with ease things ordinary, less expert craftsmen find difficult or impossible. A potter, for instance, may be able to throw pots with walls so thin that other potters would be unable to prevent them from collapsing. Conversely, he may be able to throw great masses of clay other potters would find impossible to control. The specific object of virtuosity varies from field to field, but always involves an extraordinary control of materials and techniques. Sometimes virtuosity also includes mastering a wide variety of techniques, being able not only to do things better than most others but also to do more things. Virtuoso craftsmen take pride in their skill and are honored for it in the craft and sometimes by outsiders.

That an object is useful, that it required virtuoso skill to make—neither of these precludes it from also being thought beautiful. Some crafts generate from within their own tradition a feeling for beauty and with it appropriate aesthetic standards and canons of taste. Both makers and users think that some furniture is beautiful in addition to being useful and that they can tell the difference. Not many people care to make these fine distinctions among household craft objects, but those who do (Japanese, for instance) add beauty to utility and virtuosity as a third criterion of judgment which informs their daily activities. Beauty becomes an additional criterion connoisseurs use in making judgments and workers try to satisfy.

By accepting beauty as a criterion, participants in craft

activities take on a concern characteristic of the folk definition of art. That definition includes an emphasis on beauty as typified in the tradition of some particular art, on the traditions and concerns of the art world itself as the source of value, on expression of someone's thoughts and feelings, and on the relative freedom of the artist from outside interference with the work. (Concerning the last element, the folk definition acknowledges, implicitly though usually not explicitly, that other participants in the art world—patrons, dealers, curators, and critics, for instance—will in fact if not in theory constrain the artist's expressive freedom substantially.)

Because some craftsmen accept beauty as a criterion, the organizational form of craft worlds becomes more complicated and differentiated than it would otherwise be. Crafts ordinarily divide along the line between ordinary craftsmen trying to do decent work and make a living and artist-craftsmen with more ambitious goals and ideologies. Ordinary craftsmen usually respect artist-craftsmen and see them as the source of innovation and original ideas. The two types not only carry on the craft in distinctive ways, but also constitute distinct groups of people, since workers tend to identify themselves as one or the other and to adopt one or the other mode of activity fairly exclusively.

The ordinary craftsman probably does not take the criterion of beauty very seriously. Busy satisfying the demands of a variety of jobs and customers, he contents himself with making sure that the pipes he installs carry water, that the bookcase he builds is sturdy and fits in the space he measured for it, that the meal is served expeditiously. I have, of course, deliberately chosen examples from crafts in which the idea of beauty seldom enters anyone's calculations, at least in the conventional sense connected with such high arts as painting and sculpture.

Some craftsmen (a current list would include potters, weavers, glassblowers, and furniture makers, to cite the most obvious cases) speak of themselves as artist-craftsmen (Sinha, 1979). The distinction means something in these craft worlds. The American Crafts Council identifies itself as the organized voice of the artist-craftsman. The influential magazine it once published, *Craft Horizons*, emphasized questions of beauty and artistic merit, in contrast with a then more purely craft-oriented magazine like *Ceramics Monthly*. Similar purely craft-oriented magazines serve most crafts.

Work by artist-craftsmen, with some claim to be considered art by the custodians of conventional art—collectors, curators, and gallery owners—finds new organizational settings, which partially free the artist-craftsman from the constraints embodied in the employer-employee relationship characteristic of the pure craftsman's position. Under the heading of "minor arts," beautiful craft objects are displayed in shows and museums, win prizes for their beauty, contribute to the reputations of the craftsmen who make them, become the subject of books and the occasion for demonstrations of "how to do it," and even furnish the basis on which teaching jobs are given and held. In short, not only do some people care to make the distinction between beautiful and ordinary craft objects, but there are substantial rewards for making more beautiful objects while adhering to craft standards.

Artist-craftsmen have higher ambitions than ordinary craftsmen. While they may share audiences, institutions, and rewards with ordinary craftsmen, they also feel some kinship with fine-art institutions. They see a continuity between what they do and what fine artists do, even though they recognize that they have chosen to pursue the ideal of beauty they share with fine artists in a more limited arena. What constitutes beauty can of course be the subject of considerable controversy, but it is the third major criterion according to which people judge work and to which they orient their own activity.

We might imagine the differentiation of craftsmen and artist-craftsmen as a typical historical sequence. A craft world, whose aesthetic emphasizes utility and virtuoso skill and whose members produce works according to the dictates of clients or employers operating in some extracraft world, develops a new segment (Bucher, 1962; Bucher and Strauss, 1961). The new segment's members add to the basic aesthetic an emphasis on beauty and develop some additional organizations, which free them of the need to satisfy employers so completely. These artist-craftsmen develop a kind of art world around their activities, a "minor art" world. The world contains much of the apparatus of full-fledged major arts: shows, prizes, sales to collectors, teaching positions, and the rest. Not all craft worlds develop such an artistic, beauty-oriented segment (plumbing has not). But where an art segment develops, it usually coexists peacefully with the more purely utilitarian craft segment.

Another sequence occurs when members of an established world already defined as art, people involved in the typical activities and ideologies of the contemporary art world, invade (and the military metaphor is appropriate) an established craft world, especially its art segment. The sequence begins when some fine artists look for new media in which to explore a current expressive problem. These artists happen on one of the crafts and see in its materials and techniques a potential for artistic exploitation. They see a way to do something that will interest the art world to which they are oriented and to which they respond. They have no interest in the conventional standard of practical utility; their notion of beauty is likely to be very different from and more advanced than that of the craft they are invading and the kind of skill and control that interests them quite different from that prized by the more traditional practitioner.

The new breed of artists in the craft devise new and aggressively nonutilitarian standards. Only the utilities defined by the art world in which they participate interest them. Art utilities typically include usefulness as objects of aesthetic contemplation, as objects of collection and ostentatious display, and as items of investment and pecuniary gain, but not the practical utilities defined by the purposes and organization of other worlds. Artists invading a craft want to make sure that the works they produce cannot be used as people have been accustomed to using them. Robert Arneson, for example, one of the leading spirits in the movement which claimed pottery as a fine-art field (Zack, 1970), made a series of large plates, technically competent, whose utility was destroyed by the large brick which sat in the middle of each one, slowly sinking into the surface as the series progressed (see figure 28). In another instance, a group of artists gained control of a ceramics department in an art school. The new chairman announced decisively that from then on no one in the department would make high-fire pottery. He meant that they would no longer make clay objects that had any utility, because only high-fire pottery will hold water and thus be useful for domestic purposes: cups, glasses, dishes, vases. By insisting that only low-fire pottery be made, he in effect announced that what they did from then on would be some version of contemporary sculpture. Lest anyone miss the point, he elaborated: "We are not going to make any vessels."

Just as the standard of utility is devalued, so, too, are the old craft standards of skill. What the older artist-craftsman has spent a lifetime learning to do is suddenly hardly worth doing. People are doing his work in the sloppiest possible way and being thought superior to him just because of it.

Instead of adhering to the conventional craft criteria, which of course turn up in somewhat different form, the artists who enter a craft field propose, rely on, and organize their work according to criteria characteristic of worlds conventionally defined as high art. In the art versions of any of these media, for instance, uniqueness of the object is prized. Artists and their publics think that no two objects produced by an artist should be alike. But for good craftsmen that is not a consideration; on the contrary, the artist-craftsman's control shows in his ability to make things as much alike as he does. People who pay $200 for a small, beautifully turned bowl will not feel cheated if they find there is another more or less like it. What they bought exhibits the virtuoso craftsmanship they paid for. Had they bought the same bowl on the assumption that it was a unique work of art, they *would* feel cheated to find that there were two. So artists who work in these media sell their conception and its execution in that medium and take care to be obvious about how each of their pieces differs from all others. No one wants to buy a copy from an artist, only from a craftsman.

FIGURE 28. *Robert Arneson,* Sinking Brick Plates. *When artists invade a craft medium, they deliberately make work that is non-functional as a way of showing that, though the medium is associated with a craft, the work is art. Ceramic, 1969. (Photograph courtesy of the Hansen Fuller Goldeen Gallery.)*

The new standards artists create insure that a work's only utility will be as art—to be admired, appreciated, and experienced. The artists denounce the mere virtuosity of the old school of craftsmen. They discover and create a conscious continuity with work in other areas of art, especially the traditional areas of painting and sculpture. They announce their independence of others' ideas of what their work should consist of and denounce any attempt to saddle them with the requirements of utility. What they do usually requires a great deal of skill and control, but the skills needed are usually deliberately different from those prized by ordinary craftsmen or artist-craftsmen and often are hidden as well. Marilyn Levine achieved a considerable reputation by making ceramic sculptures of shoes, boots, and other leather objects, which looked so much like real leather that you had to tap them and hear the ring to be convinced that they were clay (see figure 29); that takes considerable skill, but not the kind ceramicists usually prize. It becomes a virtue not to display conventional craft virtuosity, and artists may deliberately create crudities (the making of the crudities may itself involve considerable virtuosity, though not the same as the craftsman's), either for their shock value or to show their freedom from that particular set of conventional craft constraints.

Defining their work as art, the artists who adopt craft materials and techniques create and accommodate themselves to a social organization different from that which grows up around a craft. Craft organization subordinates the craftsman to an employer, at whose insistence and for whose purposes the work is done. But the contemporary folk definition of art presumes that the artist works for no one, that the work is produced in response to problems intrinsic in the development of the art and freely chosen by the artist. Organizationally, of course, the artist is no such heroic individualist, but operates in a setting of institutional constraints, which vary from time to time and place to place. Artists whose work was distributed through systems of church and royal patronage found it expedient to take account of their patrons' tastes and desires to the point that, as we saw in

FIGURE 29. *Marilyn Levine,* Brown Satchel. *Artists taking over a craft medium cultivate skills different from those of craftsmen—for example, the ability to imitate the surface look of leather. Ceramic, 6 × 9 × 13–1/2 inches, 1976. (Photograph courtesy of the Hansen Fuller Goldeen Gallery.)*

chapter 4, the patrons might on occasion reasonably be thought of as collaborators. Contemporary artists, enmeshed in a world of collectors, galleries, and museums, typically produce with no particular purchaser in mind and expect their work to be marketed through the conventional apparatus of dealers and museums, the purchaser exercising control by buying or refusing to buy. Whatever the organizational form, the folk definition further presumes that these purchasers and intermediaries are as concerned as the artist with the utilities defined by the art world and therefore with problems and topics defined within, rather than outside of, the current art world. These presumptions are often violated, but artists orient themselves to that model.

Fine-art photographers, for example, do a greater variety of work, less constrained by the requirements of organizations in which they work, than do photographers who work in such craft-oriented areas as advertising, fashion photography, or photojournalism (Rosenblum, 1978). Similarly, artists working in conventional craft media are relatively freer than artist-craftsmen who work in the same media, both in the diversity of the objects they make and in the variety and whimsicality of the talk with which they explain their work. The objects typically resemble current work in such contemporary high-art worlds as painting and sculpture, and the talk both calls attention to the resemblance and displays at least superficial indifference to being intelligible or rational. The latter characteristic expresses an indifference to public acceptance characteristic of many contemporary artists.

Here are some examples. Arneson has made many pieces which are in fact sculpture: a typewriter, somewhat sagged out of shape and rough around the edges, whose keys are red-painted fingernails (see Zack, 1970, for other examples, and see figure 30); a series of self-portraits, smoking a cigar or with the skull opened to reveal various contents; an enormous table covered with dishes of food, standing in front of a life-sized portrait of the artist in a chef's hat, all glazed a pure unrelieved white. To an observer familiar with the conventions of contemporary sculpture and ceramics, these pieces look not quite like sculpture, but more like ceramics. Aggressively not utilitarian pottery, they nevertheless call attention to themselves as pottery through the rough modeling of the clay and the gaudy glazes. Some of their effect lies in the ambiguity so created. Other pieces are utilitarian in principle but not quite in fact. An example is Arneson's teapot whose spout is a realistically modeled penis; you can pour tea from it, but not for everyone (see figure 31).

To turn to the talk that accompanies such work, here is Arneson explaining himself:

FIGURE 30. Robert Arneson, Typewriter. *Artists taking over a craft medium emphasize the continuity of their work with that being done in more conventional media. This work reflects the concerns of Pop Art sculpture. Ceramic, 6–1/8 × 11–3/8 × 12–1/2 inches, 1965; collection of the University Art Museum, University of California, Berkeley; gift of the artist.*

My recent ART WORKS IN PORCELAIN, GLAZED IN ALL THE COOL-NESS OF CELADON, are like a 9th Century southern Chinese Sung Dynasty potter explaining the TRUTH of art, non-art, not-art and their significance in a precious and free sense way with added footnotes and trivia culled from folks like Steve Kaltenfront, the Duncan Mold Company, and my own astro-logical signs for a Virgo artist who thought his Scorpio was rising until his astro flashed the truth from the depths of the station. But that was long after the fires went out and the kilns had cooled, so I figured in light of the evidence presented, and

FIGURE 31. *Robert Arneson,* A Tremendous Teapot. *Artists can make works socially as well as technically nonfunctional. This teapot can be used to pour tea, but not for everyone. Lustered earthenware, 8 inches tall with base, 1969. (Photograph courtesy of the Hansen Fuller Goldeen Gallery.)*

depending on where you stood, that it all didn't seem to make too much difference anyway—just a lot of work in white mud calling itself art. (Quoted in Slivka, 1971, p. 42)

Arneson ridicules the idea of art and conventional artists' explanations of their work in a way now common among "advanced" artists. He is not the only one. Roger Lang explained his sculpture of a piece of pie on a plate similarly:

Pie was interesting to me first of all as food—then I found some triangular associations, geodesic, mathematical, sexual, using a pie wedge as a basis for plate decorations. Later, high in the sky, chicken pot pie, apple pie, cherry pie, and pie-eye thoughts pushed me into 3-dimensional usages. Fruit Pie is, after all, a very American food. Gradually, things accumulated and I came to think of pie as a vehicle for associations, things that come along for nothing, free. In addition, there are the visual changes which I impose, and I haven't even begun explorations of one-crust pies yet. Taking everything into account, pie is very rich. (Quoted in Slivka, 1971, p. 43)

Similar examples, visual and verbal, could be collected for weaving, glassblowing, furniture making, and clothing design.

I have spoken of artists invading and taking over a craft world, bringing new standards, criteria, and styles to an activity previously dominated by craftsmen and artist-craftsmen. All the conventional crafts have an apparatus of exhibitions and shows, usually held in specialized craft galleries and smaller museums (the biggest annual ceramics show is held in the Everson Museum in Syracuse, New York) or in out-of-the-way corners of more important museums. Artist-craftsmen usually busy themselves fighting for more exhibition space in better museums for their craft and rejoice when "one of ours" makes it into a more prestigious space (see Christopherson, 1974a). Museums tend to be especially sensitive to ideological and aesthetic fashions. This sometimes results in the invaders being invited to serve on the juries of craft shows. They pick work that ranks high by their standards and ignore work done by the old standards. Soon the new, artistically oriented works are being shown, winning prizes, being written up in the magazines, perhaps even being sold. (Sales depend on the degree to which the new style of work muscles in on the already established craft market, as opposed to simply creating a new market or siphoning off some of the money that might have gone to other forms of advanced art.) The older craftsmen become enraged and often are hurt economically. They lose teaching positions to the newcomers, so that a whole new generation of students and potential consumers adopts the movement's standards as both producers and purchasers of work.

In part, then, one group—the new artists—simply replaces

the older group of artist-craftsmen. As that happens, a great deal of conflict occurs. The craftsmen feel that a bunch of incompetent savages is taking over what they have no right to. The artists feel that they are getting rid of some fuddy-duddies who stand in the way of artistic progress. A pair of quotations from *Craft Horizons* illustrates the emotional tone and ideological content of the polemic. In 1960, Mary Buskirk, a well-known traditional weaver, said:

> Too many times an object overshadows the purpose for which it is designed. Draperies, for instance, which are to serve as a background, should be just that—a backdrop to pull together all the objects in the room. As for rugs, they should invite you to step on them. Too often you find people walking around a rug and, when this happens, it is safe to say that design and function have gone out of focus. This doesn't mean you can't use color and pattern, but it does mean you should use those elements to create something which is inviting to step on. (Quoted in Halverstadt, 1960, p. 10)

Ten years later, Virginia Hoffman, representing the artist group, spoke to the question, "When Will Weaving Be an Art Form?" and made clear the kind of conceptual transformation which occurs as the new group takes over, as well as the degree to which one such movement may serve as the model for others:

> The controversy regarding the status of weaving as an art form, efforts to justify its placement among the hallowed media, labels such as stitchery, appliqué, macramé, woven, nonwoven, unwoven, loom-free, built-in loom, ad infinitum, may indicate that a transition in thinking has not occurred. . . . one hears echoes of the past, as when the ceramists were searching for a raison d'être for nonfunctional pots. . . .
>
> If one accepts the lack of need for minute classification of media and processes, how may one refer to different ways of causing concepts to materialize? Ron Goodman's "Genesis" in "Young Americans 69" pointed to the obvious nomenclature: soft sculpture. Such a large category could logically include any three-dimensional form made by flexible joinings, fibrous materials, modules with no fixed beginning or end, soft materials made hard and vice versa, strength through tension, counterbalancing, spacing, and forms created by use

of invisible forces such as weightlessness and gravity. One thinks of the metal tubing and cable structures of Kenneth Snelson, some works by Gabo, architectural structures such as the Sports Palace in Mexico City and Fuller's Geodesic Domes, works by Eva Hesse, Alan Saret, Robert Morris, Alice Adams, and a growing group. (Hoffman, 1970, p. 19)

This statement also illustrates the striving to change the standards of the craft, even to change the name, and to establish a continuity with work by serious artists in other fields.

But the change is not simply a matter of one group replacing another. Artists do not replace craftsmen completely, for the craftsmen continue to exist, produce, sell, make reputations, have careers, and construct and maintain a craft-oriented world. Instead, a new and more complicated world comes into being, in which craft segments, artist-craftsmen segments, and art segments coexist. You can work solely in the confines of one such segment or orient yourself to some combination of them; most of the possibilities for orientations, modes of action, and careers that existed in the craft world still exist, together with a variety of new combinations.

ART BECOMES CRAFT

As the years pass, these worlds settle down and begin to experience their own segmentations, differentiations, and splits. An already developed world commonly defined by insiders and outsiders alike as an art world, complete with appropriate ideologies, aesthetics, and forms of social organization, often (in another characteristic sequence) changes in the opposite direction. The originally expressive art works and styles become increasingly more organized, constrained, and ritualized; organizational forms subordinate the artist increasingly to partially or entirely extraneous sources of control; and the world and its activities begin to resemble conventional craft worlds. In this sense, an art turns into a craft. The process takes two forms. One leads to what is usually called "academic" art, the other to what is usually called "commercial" art.

Academic Art

Academicism consists of an increasing concern with how things are done, with the skill the artist or performer exhibits, as opposed to what is done, the ideas and emotions the works embody and express. Since all arts require some substantial measure of skill, academic art is clearly an intermediate and ambiguous case of a tendency that emerges full-blown in commercial art. Most participants in any art world don't worry about being expressive or creative; they are content to work within conventionalized formats. But they, and those who support their art world as patrons or customers, generally orient themselves to expressiveness and creativity as the valuable components of art works.

We can speak of academic art as art produced in a world in which artists and others shift their concern from expressiveness and creativity to virtuosity. That concern, paralleling the craft concern with skill, is a step away from the standards conventionally accepted as developing out of the history of an art and toward the standards characteristic of crafts, but it is only a step, not the full trip, for the utilities toward which the work is pointed are still those of the art world—appreciation, collection, and display. Sixteenth-century engraving exemplifies the development of such academicism:

> Thus, in engraving there were performers who made great specialties of the rendering of glass and shiny metal, of silks and furs, and of foliage and whiskers. It is impossible to think that even so great an artist as Dürer was not tainted by this sort of virtuosity. The virtuoso engravers chose the pictures they were to make or reproduce not for their merit but as vehicles for the exhibition of their particular skills. The laying of lines, swelling and diminishing, the creation of webs of crossed lines, of lozenges with little flicks and dots in their middles, the making of prints in lines that all ran parallel or around and around—one engraver made a great reputation by the way he rendered the fur of a pussy cat, and another made a famous head of Christ that contained but one line, which beginning at the point of the nose, ran around and around itself until it finally got lost in the outer margin—stunts such as these became for these exhibitionists not a way of saying something of interest or importance but a method of pos-

turing in public. Naturally the great show men became
the models of the less gifted but equally stupid routine performers, for all these trick performances contained far more
of laborious method than of eyesight or of draughtsman-
ship. (Ivins, 1953, pp. 69–70)

Classical ballet and the virtuoso playing of concert instrumentalists also furnish examples: for long periods, criticism in both dealt largely with whether any mistakes had been
made, whether the performer had been faster or surer than
others, and other craft concerns.

The conventional style which marks the turning of art into
craft is precisely what "academic art" means (Pevsner, 1940).
That it is academic does not mean that it cannot be beautiful
or effective, but effectiveness and beauty become harder to
achieve because there are so many rules of good procedure
and form to follow. Every high art shows examples of the
tendency. In certain periods poets must know a great variety
of forms, many of them as demanding or constraining as the
sonnet, just as composers have sometimes had to know and
use such constraining forms as the fugue and canon. At the
extreme, there is a right way to do everything: to draw a tree,
to harmonize a theme, to portray Lear. The subject becomes
more and more the skill and craft of the artist, whatever the
work is ostensibly about. Such work appeals only to serious
audience members, who understand the conventions, rules,
and skills almost as well as does the artist.

Innovations are quickly assimilated into the conventional
vocabulary and become the basis for lay criticism and complaint, even directed against these who pioneered the innovations. Stravinsky suffered from just this when he premiered his comic opera *Mavra*. It used much simpler musical
language than the earlier ballets—*Petrushka* and *Rite of
Spring*—which had made him famous. According to his son,
who witnessed the premiere of *Mavra*:

> The modest and intimate character of *Mavra*, together with its
> melodic idiom, which is related both to gypsy songs and to
> Italian *bel canto*, was bound to upset a public which over a
> period of years had become accustomed to look on Stravinsky

as a rebel; it could not, and would not, expect each work to be other than "sensational." Such a public was bound to feel frustrated, and to look on Stravinsky as having failed his duty. The disappointment was great; and the most annoying part of it was that *Mavra* contained absolutely nothing to justify such an uproar. (Quoted in White 1966, pp. 59–60)

The American photographer Edward Weston suffered from similar complaints that he had failed to meet his own compositional and technical standards, as embodied in his earlier photographs. Those who admired his still lifes and landscapes were scandalized when he produced a series of bitter and unusual pictures during World War II, typified by "Civilian Defense," an image of a nude woman lying on a sofa wearing a gas mask. He wrote to a friend who had complained about these pictures:

> Your reaction follows a pattern which I should be used to by now. Every time that I change subject matter, or viewpoint, a howl goes up from some Weston fans. An example: in the E. W. [Weyhe] book is a reproduction of "Shell and Rock —Arrangement"; my *closest* friend, Ramiel, never forgave me for putting it in the book because it was "not a Weston." Another example: when I sent some of my then new shell and vegetable photographs to Mexico, Diego Rivera asked if "Edward was sick." And finally (I could go on for pages) when I turned from shells, peppers, rocks—so called abstract forms—Merle Armitage called my new direction the "hearts & flowers" series.
>
> So I am not exactly surprised to have you condemn . . . work which will go down in history. (Quoted in Maddow, 1973, p. 269)

Commercial Art

Subordination to the requirements of audiences and employers occurs in a more coercive and complete way in commercialized arts (see Becker, 1963, pp. 79–119; Griff, 1960; Sanders, 1974; Lyon, 1975). The employer chooses a use, just as in craft worlds, and the artist uses his virtuoso skill to meet the employer's requirements. An artist who has more interest in the display of virtuosity than in the expres-

sion of personal ideas or emotions is more open to suggestion, influence, or coercion and more prepared to take on any
of a variety of assignments proposed by others. The craft
interest in utility appears in a somewhat different form, as
the artist begins to pride himself on being able to do whatever he might be asked to do. Thus a commercial actor might
be proud of his ability to play a variety of roles—people of
different ages, classes, nationalities, and character types. A
musician might be proud of his ability to play a great variety
of kinds of music, from ethnic specialties like the polka to
jazz, symphonic, and avant-garde music and perhaps even
music from cultures using unfamiliar instruments. These
highly developed skills make such artists attractive to a variety of employers, who find those varied abilities useful.

Artists who master such technical skills usually begin to
think, talk, and act like craftsmen. Proud of their virtuosity
and control, much more than of the content of the art they
happen to be producing, they boast of their ability to handle
whatever comes up. The musicians who record sound tracks
for films and television programs epitomize this attitude
toward artistic work (Faulkner, 1971). The work is well paid
and requires great skill. Most of what these musicians play is
very simple. But they must be prepared to play tremendously
difficult material at a moment's notice. Faulkner quotes a
cellist:

> Ninety-eight per cent of the time is just simple and dull. But
> one or two per cent . . . it's demanding and you have to do
> it . . . Now tomorrow at 9:00 I have a call I don't have the
> vaguest idea who I'm working for, or what it is, how big the
> orchestra is, or who else is with me in the section. It may be X,
> Y or Z studio . . . 9:00. Now a cue might come up from a cello
> concerto, which if Leonard Rose or Pablo Casals had for a
> goddam concert, they'd have to study it for two months. And
> we have to knock it off . . . just like that on the spot—two runs
> and then a take. . . . That's why they're paying me more, and
> that's why you are known as a soloist in the business; that's
> why you're in demand. And we better do it. So those kinds,
> like I say, two per cent of the time . . . you get 'em. . . . Those
> moments are rare, just here and there . . . a couple of weeks

that you have to use every bit of talent and tricks and whatever learning from past experience has taught you. (Faulkner,
1971, p. 120)

Not only is the music these men have to play difficult, but
they have to play it under the most trying conditions—without benefit of prior study, according to a rigid rhythm already recorded on a previous sound track, and with no more
than two run-throughs before they make the final recording,
all because of economic pressures. The musicians who play
and record these scores have great technical competence.
They know it and feel a great pride. Faulkner quotes one
"elder statesman": "I believe it is necessary to play commercial music, no matter how poor, no matter how poorly
written, or how poorly starved a film score is for good ideas,
I feel that for my own private pride of performance, it deserves the best I can give it. I never compromise on that"
(Faulkner, 1971, p. 129). A few musicians bragged about their
versatility:

Many reed players don't bend, they're not flexible. Some don't
even get the right sound in the studio or they refuse to play
different. So [a composer] wants a light, French sound on the
oboe for example, and [another composer] prefers a dark,
flat German sound and you have to bend, to be able to play
them all. . . .

I doubt whether symphony players or other guys really have
all the things down, all the experience that comes with knowing every style, of having gone through the mill. . . . I have to
be funny, be a clown, be serious, play jazz, there's all types of
music and all types of challenges. You have to improvise, the
composer will even tell you to do anything you want. . . .

You're pounding on high notes like we were last week for a
couple of hours and all your blood has gone out of your lips
and then they have you turn right around and play something
soft and delicate, in the upper register, or play a little jazz, or a
bugle call with finesse. Not many can make it come on. . . .
(Faulkner, 1971, p. 140)

a

b

FIGURE 32. *Two stages in the development of American art photography. (a) Gertrude Kasebier, untitled photograph. Members of the Photo-Secession, around the turn of the century, made romantic, painterly photographs. Undated, gum print. (Courtesy of the Art Institute of Chicago.) (b) Robert Frank,* Covered Car, Long Beach, California. *Robert Frank's work returned, in some ways, to the painterly and symbolist concerns of an earlier era, although it used a more modern language and subject matter. These photographs illustrate a continuing process of solidifying technical standards and rebellion against them. Undated, black and white photograph. (From* The Americans, *1959; courtesy of the Art Institute of Chicago.)*

People usually refer to this mode of working in the visual arts, music, or theater as "commercial." Commercial arts use more or less the same skills and materials as fine arts but deliberately put them to uses no one regards as artistic, uses which find their meaning and justification in a world organized around some activity other than art. When visual artists make drawings for an advertisement or an instruction manual, they serve ends defined by business or industry, as do musicians when they record the background for a television jingle. Musicians work to serve ends defined by ethnic cultures and family display when they perform at wedding celebrations. Workers and consumers judge the product by its utility as that is defined by some world other than the art world, in relation to some other form of collective action than that defined by the art world. Art academies (Pevsner, 1940) teach the range of techniques necessary to be able to do that well.

Of course, whole art worlds do not turn to a craft orientation in this way. Instead, they gradually spin off a segment composed of people who devote themselves primarily to craft-commercial activities. Because these people are skilled craftsmen, they can (and often do) also devote themselves to creating fine art on occasion. The players Faulkner interviewed furnish personnel for avant-garde concerts and jazz groups in Los Angeles when they are not recording.

Revolt

As an art becomes conventionalized, standards become more and more rigorous. Most artists accept that rigor, satisfied with the expressive possibilities of conventionally acceptable forms. They are integrated professionals, analogous to the scientists who produce "normal science" in nonrevolutionary periods (Kuhn, 1962). But others find the rigor constraining and oppressive. They feel that, to demonstrate their competence, they have to spend so much time acquiring the conventional wisdom and skills that they can never get to the production of the art which interests them. They sometimes also feel that they will never be able to outdistance the traditional knowledge and technique of those now acclaimed.

In addition, they find that every innovation they make provokes the criticism that it fails to meet current standards of competence. Artists who give no evidence of knowing any of the right ways of doing things are thought by critics, audiences, and other artists to be bunglers and incompetents, even though they deviate from standard forms deliberately. The tyranny of such proper models of artistic work can be found in every field. Photographers who experiment with such outmoded devices as a soft-focus lens may be berated for their apparent inability to get a picture in focus. Many dance and jazz musicians found the Beatles incompetent because of their apparent inability to compose and play songs in the strict forms of contemporary popular song, the eight-bar sections to which such musicians were accustomed; it did not occur to them that composers like Lennon and McCartney were creating nine-bar phrases deliberately. (This is a particularly painful example for me, since I was one of the reactionaries who objected to the Beatles' inability to count to eight.)

Critics, patrons, and artists who find the constraints of convention intolerable fight back using a variety of invidious descriptive phrases. They call work which accepts the constraints "academic" or speak of "mere" technical virtuosity or "mere" craft.

So the end point of the sequence in which an art turns into a craft consists of younger, newer, rebellious artists refusing to play the old game and breaking out of its confines. They propose a new game, with different goals, played by different rules, in which the old knowledge and techniques are irrelevant and superfluous, no help at all in doing what is to be done in the new enterprise. They produce or discover new exemplars, new great works that furnish a new standard of beauty and excellence, works which require a different set of skills and a different kind of vision. In short, they make a revolution, of the kind discussed earlier in this chapter.

Photography has gone through many such revolutions in

its short history (see Corn, 1972; Newhall, 1964; Taft, 1938). At one time the object was to make sharp, clear renditions of whatever was there to be photographed and documented; perhaps at that point photography was a craft whose end was to serve the purposes of those who needed information in pictorial form. Later on, more artistically oriented photographers made romantic, painterly photographs; Edward Steichen, in the early part of his career, Alvin Coburn, and Clarence White took this tack. They were replaced by the f64 group, who insisted on a standard of sharp focus and clear light, who were replaced in turn by a variety of photographers, including Cartier-Bresson and Robert Frank, concerned with capturing moments of real life. But Frank's notion of real life was more symbolic than most and in some ways might even be seen as a return to the painterly concerns of the early Tonalists (see figure 32). The game of solidifying technical standards and rebelling against them goes oñ endlessly.

In discussing the oscillation between the solidification of standards and the development of new approaches, I do not intend to present a picture of lonely, inventive geniuses fighting against smug artistic establishments (although that happens, too). The shift from art to craft and back is not carried out by individuals acting independently; such shifts are successful only insofar as they involve enough people to take over an established art world or to create a new one. Most of the people involved in such transformations experience them as a choice among alternative institutional arrangements and working companions rather than as an inventive and creative leap.

SOME FINAL THOUGHTS

Most contemporary high art probably started out as some kind of craft (see Baxandall, 1972; Harris, 1966; Martindale, 1972). The composition and performance of European art music started as an activity subservient either to the requirements of the church (as in the composition and performance of the Mass and plainsong), or to the desires of a royal

patron and his court for entertainment and music for dancing or of the ordinary members of a community for some
kind of entertainment. All the fine arts we now enjoy may
have begun in just this way, going through some such change
as I have described in the case of weaving and ceramics.

In this sequence of changes, as in those considered previously and those to be taken up in the next chapter, change
in itself counts for very little. What makes the changes important—for artists, for audiences, for support personnel,
and for analysts of the arts—is the way they involve, generate,
and in turn depend on changes in organization. When all
these kinds of people change the conventional basis on
which they interact, then a real and lasting change occurs in
the medium and in the world it is produced in.

10 • Change in Art Worlds

The early parts of this book emphasized the way the activities of an art world fit together, focusing on the way people cooperate to produce an art world's characteristic products. The discussion of mavericks pointed out the ability of art worlds to repel change, to keep people whose innovative ideas would force art world participants to devise new forms of conventional practice on the outside where they could not make trouble. That may have suggested to some readers that I intended some conception of a system in equilibrium, which does not change or automatically reacts to external changes so as to minimize change within.

I do not want to suggest that at all. Art worlds change continuously—sometimes gradually, sometimes quite dramatically. New worlds come into existence, old ones disappear. No art world can protect itself fully or for long against all the impulses for change, whether they arise from external sources or internal tensions.

But I do want to insist on the crucial importance of organizational development to artistic change. Artistic mavericks show what happens to innovators who fail to develop an adequate organizational support system. They can make art, but they do not attract audiences or disciples, and found no schools or traditions. If they find a place in the history of their medium (and most do not), it is in a footnote rather than a chapter heading. Most history deals with winners. The history of art deals with innovators and innovations that won organizational victories, succeeding in creating around themselves the apparatus of an art world, mobilizing enough people to cooperate in regular ways that sustained and furthered their idea. Only changes that succeed in capturing existing cooperative networks or developing new ones survive.

The analysis in this chapter considers artistic change from this point of view, seeing how art worlds change and how they are born and die. It looks especially for how changes find an organizational base and thus last. Keep in mind that lasting is the major criterion by which people recognize great art. The connection between reputation (in this case, for greatness) and organization will concern us in the next and final chapter.

CONTINUOUS AND REVOLUTIONARY CHANGE

The art works art worlds produce, the cooperative activity through which they are produced, and the conventions by which people coordinate their cooperation all change more or less continuously. If for no other reason, practices and products change because no one can do anything exactly the same way twice, because materials and surroundings are never exactly the same and because the people you cooperate with do things differently.

Artists, and ideologists of art, often insist that such uniqueness is one of the important features of art works, which, expressing the artist's thought and mood exactly, necessarily vary. They mean thus to indicate how art works differ from the work of nonartists, industrial workers, workers in the crafts, and folk artists, all of whom (so the argument goes) produce the same object or performance over and over with no discernible change. But the works produced by all these people vary too; the difference is that no one cares about the variations in what they produce, only about the similarities. The differences and changes go unremarked. If the objects industrial workers produced really were all alike, factories would not need quality control, nor would some automobiles be "lemons" while others operate as advertised. Similarly, careful students of the crafts and folk arts have no trouble distinguishing different versions of the same object, either made by the same maker or by others working in the same tradition (Glassie, 1972, gives some examples). Log cabin quilts look alike only if you don't look closely.

In the same way, we may attend to or ignore the differences between similar art works, "we" including audiences, critics, historians, and the person making the work. Differences that might provide the basis for some major innovation can go unremarked or, if they are noticed, be interpreted as mistakes, slips, things to be cleaned up in a final version, or random variations that make no difference. K. O. Newman (1943)* describes how he attended every performance of a London play in which a friend was acting and his reactions to seeing it some eighty consecutive times. At first, like any casual theatergoer, he was incredibly bored. As time went on, however, he found that no two performances were alike. Sometimes the actors were "up" and the performance more exciting; sometimes they made mistakes which altered the sense and feeling of the play; sometimes they altered their interpretation on the spur of the moment, with varying success. When the play finally closed, he was sorry to leave the adventure of discovering the play anew every night.

Like Newman, at first people ignore most of the changes, intentional or otherwise, which occur in the doing and redoing of art works. If a dancer learning a new dance slips or stumbles, the choreographer will probably go over the sequence again until the roughness has been eliminated. Ignoring the changes does not mean that they do not persist. Language changes almost entirely through the accumulation of a series of small, unremarked changes in pronunciation and usage. No one consciously decides that from now on we

*Philip Ennis called this book to my attention.

will all drop the terminal g's of gerunds, or speak of the results of an action as "the bottom line." Instead, a few people experiment with the change, others imitate, those changes lead to other new pronunciations and clichés, and after awhile the language is noticeably different, through a series of almost imperceptible shifts for which the metaphor of "drift" is entirely appropriate.

Some drift is more conscious than this makes it sound. If we think of an artistic tradition as a connected series of solutions to a commonly defined problem (Kubler, 1962), we can see that the solutions and the problem they are meant to solve can change in this gradual way. Each consciously sought solution alters the problem somewhat, if only by altering the range of possible solutions to problems of that kind. After a while, both problems and solutions have changed substantially, though people involved in the process would probably think of these movements as logical developments in the tradition. Practice and artistic result change, but no one thinks anything special has happened. A choreographer, seeing a dancer stumble, might decide to enlarge the dance vocabulary by including stumbles as one of the expressive movements dancers can do (Paul Taylor and others since him have done just that). Such changes, at first quite surprising to performers and audiences alike, soon find a place in conventional practice. Rosenblum and Karen (1979) describe similar connected series of changes in techniques of film editing.

Leonard Meyer (1956, p. 66) gives a nice example of drift in his description of the use of vibrato by string instrument players. At one time string players used no vibrato, introducing it on rare occasions as a deviation from convention, which heightened tension and created emotional response by virtue of its rarity. String players who wanted that emotional response began using vibrato more and more often, until the best way to excite the emotional response it had once produced was to play without vibrato, a device Bartok and other composers exploited. Meyer describes the process by which deviations from convention become accepted conventions in their own right as a common one.

Art worlds do not define drift as change because it does not require any troublesome reorganization of their cooperative activities. No one is inconvenienced because someone else insists on doing things differently. No support personnel have to produce a new kind of material or perform in a wholly new and uncomfortable way. No audience has to pay more, to stay longer, or to exert itself in an unaccustomed way to enjoy the work. No one loses rank in a system of esteem or power; no one's livelihood is threatened. The people who cooperate to produce work will continue to do so, even though the work they produce is different.

Other innovations require some participants to learn and do different things, inconveniencing them and threatening their interests. Members of some art world segments, having insulated themselves from these drifts and minor changes, may fall behind current practice and suddenly find that they cannot do what is required of participants like them. Musicians find that they cannot easily execute parts younger players routinely play. When large segments of an art world get out of step in this way, some realignment of patterns of cooperative activity will take place. Change of this kind is usually viewed by everyone (except perhaps those who have fallen behind) as normal and to be expected.

Other innovations disrupt routine patterns of cooperation, involving what, with some stretching of Thomas Kuhn's (1962) usage, could be called a "revolution." People can no longer cooperate with others in the accustomed way, and cannot produce as usual the kind of works they know how to make. Revolutionary innovations, involving deliberate changes in the conventional language of the art, inevitably change who can act together to do what. Art world participants understand that the changes are intended to be major, and to affect cooperative networks, as they do. In this, revolutions differ from the gradual shifts in interest, attention, and convention just discussed. They attack, ideologically and organizationally, the standard activities of that art world at that time. The ideological attack takes the form of manifestos, critical essays, aesthetic and philosophical reformulations, and a revisionist history of the medium, denouncing old idols and exemplars and celebrating new work as the embodiment of universal aesthetic values. The organizational attack aims to take over sources of support, audiences, and distribution facilities.

Artistic revolutions make major changes in the character of the works produced and in the conventions used to produce them. Thus, impressionists and cubists changed the existing visual language, the way one put paint on canvas so that it could be read as a representation of something. Schoenberg, Berg, and Webern fundamentally changed the logic of relationships between musical tones when they introduced the twelve-tone system of composition. What is fundamental depends on what the attacked art world can accept and incorporate. Cubism and serial composition were fundamental changes because they required people to do what none of them knew how to do, so that they could not perform their parts in the collective action without substantial efforts to learn new materials and ways of doing things. Audiences had to learn to respond to unfamiliar languages and to experience them aesthetically.

Every convention implies an aesthetic which makes what is conventional the standard of artistic beauty and effectiveness. A play which violates the classical unities is not just different. To those for whom the classical unities represent a fixed criterion of dramatic worth, it is distasteful, barbaric, and ugly. An attack on a convention attacks the aesthetic related to it. Since people experience their aesthetic beliefs as natural, proper, and moral, an attack on a convention and its aesthetic also attacks a morality. The regularity with which audiences greet major changes in dramatic, musical, and visual conventions with vituperative hostility indicates the close relation between aesthetic and moral beliefs (Kubler, 1962).

An attack on aesthetic beliefs as embodied in particular conventions is, finally, an attack on an existing system of stratification. Hughes (n.d.) argues, following William G. Sumner (1906), that folkways and mores create status. Sects —religious, political, or artistic—are at war with the mores. An attack on the mores (for which, in this case, read conventions) is thus an attack on social structure (for which read the organization of an art world), and sects or innovators in art worlds are at war with the systems of rank current in the worlds whose conventions they attack and attempt to replace.

Remember that the conventional way of doing things in any art utilizes an existing cooperative network, which rewards those who manipulate the existing conventions appropriately in light of the associated aesthetic. Suppose that a dance world is organized around the conventions and skills embodied in classical ballet. By learning those conventions and skills, I become eligible for positions in the best ballet companies; the finest choreographers will create ballets for me, just the kind I know how to dance and will look good in; the best composers will write scores for me; theaters will be available; I will earn as good a living as a dancer can earn; audiences will love me; and I will be famous. Anyone who successfully promotes a new convention requiring skills he has and I don't—stumbling, for instance—not only attacks my aesthetic but also endangers my position in the world of dance. I resist the new both because I find it aesthetically repellent and thus morally outrageous and because I stand to lose if it replaces the old.

Others besides the artist have something invested in the status quo which they stand to lose through a change in accepted conventions. Consider an earthwork sculpture made by a bulldozer in a square mile of pasture. You cannot collect it (though a patron might pay for its construction and receive signed plans or photographs as a document of his patronage), or put it in museums (though the mementos the collector receives can be displayed). Suppose earthworks become an important art form. Museum personnel, whose evaluations of museum-collectable art have had important consequences for the careers of artists and art movements, will lose the power to choose which works will be displayed. No one needs their museums to display such works. Everyone involved in museum-collectable art (collectors, museum curators, galleries, dealers, and artists) loses something. Since every art world creates value by the agreement of its members as to what is valuable (Moulin, 1967; Levine, 1972; Christopherson, 1974a), when someone successfully creates a new world which defines the mastery of other conventions as the mark of artistic value, all the participants in the old world who cannot make a place in the new one lose out.

Revolutions do not change every pattern of convention-mediated cooperative activity. If they did, we would not call them revolutions but rather would see them as the development of an entirely new art world. As with political revolutions, no matter how much changes, much stays the same (as we saw in our discussion of mavericks). Composers may use new sounds and notations; musicians may play their instruments in unfamiliar ways and use new kinds of equipment. But composers still produce scores which, however unconventional, function as parts that the performers read and use to guide their performance; performers play in public events called concerts or recitals, lasting a conventional two hours or so; audiences attend at a specific time and sit quietly while the performers play, frequently having bought tickets to the event as a result of learning about it through publicity and newspaper stories. So composers, performers, audiences, ticket sellers, renters of halls, and publicity people still cooperate to produce these events, even though the nature of the event has changed. We think of the changes as revolutions when one or more important groups of participants find themselves displaced by the change, even though the rest remains much the same. Thus, earthworks create a revolution when they threaten the position of curators and dealers, who formerly had substantial control of the public displays which legitimated artists and their work. Earthworks threaten the critics and audience members who do not alter their past aesthetic and make room for the new work in their experience. But for participants who make the change and thus preserve their positions in the cooperative network, the change is not so revolutionary after all.

We cannot distinguish continuous from revolutionary change on the basis of the change itself. Changes in the tonalities used in musical composition or in the conventions of realistic representation in visual art are only revolutionary if the contemporary art world cannot absorb them without important members losing their positions and prerequisites. Furthermore, a change may be revolutionary for some people involved in the existing system, but not for others. There is no simple way to sum up all the changes and decide that so much change, but no less, is revolutionary. Nor is there any good reason to make the distinction so clear-cut. What is important to understand is the process by which participants ignore, absorb, or fight change, for those responses define the seriousness and extent of the change, which make it a revolution or something less dramatic.

Revolutionary changes succeed when their originators mobilize some or all of the members of the relevant art world to cooperate in the new activities their vision of the medium requires. When actors will perform in new ways (appear nude, for instance) for directors; when pianists will reach inside to pluck strings directly if a composer directs them to; when printers and publishers produce books that are longer or shorter or set more unconventionally than books used to be—when innovators succeed in so mobilizing people, they have changed the terms of cooperation in that art world. From then on, competent participants must know and be able to do, in addition to whatever was formerly required of them, what the innovation makes conventional. If participants can simultaneously forget some of what they used to know because it will no longer be used, we might say that the innovation has replaced the older forms. But the innovation is usually added to what competent participants need to know and do. When you learn to play the violin in a new way, because your orchestra is going to perform a work by John Cage, that does not mean that you can forget the techniques necessary for Bach, Mozart, or Copland. You will play their works during the season as well.

Just as some older participants fall so behind that, no longer knowing or able to do what is needed, they can no longer participate, some innovators can leave the bulk of what the conventional art world requires behind, specializing in what an innovation has made possible. An art dealer might specialize in conceptual art, a publisher in avant-garde poetry, a pianist in the performance of aleatory works. Participants can only do this if enough others join them to support the new activity. Dancers who specialize in contemporary dance may have only a four- to six-week season, compared with conventional dancers' twenty to thirty weeks; the audience for contemporary dance will not support more performances than that. Not every locale can support such specialization. An instrumentalist in New York or London can specialize in Renaissance and baroque music, but an equally skilled player in Kansas City, to make a living, will play every variety of classical music and probably moonlight in a dance orchestra as well.

Innovators who command the cooperation of everyone needed for the activities the innovation requires have an art world at their disposal, whether they take over existing institutions, replacing the people who formerly made use of them, share the use of those facilities, or simply create an entirely new network. Rock-and-roll musicians illustrate all these possibilities. They pushed conventional dance bands out of some kinds of work, gaining an almost exclusive monopoly on teenage dances, got their share of the popular record business, and created a new network of performance facilities in indoor and outdoor rock concerts and rock-and-roll night clubs. While they use some conventional instruments, an entire industry has grown up to provide the new instruments and accessories they need. Most substantial changes in art worlds have this mixed character.

In short, changes in art occur through changes in worlds. Innovations last when participants make them the basis of a new mode of cooperation, or incorporate a change into their ongoing cooperative activities. Changes can occur piecemeal and peacefully, almost unnoticed, or occasion substantial conflict between those who stand to profit and gain in public esteem by the change and those who will lose. Innovations begin as, and continue to incorporate, changes in an artistic vision or idea. But their success depends on the degree to which their proponents can mobilize the support of others. Ideas and visions are important, but their success and permanence rest on organization, not on their intrinsic worth.

BIRTH AND DEATH

From time to time new art worlds appear, grow, and prosper, eventually achieving sufficient stability that they can go through some of the sequences of internal change we have already considered. An art world is born when it brings together people who never cooperated before to produce art based on and using conventions previously unknown or not exploited in that way. Similarly, an art world dies when no one cooperates any longer in its characteristic ways to produce art based on and exploiting its characteristic conventions. We cannot clearly separate new art worlds from those which have changed substantially by virtue of an artistic revolution, nor can we easily decide when an art world has died, as opposed to being changed or taken over by new people. We need not make these distinctions definitively, since our interest is in the growth and decay of forms of collective action rather than in the development of logical typologies. We will look for the mechanisms which help art worlds to operate and whose disappearance interferes with that operation.

We should not confuse innovation with the development of an art world. New worlds develop around innovations—technical, conceptual, or organizational changes—but most innovations do not produce new art worlds. We have seen how mavericks can create interesting innovations which become dead ends and blind alleys, not because the innovation could not sustain continued experimentation and development, but because the innovator could not find sufficient numbers of people to join in that development. What might have been an art world remains an unexplored possibility. Most substantial innovations which someone has deliberately made, hoping to persuade others to join in their exploitation, share that fate. To understand the birth of new art worlds, then, we need to understand, not the genesis of innovations, but rather the process of mobilizing people to join in a cooperative activity on a regular basis.

New art worlds grow up around something that has not been characteristic practice for artists before. Since art worlds have many characteristic modes of practice, ranging from conventions for making works to methods of display and technical and material components, a new way of doing any of these might be the basis for a new world.

Some art worlds begin with the invention and diffusion of a technology which makes certain new art products possible. The technical development will likely have originated for nonartistic purposes, for art is seldom important enough to attract serious inventors to its problems. Tinkerers abound, but the sustained investment of time, money, and other resources required for the practical development of a new technical possibility is rare. The inventions and developments which made still photography and motion pictures possible did not arise from anyone's desire to make art, but from the scientific, commercial, and entertainment possibilities of these media. Much, much earlier, people invented ways of working with metal, which incidentally made sculpture and artistic jewelry possible, although that was not the purpose of those inventions either (see Smith, 1970).

We notice these technical developments most in contemporary art, where they create serious ambiguities as to whether we are seeing new art worlds develop or only new segments of old ones. The invention of the tape recorder and other electronic devices (from oscillators to synthesizers) created a way of making music without human performers. Nevertheless, much electronic music is created by people trained in music, who use the machines as an adjunct to live human performance, is heard by audiences raised on more or less conventional concert music, and is judged by critics who use the same standards they apply to other serious, composed music. All this suggests that no new art world has arisen around these electronic inventions.

Other creators of electronic music, however, come out of the world of computer electronics and mathematics. Oriented toward computing and machinery rather than music, they have begun to make music with the machines alone, dispensing with human players. Not only does the music differ in various ways—using random noise or machine-generated pure tones as raw material, for instance—but the composers are less performance oriented, more interested in mailing tapes to each other and in having them available for others to hear. Not having been trained to see public performance as the proper way to hear music, anything else being merely a record of that public event, they treat tapes as an author treats books, as objects containing the work itself, any copy being as good as any other, and do not regard the work as being improved in the slightest by being done in public, any more than a literary work's essential merit lies in how it sounds when its author reads it aloud. This version of electronic music makes the development of a new art world more likely.

Some art worlds begin with the development of a new concept, a new way of thinking about something, whose possibilities can be explored and exploited just as a technical development is. Ian Watt describes the development of the novel as partly due to the new idea of "formal realism" as an appropriate mode of discourse in fiction. Such inventors of the novel as Defoe, Richardson, and Fielding substituted, for the stylized plots and characters of earlier fiction, a fidelity to the details of ordinary experience that showed itself in realistically complex, original, and not completely designed plots, in the particularity (as opposed to universality) with which characters and environments were drawn, and in the plain, everyday language in which the story was told (Watt, 1957, pp. 13–30). A story so told differs in more than minor details from a romance with an artificial plot, characters (like Gargantua) whose names insist that they are universal types, and a language none of the characters could have managed in real life—it differs in its conception of what a work of fiction ought to strive for and what it might accomplish. Around that new conception a new world of writers and readers gradually arose.

Some art worlds begin with the development of a new

audience. The work they produce may not differ much from work in similar genres which preceded it, but they reach a new audience through new distributional arrangements. The "new" rock music of the 1960s resembled what had preceded it: white imitations of black blues and rock-and-roll, mixed with country-and-western music. But it employed new organizations to reach young people: the outdoor concert (Peterson, 1973), which, like Woodstock, went on for hours or even days, and working-class ballrooms, like the Fillmore Auditorium, whose "Over Thirty" crowd had deserted them. Instead of drawing customers from already-existing audiences, it reached into an age group that had never consumed much live or recorded music. Major elements of the radio and recording industries soon began to distribute the music, too (Denisoff, 1975), so that one cannot say that it developed an entirely new set of institutions. Nevertheless, so many new groups and kinds of people were cooperating in the production and consumption of rock-and-roll that we can reasonably speak of a new world having come into existence.

Watt (1957) makes a similar point with respect to the development of the novel. A new audience developed along with the new conception of fiction, and that made the continued production of realistic fiction possible. The spread of literacy in eighteenth-century England produced more readers, of a new class which did not share the earlier aristocratic conception of proper fiction. The new audience, swelled by the addition of middle-class people involved in commerce and manufacture (in many cases, by their apprentices and house servants as well), did not have the classical education needed for appreciation of the more formal and allusive style which preceded the novel. Not interested in moral edification, they looked instead for easily absorbed entertainment, which the novel provided. The new work for the new audience was distributed through new institutions: magazines and new forms of book publication, in which printers made the editorial choices previously made by publishers.

Innovations of this kind, around which new art worlds

may develop, usually arise simultaneously in a number of places. Except for isolates like the naive artists considered earlier, whose visions and methods are relatively idiosyncratic, the people who develop new art worlds participate in the broad currents of intellectual and expressive interest growing out of extant tradition and practice. The musicians and promoters who developed rock-and-roll knew the black and white popular musics which could be combined to produce rock. The people interested in the possibilities created by the invention of photographic and film equipment probably share many other interests—recording the landscape or making portraits for sale, for instance. Because they share traditions and interests, what they do with the innovation's possibilities, while it varies, varies within a relatively small range.

A new technique, conception, or audience suggests new possibilities but does not define them fully. So the first people involved experiment with it, seeing what it can do and what they might want to do with it. What people actually do with the innovation depends on what it makes possible, on what version they have of contemporary traditions and interests, and on the people and resources they can attract. Innovations, with their associated possibilities, often spread quickly. It takes longer for the people who experiment with them to find each other and to establish communication. Technology, for instance, may appear in many places simultaneously. People can order equipment and supplies from a catalogue and teach themselves to use it, but they do not know what the other people who have ordered from that catalogue are doing. Each experimenter develops, with experience, a technique that produces a result someone finds pleasing. Each experimenter's result, within the limits of what the innovation makes possible, differs from the others'. Whether the experimenters work entirely alone or with a small circle of professional or amateur local colleagues, they produce what might be called a local art world, one whose circle of cooperation does not go beyond the face-to-face interaction of a local community.

Consider two extended examples of this process. One, the

development of the stereograph, the three-dimensional photograph, at first produced a successful art world, but it did not last. The second, the development of American jazz, produced a music that succeeded on an international scale.

Because the principles and technology of stereography developed at about the same time as the two-dimensional photography which did become successful, it is useful to think of the two as competing ways of producing visual imagery, either or both of which might successfully have produced an art world. Two dimensions won that contest.

At first, hand-drawn images illustrated the stereographic effect; later daguerreotypes and various versions of the negative-positive process were used. The technology was simple, and anyone who could control the cumbersome equipment and complicated techniques of early photography could make stereographs. The early versions of the process, however, made it somewhat difficult to produce large quantities of work. That limited circulation. Images usually circulated where they were made, to a local audience interested in local events, places, and people. Local practitioners made portraits, scenic views, and pictures of local disasters, probably more or less exclusively for local consumption.

Not much is known about the practices of early stereographers. Did they, for instance, make small numbers of items of local interest, which then circulated primarily in the local community? Fragments of evidence, such as this letter to the *Photographic Times* (1871) from an Illinois photographer who had purchased a "Philadelphia Wilsonian Stereoscopic Box Camera" with "Ross' Stereoscopic Doublet Lenses," suggest that.

> I have awakened to the necessity of making stereoscopic pictures. Several good orders lost have taught me to believe that it will pay to give a little attention to that growing branch of our art. . . . I am not blessed with a continual rush in my studio, so I have always had a little spare time. The first spare hours I had, I put out, and made a few views of some of the prettiest residences in our suburbs. As I returned home I found the light just right on our new bank building, and I

banged away at that. I made some good prints, showed them to the parties, who did not know that there was an apparatus in town that could give them such a surprise, and made that information cost exactly forty dollars for negatives made in one short morning. Those pictures have brought me several more orders, which I shall fill during the next spare hours. Our people said they had often wished for such views of their places, and the introduction of your 5 x 8 boxes has caused more excitement among our three thousand inhabitants in our quiet village than you have any idea of. I only hope it won't raise the price of 'scopes. ("Southern Illinois," 1871, p. 91)

William Culp Darrah lists the variety of photographers who produced the early stereographs:

1. The photographer who specialized in the production of stereographs but confined his practice to local subjects.
2. The resort photographer (there were hundreds of them at Niagara Falls, Saratoga, the White Mountains, Catskills, etc.) who virtually limited his work to the tourist trade.
3. The studio photographer who, as a side line, occasionally produced stereoscopic portraits, poses, interiors of churches and public buildings, commonly including a small series of local town views.
4. The opportunist who produced a few views when some unusual event—flood, fire, train-wreck, parade, or such—created a transitory market for souvenirs. (Darrah, 1977, p. 44)

A variant of these occurred in the Shaker religious communities, which did a large business with the outside world, not only in furniture and food, but also in stereographic records of their community life:

One of the chief diversions of visitors to fashionable vacation retreats, such as Lebanon Springs, New York, near the Mt. Lebanon Shaker community, and Poland Springs, Maine, near the Sabbathday Lake village, was a trip to visit the Shaker stores and purchase mementos of their trip. Recognizing the need for items that tourists would find both interesting and informative, the Shakers in these areas sold sets of stereo views of the Shaker community. They also offered them to other Shaker villages at wholesale prices. (Rubin, 1978, pp. 56–57)

Audiences also had to acquire a technical skill, that of looking at stereographs. Anyone who has only recently had the opportunity to look at them can recall the difficulty (perhaps only momentary, perhaps longer) of making the two images come together so that you get the "stereo" experience of depth. It doesn't take long to learn to do it, but you must acquire the ability. An occasional article (Oliver Wendell Holmes produced one of the early ones) suggested exercises for accustoming the eyes to the phenomenon, and explained the particular pleasures to be gained from using the new skill. It would be interesting to know how people learned these skills and what difficulties they had. Who taught the skills and to whom? Could some people simply not get the knack? A particularly critical article of the 1890s suggests such possibilities:

> The present limited popularity of the stereoscope seems to be due to several causes. First of which is probably the great number of cheap and miserably made pictures and stereoscopes which have been offered to buyers, only to give disappointment to, and to strain the eyes of those attempting to use them. (Luders, 1892, p. 227)

In addition to learning to read the stereographic image, viewers must have learned a taste for its unique pleasures. The early appreciative articles dwell on these—the illusion of solidity, of feeling yourself actually present and immersed in a scene. Some stylistic features of stereographs must have been designed to accent that illusion of three dimensions. Just as 3-D movies always had a scene in which an airplane flew directly at the audience or a trapeze artist swung back and forth over their heads, so stereographs used devices which emphasized the feeling of depth. (The same compositional features may also have been characteristic of two-dimensional photography of the period; stereographs often, for instance, used a long, slanting line which went far back into the distance, or placed a figure in the foreground to emphasize the distance between the foreground and the mountain or other scenic wonders at a distance [see figure 33].) Even comic views and funeral pictures used tricks which made the depth explicit (portraits of the deceased were sur-

FIGURE 33. *James M. Davis,* The Railroad, 'Tis Like Life. *Stereographs emphasized the three-dimensionality of the image by including diagonals that ran into deep space. (Courtesy of the Visual Studies Workshop.)*

rounded with floral wreaths that stood out in strong relief). The makers anticipated the complaints of customers who had paid for three dimensions, and found that they might as well have been seeing the image in two. Thus, the critic quoted earlier speaks of "... unsuitable subjects, or rather not selecting suitable ones ... any subject composed of straight lines will be nearly as well rendered by a single view." (Luders, 1892, p. 227).

Thomas Hennessey (1973) has made a similar analysis of the successful development of jazz in the period from 1917 to 1935. He notes that wherever jazz arose, it combined Afro-American and Euro-American elements in music that was performed for an audience rather than accompanying someone's work or being made within a folk community. His analysis shows the connections, in the several centers in which jazz arose, between the musical traditions drawn on, performance situations, performance spaces, and the kinds of musicians recruited, and deserves quoting at length:

> Jazz did not begin as a single musical tradition in New Orleans or elsewhere. The reality of early jazz history is the emergence

in several parts of the country of independent popular musical styles, all linked by the common bonds of a mixed Euro- and Afro-American musical parentage and a performance orientation. They developed in response to specific situations and thus each strain had its particular mixture of individual elements. In the Southwest, the blues and piano ragtime had a strong influence on the style. In the Midwest and Southeast, the brass band tradition of the circus and tent show musicians emerged in an instrumental ragtime style. In Chicago and New York, established black communities sought legitimacy with a style heavily-weighted with Euro-American elements. In the Northwest and West Coast, the lack of any strong input from black folk tradition saw a very weak musical style develop, closely tied to brass band and dance music tradition. In New Orleans, two very strong traditions, (a) the classically-influenced Creole and (b) the blues and church music, shaped uptown tradition, developed and intermingled.

Each area also had its own performance situation. For the scattered black settlements in the Southeast and Midwest, the touring shows; for the Southwest, barn dances and honky-tonks; for Chicago, theaters and night clubs; for New York, private dances and cabarets; for New Orleans, street parades, sporting houses, outdoor concerts, and private balls. One performance situation prevailed throughout the country. This was the local brass band, frequently with a kid band auxiliary. Although it did not play jazz in a strict sense, these groups contributed much to the style and served as a training ground for many future jazz musicians. (Hennessey, 1973, pp. 470–71)

Many pre-1917 musicians were amateurs, but that changed. Full-time professional black musicians, better trained (especially in New York and Chicago), played a higher proportion of European-influenced music. That proportion also reflected the greater opportunity black musicians had to reach white audiences at society parties, cabarets, and occasional appearances in vaudeville and legitimate theater. By 1917, for instance, New York's dominant black music was "a large ensemble style mixing traditional ballroom music and instrumental ragtime. This was remote from the five-piece contrapuntal style brought to New York in that year by the white Original Dixieland Jazz Band" (Hennessey, 1973, p. 473). A similar confrontation occurred in

Chicago, between the "loose, improvised jazz of the Chicago black cabarets . . . heavily influenced by New Orleans imports such as King Oliver, Jelly Roll Morton, Kid Ory [and] Johnny and Baby Dodds . . . small five-piece groups collectively improvising within an established framework with strong ties to the black folk tradition" and "a large ensemble, classically influenced style similar to that of New York," represented by the orchestras of Erskine Tate and others (Hennessey, 1973, p. 473).

Hennessey emphasizes the dependence of this music's success in the larger centers on the presence of a large black bourgeoisie:

> It was sophisticated and had classical roots. It was not foreign to white ears and could be judged on classical terms. Its evident musical merit seemed to raise it above the "raucous noise" of the New Orleans men. Its proponents were well-trained musicians and well-behaved gentlemen unlike the drinking, carousing, undependable "ace musicians" of the New Orleans school. (Hennessey, 1973, pp. 473–74)

Centers with a smaller black middle-class responded to and supported local, correspondingly less refined, versions of the African-European amalgam.

As both examples indicate, localized groups of various sizes (small in the case of stereography, larger in the case of jazz) produce variant local versions of the new possibilities. Experimenting groups cluster locally because they communicate largely face-to-face, hearing or seeing each other's work. That restricts colleagueship to the immediate vicinity, unless other means of communication are available to scattered experimenters who know of each other.

In addition to experimenting with the new possibilities, the pioneers also begin to construct the rudiments of an art world—networks of suppliers, distribution facilities, and collegial groups in which aesthetic questions can be argued, standards proposed, and work evaluated. Successful suppliers quickly outgrow the locality, exporting their products to other locales in which the process of local experimentation can take place. Musical instruments, cameras, and other sorts of equipment can more easily be shipped here and there than other elements of an art world. Manufacturers, where the economy makes that possible, soon develop extensive markets. George Eastman (the founder of Eastman Kodak) and a relatively few other manufacturers had sizable national markets long before there was a national photography world, and the same was true of photography's international development (Taft, 1938; Jenkins, 1975).

Colleagues, especially, seem to be local for a long time. They may cluster near the equipment they need, as electronic composers do near the studios, radio stations, and universities which have good collections of current equipment. They may find each other around, and through the good offices of, suppliers of materials, who put them in touch with one another. They often establish small organizations of like-minded people; from the beginning of photography, the ubiquitous local camera club brought together people who were experimenting with the same equipment to have exhibitions and to criticize each other's work (Taft, 1938, p. 376; Newhall, 1964, pp. 103–4; Tice, 1977). (Similar organizations occur today, in fields not yet thought of as serious art by most people, e.g., china painting.)

Audiences remain local for some time, too. The barriers to communication that prevent the geographic spread of colleagueship limit audience interest to the work produced in the locality. People cannot appreciate music that, because it is played in inaccessible places, they have never heard. (Inaccessibility, usually geographic, can also be social. Many white Americans of the 1920s could not learn to appreciate jazz because they would have had to go to places most whites did not then go to hear it. Adults were late in developing an interest in rock music because it was played in places and on radio stations totally unfamiliar to them.) But local audiences, clustering around whatever rudimentary distribution organizations exist, support the young art world's practitioners, their responses (informal, perhaps just criticism printed in a local paper) helping to produce an aesthetic appropriate to the work.

Some art worlds develop beyond the local level. They attract more participants in all the roles the world contains, attract them from farther places, and create the extended network of cooperation we might think of as a full art world, everyone using conventions developed in many different local segments but now known and understood nationally or even internationally. A number of intertwined processes produce this result, but the result is not inevitable. Most innovations which begin to develop on a local level never get any farther. They may persist at the local level, but do not become national or international.

Production

As work becomes known over a larger area, people produce more of it, either because more people get involved in production or through the introduction of industrialized methods. Jazz spread faster after the industrialized production and distribution of phonograph records allowed local players to hear and imitate what musicians elsewhere were doing.

The industrialization of stereograph production took place in a relatively short time. If a national market was going to disseminate the new art of stereo views, manufacturers had to produce them in sufficient quantity to meet the demand (see figure 34). The handicraft methods of the early producers would not do:

> Five steps were involved in the manufacture of a card stereograph:
> 1. making positive prints from the negative, including washing and drying them (usually overnight);
> 2. trimming the prints with a scissors or die;
> 3. pasting prints on the card;
> 4. drying under gentle pressure;
> 5. applying labels and imprints.
> The entire operation extended over three days and two nights, although some large establishments were able to speed the process by using drying ovens or warming tables. A single skilled workman could produce 50 or 60 card mounts a day, or up to 350 per week. If the process was carried out, with a

FIGURE 34. *Stereoscope manufacturing at Underwood and Underwood, circa 1910. With the growth of markets, production facilities were industrialized. (Courtesy of the Hastings Gallery.)*

division of labor, five operators could produce more than 3,000 per week. (Darrah, 1977, p. 7)

The industrialization of the process began almost immediately in the 1860s, assembly-line techniques raising production considerably (see figure 35). Darrah describes one of several such operations:

Kilburn Brothers (Littleton, New Hampshire) erected a large three-story factory with special rooms for printing, toning, washing, drying and mounting. The division of labor was in no way different from already-established practice. Improvements resulted from greater efficiency in passing from one

FIGURE 35. Stock room, Underwood and Underwood, circa 1905. At the height of the stereograph's popularity, manufacturers were publishing as many as a million cards a year. (Courtesy of the Hastings Gallery.)

operation to another. The only mechanization was an endless belt exposure machine which, by eliminating handling of each exposure, doubled the rate of production of prints. Employing fifty-two persons, some of whom were maintenance men and clerks, the Kilburns produced, on an average, three thousand finished stereographs per day. In other words, the Kilburn factory could easily publish a million cards per year. (Darrah, 1977, p. 45)

Some forty years later, further mechanization again upped production and completed the industrialization of the process; here is Darrah's description of the H. C. White Company of North Bennington, Vermont:

In 1907 White erected a three-story factory of brick and rein-forced concrete, which for a short period was the finest and most mechanized stereo publishing facility in the world. The entire photo-printing process was automated. The glass neg-atives were clamped in front of a lamp under which an endless belt carried the printing paper, stopped for the set time and then advanced the paper for the next exposure. Such machines had been in use since 1866. The White operations, however, mechanized developing, fixing and washing ma-chines with which it was possible to maintain uniform stan-dards of quality. Prints were trimmed with a high-speed die-cutter. Titles were printed automatically at the rate of 10,000 per hour. There were three washing machines, each with a capacity of 5,000 prints per 10 hour day. Automatic driers, utilizing piped steam, had a capacity of 15,000 prints per day. A special machine gilded the printed titles and imprint on the deluxe format of White stereographs. (Darrah, 1977, p. 51)

Distribution

New business and distribution arrangements help the growing art world spread over a larger territory. This in-volves the sale of finished work, for object-producing arts, and the development of stable contractual arrangements for performances.

The small businesses of early stereograph operators were confined largely to their own localities. Different areas traded images through "exchange clubs," whose amateur members regularly traded work. Imagery also traveled as people brought back stereographic souvenirs of their trips, but the large-scale migration of imagery began with highly orga-nized merchandising schemes, designed to move the output of the industrialized producers.

Early photographers sold views out of their studios, through such agents as opticians and art shops, and by mail. The big producers who replaced them created large door-to-door sales forces. The president of the Keystone View Company described turn-of-the-century marketing tech-niques as follows:

Salesmen were recruited primarily from the colleges and uni-versities. Most of these men worked only during the three months of the Summer vacation, and frequently were able to earn enough money within that time to pay their entire college expenses for the year. Underwood & Underwood claimed that their organization alone sent out as many as 3,000 college students in one Summer. With the other big companies, each employing more than 1,000, it is easy to understand how the countrysides of the nation literally swarmed with stereograph salesmen throughout the Summer months! . . . The method of selling was unique and effective. On the first call, the salesman endeavored merely to book an order for a stereoscope and "some views" or, if the prospect had a stereoscope, an order would be booked, if possible, for only "one view." Approximately three weeks were spent in the booking of orders, which were followed by three weeks of deliveries. On the delivery, the salesman took with him a large collection of stereographs, sometimes covering thousands of subjects. With the prospect's head in a stereoscope, he would skillfully run for him a succession of views, by sliding one in behind the view in place and then lifting the front view to expose the one behind it. The prospect would say from time to time: "I'll take that one." The close of the sale meant bringing the prospect as close as possible to paying for all of the subjects he had laid out on the original showing. (Hamilton, 1949, pp. 17–18)

Stereographs were also sold by mail. Catalogues of the major suppliers listed thousands of views—scenic, historic, educational, artistic, and comic—and mail-order houses like Sears, Roebuck advertised similar assortments in their catalogues (see figure 36). The Sears catalogue of 1908, for instance, offered sets of one hundred cards each on such topics as "The Siege of Port Arthur" during the Japanese-Russian War, "Fair Japan," "The Holy Land," "The St. Louis World's Fair," and "Hunting, Fishing, Camping and Indian Life." Underwood and Underwood, a major supplier, offered their "Travel System," collections of stereographs, maps, and written guides to such places as Egypt, Denmark, and the Grand Canyon.

Hennessey describes the analogous shift in the way black bands handled their business affairs which made possible the development of a national audience. At first, whether the

FIGURE 36. Ad for stereographs in the Sears, Roebuck cata-logue. Sears, Roebuck advertised thousands of stereographs, distrib-uting them throughout the country. (Courtesy of the Visual Studies Workshop.)

band was run by a leader, a partnership, or on some co-operative arrangement,

The band member responsible would contact the owner of a ballroom, night club, cabaret, or a dance promoter and ar-range for an appearance. The contracts were usually informal and flexible. The musicians' union was repeatedly unsuccess-

> ful in requiring black bands to follow union standards in the contract arrangements. These informal arrangements were usually simple involving merely a long location stand or a set local tour pattern. (Hennessey, 1973, p. 484)

This kind of informal arrangement inevitably limited bands to engagements in an area small enough that they could know the people they were dealing with personally.

Between 1929 and 1935, changed business procedures, combined with the changes in transportation and communication to be considered below, made national reputations and contractual arrangements on a national scale possible for black bands.

> Using one location as a base, a band built a national reputation through records and radio appearances. This reputation was then exploited for financial gain with nationwide tours which took the band to ballrooms, hotels, theaters, anywhere where the public which had learned to like the band's style from the media would be willing to pay good prices to see the group live. (Hennessey, 1973, p. 487)

Whether through changes in manufacturing and sales or changes in contractual arrangements for performances, the work characteristic of one locale comes to be exportable. There is enough of it, and distributors and others have been persuaded to cooperate so that audiences and practitioners in other locales can become familiar with it. One locale may become dominant, other local worlds modeling themselves on its example, or the work of many locales may become exportable simultaneously.

In the development of stereography, the combined manufacturing and selling operation described earlier created an enormous demand for stereoscopic photographic images. No local photographer or group of local photographers could supply so much imagery. To feed the operation, the large publishers used images from everywhere. They bought negatives from local photographers, made copy negatives from available material (often without paying for the rights), produced series of comic or narrative images, and sent their own staff photographers out on assignments.

And so skilled stereoscopic photographers were sent to bring back high-class negatives of places, monuments, and shrines, famous in history and literature. Nor was Scenic America—from Bar Harbor, Maine, to the Golden Gate on the Pacific shores—neglected. Great expositions like the Centennial Exhibition in Philadelphia, the World's Columbian Exposition in Chicago, and the World's Fair in St. Louis were photographed—large sums of money being paid for exclusive rights, which were not always honored by competing photographers. At any rate, culture was being provided for the farm homes of America. . . . They instructed their photographers to look always for scenes of high educational significance. Industries were photographed, specimens from science laboratories received attention, and scenes of historic possibilities were not overlooked. Among the first photographers to make pictures of the early experimental airplane flights of the Wright brothers were stereoscopic photographers—leaving to history priceless studies of the details of the earliest airplanes in flight. (Hamilton, 1949, pp. 19–21)

In the case of big band jazz, nationally known bands came to dominate even local music worlds. But the developing jazz world of clubs, recordings, vaudeville, ballrooms, and radio needed a lot of musical material, and found it everywhere: Ellington from Washington, D.C., Count Basie and Andy Kirk from Kansas City, and others from Chicago, New York, and elsewhere.

Typically, no one small locality, however metropolitan, can furnish a sufficient amount and variety of work to serve a national or international market. For that reason, what happened to both stereographs and jazz is probably common: the organizations that distribute work begin to look everywhere for material and thus breach the walls around the local, provincial art world.

Communication

Those walls, insulating local artists from the influence of workers in other localities who are producing a different version of the innovation, will already have begun to fall, because of the increased communication between local art worlds. Communication may increase technologically or simply because artists and audience members travel.

The great patrons of Renaissance Europe attracted artists from countries other than their own, and painters traveled, as well, to see the work of others they had heard of (Haskell, 1963). Similarly, composers and musicians traveled from one European country to another, in the service of the church or of some rich or noble patron (Reese, 1959). These travels let artists learn firsthand what had developed in other locales and pass on what they knew from their own locale. Audience members who traveled likewise learned to understand and appreciate work that differed from what they were used to at home.

On a more homely scale, experimenters with a new artistic possibility who travel to where similar experiments have produced different results can show other practitioners what they know and can learn from them at the same time. Both parties, having acquired something new in the process, can exchange ideas in a way not formerly possible. Whatever increases the ease and likelihood of travel—politically open borders, available travel routes and carriers, plenty of money, cosmopolitan attitudes—promotes such exchange. New train routes, telephones, discount fares on airplanes, and a booming economy all help in the process.

Technical developments have the same effect. When printing techniques made possible "exactly reproducible copies" (Ivins, 1953), artists everywhere (and audience members, too) could see work that previously they had only heard about. Of course, they could only see the work itself if it was a work of graphic art—an etching, engraving, or lithograph. When those techniques were used to reproduce a painting or drawing, then the original work was filtered through a set of conventional translations from oil or charcoal to engraving tool and ink, and the result was not the same as the original, any more than a photograph (which now performs this service for art worlds) is the same as the original it portrays (Ivins, 1953). But, true to the original or not, the reproduction brought some semblance of it to people who previously had only word of mouth to depend on for an understanding of what artists were doing elsewhere. It thus helped spread the word across a larger territory.

The phonograph record did the same thing for the development of jazz:

> Jazz was an improvised flexible form which could not be readily captured in standard notation or spread through sheet music. Records allowed this ephemeral style to be frozen and held. This made it much easier to learn. It also meant that the style could be learned without direct personal contact with the performer. The influence of a particular regional or individual style could thus be extended considerably through this media. (Hennessey, 1973, p. 477)

Radio made available a much wider variety of performances, even to people who could not afford large record collections. From the late twenties on, local radio stations filled the late evening hours with broadcasts of big bands playing at local nightclubs and ballrooms, some of them big jazz bands, some of whose players were well-known jazzmen. Late at night, when smaller stations went off the air, some powerful stations could be heard thousands of miles away. As an aspiring teenage jazz musician, too young to afford or even be admitted to the places jazz was played, I could thus hear all the well-known bands and soloists performing live. Hearing the same numbers night after night, I could study the differences between improvisations on the same themes, as they came out of my bedroom radio. Many musicians who grew up in the thirties and forties learned some of what they knew this way. Unlike records, the radio let you learn the amount of leeway allowed by performance practice; instead of learning someone's recorded solo note for note, you learned what kinds of solos were possible.

An interesting instance of the internationalization of an art world occurred as a result of World War II. U.S. soldiers, some of them musicians, stayed for extended periods in many European and Asian countries. Local musicians who had studied jazz only from recordings could now hear and play with American players. The Americans need not have been exceptionally good players; few were. But they were unquestionably authentic, and Europeans learned, as they had not been able to from records and from the few Americans who stayed in their countries, the tradition of jazz performance practice. The lessons made an astounding difference. Prewar recordings by Europeans are clearly by non-Americans. After the war, you cannot tell Americans from Europeans or Japanese.

Records and the radio continue to have this importance in the development of new music worlds. Bennett's study (1980) of the way young rock musicians learn to play their instruments and to combine forces to produce rock music emphasizes their reliance on recordings as a functional substitute for a written score. They are so dependent on records, in fact, that most never learn to read written music. But recordings keep them in touch with what has been done and what can be done in their field.

Interchangeable Personnel

As a result of all these changes, the personnel of an art world all share knowledge of its basic conventions. The work of people experimenting with an innovation is so provincial that people from outside their locality cannot cooperate in its production or consumption. With increased communication, a variety of work becomes available for study, and practitioners from almost anywhere, having seen or heard the work of others, can collaborate with those from anywhere else with little difficulty. Audiences likewise no longer need to be from the local area to understand what is being done. They, too, have had contact with a greater variety of work and can respond to art from any of the places where the new work is being done.

Once the skills necessary to participate in any of an art world's important activities are no longer linked to a specific locale, the art world in question can reproduce itself endlessly and can recruit personnel from anywhere, no longer being dependent on chance misfortunes that might affect one area. Once the people who participate in the production of the work can be interchanged without regard for their local origins, the world has become semiautonomous. What cannot be done here can be done there. When its members travel they know they will find people who know how to do what needs to be done so that the art world's work can go on.

Hennessey says that the nationalization of jazz meant that players from any of the once separate territories now could play in the same band with one another without difficulty (see figures 37 and 38). They would know several styles, especially the more European-based style that used written arrangements and thus required musicians who could read music. When the bands grew in size:

> these extra men were more often section players to provide a setting for the soloist than new solo voices. The main selling points for these sectionmen were not their improvisational abilities, but their technical ability and dependability. . . . The twenties had seen a gradual blending of regional styles as the media allowed musicians to learn styles across territorial lines so that by the early thirties only the Southwest and to a lesser extent the Southeast still retained styles drastically different from that of the New York-based national bands. Thus, when the national bands invaded the territories, their style was not very different from that which most territory bands had been playing. Moreover, with musicians drawn from all over the country, national bands could often trot out a local product to appeal to regional pride wherever they might play. (Hennessey, 1973, pp. 486–89)

Jazzmen, and audiences, had come to share a body of conventions and practice through which they could cooperate to produce the jazz world's characteristic works. Sharing that knowledge made possible the spread of those patterns of cooperative activity.

A major component of the conventional knowledge whose spread makes personnel interchangeable is the spread of the basic imagery the new form utilizes. Art works manipulate materials more or less known to people who experience and appreciate them, as we have seen: some of the material a work uses is well known to most members of a society; some is known only to those with special training; some has to be learned by almost everyone other than the maker in order to appreciate the work. When an art world spreads so as to

FIGURE 37. *The Buddy Petit Jazz Band of New Orleans. Early jazz groups were locally based, and reflected the character of the black population in their locality and the kinds of occasions for which they performed. This band might have performed for street parades, outdoor concerts, and the like. (Photograph courtesy of the Institute of Jazz Studies, Rutgers University.)*

achieve national or international coverage, many people must learn new conventions, learn to organize unfamiliar sights, sounds, and ideas into aesthetic experiences. The rapid spread of the stereograph both produced and depended for its success on a widespread familiarity with and responsiveness to imagery which had hitherto been of interest only to a relative few. Much of the imagery, as we have seen, had a purely local interest.

To pursue that example, the sales efforts which spread stereo cards and viewers across the country must have produced an homogenization of national taste as what were

FIGURE 38. The Jimmie Lunceford Orchestra, circa 1936. As the
world of big band jazz became national, players became better
schooled, better clothed, and more disciplined. (Photograph courtesy
of the Institute of Jazz Studies, Rutgers University.)

originally local peculiarities, becoming familiar, were incorporated into the body of conventions producers and audiences alike knew and responded to. Imagine that, as these
ways of making images became familiar and standardized,
producers developed a shorthand for describing the compositions and topics they wanted their photographers to shoot.
These directions, if we had access to them, would probably
resemble, though not so detailed or theoretically oriented,
the "shooting scripts" Roy Stryker prepared for his Farm
Security Administration photographers (Hurley, 1972, pp. 56,
58); they would show us how codified conventions, lending
themselves to shorthand description, became constraints for
the photographers. The variety of available imagery must

have increased with the industrialization of stereography, though this has not been demonstrated (see Earle, 1979, and Darrah, 1977). We might assume that personal and idiosyncratic styles of expression became rarer as the manufacturer-based conventions spread, and yet the styles assimilated by the large manufacturers must have included a greater variety than any local stereographer or group commanded.

The industry thus offered consumers an immense amount of material dealing with a great diversity of subjects. Consumers, in turn, acquired an interest in that diversity they probably had not had before. At first interested mainly in local subjects, audiences became cosmopolitan just as the producers had. Pious farmers learned to enjoy views of the Holy Land, not surprisingly, but they also acquired a taste for views of the Tomb of El-Bartouk in Cairo (advertised in the catalogue of L. M. Melander and Brothers of Chicago, circa 1880). Just as they learned to master the technique of viewing three-dimensional pictures and to value the illusion of depth they provided, they acquired an interest in subjects which were not part of their immediate experience and had little effect on their own lives. They learned (as much from such other media as magazines, posters, and lantern slides as from stereographs, of course) to be interested, not only in Egyptian exotica, but also in the rest of their own country. You could buy views of Hurley, Wisconsin, or the Custom House in Atlanta.

Although it is reasonable to argue that the suppliers of stereo cards could have trained their audiences to enjoy any kind of image, it was probably easier, in late nineteenth-century America, to interest people in some topics more than in others. Jokes about "darkies" and other ethnic groups probably found a ready audience among white Anglo-Saxons, who saw their country and culture being swamped by immigrants and minorities, and slightly naughty jokes respected the proprieties of the times (see figure 39). American notions about mastery over nature and the continent found expression in an interest in majestic scenery. As

FIGURE 39. *Unknown photographer*, A Dewy Morning—the Farmer's Surprise. *Mildly risque images—showing a bit of leg— suited the national taste. (Courtesy of the Visual Studies Workshop.)*

America became one country, united by the railroad and the telegraph, people learned to see events in far places as relevant to their own lives. They learned to be as interested in the Chicago Fire and the San Francisco Earthquake (even, internationally, in the siege of Port Arthur) as they were in hometown disasters.

In addition, it was probably easy to learn to enjoy stereograph viewing because the activity meshed well with several already conventional American interests. At the height of its greatest popularity, most entertainment took place in the home, and viewing stereo cards was one way a family, a courting couple, or a group of friends could amuse themselves. (We look through family albums and see slides of friends' vacations that way today.) Stereographs also symbolized conspicuous consumption, both in their possession and in the claim to refinement and culture their use implied. Significantly, they provided a means of education (see figure 40) at a time when education was becoming an increasingly important route of social mobility. (Underwood and Under-

FIGURE 40. *Stereoscopes in the schoolroom. One reason for the wide popularity of stereographs was that they fit well into standard American activities. For instance, they were widely used for educational purposes during the rapid expansion of educational facilities. (Courtesy of the Visual Studies Workshop.)*

wood, for instance, promoted their "Travel System" by citing the schools and universities that used it as a teaching device and quoting endorsements by prominent educators.)

Art World Institutions

When an innovation develops a network of people who can cooperate nationwide, perhaps even internationally, all that is left to do to create an art world is to convince the rest of the world that what is being done is art, and deserves the rights and privileges associated with that status. At any particular time and place, certain ways of displaying work connote "art," while others do not. Work that aspires to be accepted as art usually must display a developed aesthetic apparatus and media through which critical discussions can take place. Likewise, aspirants to the status of art have to dissociate themselves from related crafts or commercial enterprises. Finally, aspirants construct histories which tie the work their world produces to already accepted arts, and emphasize those elements of their pasts which are most clearly artistic, while suppressing less desirable ancestors. These processes can be seen clearly in the history of photography in the United States (Taft, 1938; Newhall, 1964).

Within a few years of Daguerre's publication of his method for fixing photographic images on a metal plate, the United States was a hotbed of photographic activity. Professionals offered their services, selling scenic views, portraits, and whatever else customers were willing to pay for. As the daguerrotype was replaced by the tintype and then by many versions of the negative-positive process, the uses people found for photography multiplied. Some people thought the new processes could produce art and devoted themselves to that attempt. Art photographers have fought ever since to be recognized as artists. They have had some of the apparatus of an art world but, until recently, not the recognition, and have worked hard to produce the organizational elements that might persuade others they deserved it. Making visual artifacts gave them a prima facie claim to making art. But that was compromised by such ideological problems as "Can art be made by machines?" (Christopherson,

1974a and 1974b) and, more importantly, by the evident and continuing involvement of photography in nonartistic enterprises. Photography developed a national and international art world through the efforts of pioneers in the field, who fought free of those entanglements and created basic art world institutions as they did so.

Art photography first had to cut its ties to the world of commercial photography, which constrained photographers to work as craftsmen, assisting the businesses they made pictures for. Another source of essentially craft pressures, commonly seen as such by the more serious artists photographers wanted to impress, were the large number of amateur photographers organized in local camera clubs. The clubs exhibited members' work in salons, "established for the great number of photographers who had no opportunity to show their work" (Doty, 1978, p. 36). The clubs fostered a craft-oriented competition, explained this way by a contemporary participant in the club world (memorialized in Tice, 1977):

> Every month we would have black and white print competition. It was always a challenge to try to win *Print-of-the-Month*, and at the end of the year—get the trophy. That's what kept me in it. . . . I did alright in the salons, better than in the club competitions. I was a one-star exhibitor, working for two when I stopped. After you get so many prints accepted in international salons, you get a star from P.S.A. You can get up to five stars. That's the maximum. (Tice, 1977, pp. 41, 50)

That view, enforced by face-to-face criticism of the local club, constrains the freedom artists usually insisted on:

> My pictures aren't made to please me. They're tailormade for the judges. The only trouble is they don't seem to go for my stuff lately. Whenever I do enter some prints, I hear them whispering in the background: "Oh, Artie's trying to make a come-back." I don't compete much in the club anymore. (Tice, 1977, p. 47)

Alfred Stieglitz (Norman, 1973), a pioneer of American photography, made the decisive organizational moves that freed art photography from being confused with the camera clubs. When he began, commercial photography tied to advertising had hardly appeared, and photography and journalism were not yet strongly connected. But the salons, competitions, and organizations of essentially amateur photographers were numerous and strong, nationally and internationally. Stieglitz himself, deeply involved as an exhibitor, editor of the *American Amateur Photographer*, and vice-president of the New York Camera Club, pushed for a more serious and artistic approach. His early pictures drew on the amateur tradition, but he soon broke with the clubs, partly because his own vision outstripped their conventional standards (Doty, 1978, p. 26) and partly because he liked to run things without interference from well-meaning amateurs. Free from camera club politics, he organized the Photo-Secession (1902), began publication of *Camera Work* (1903), and opened a gallery exhibiting photographs as works of art (1905). He had already, ten years earlier, begun to make the photographs of the buildings, machines, and people of New York which were to make him famous.

In a brief time, then, Stieglitz produced (on a small scale, to be sure) much of the institutional paraphernalia which justified photography's claim to be an art: a gallery in which work could be exhibited, a journal containing fine reproductions and critical commentary which provided a medium of communication and publicity, a group of mutually supportive colleagues, and a subject matter and style departing definitively from the imitations of painting then in favor (see figure 41). Stieglitz, a difficult man, soon fell out with his colleagues of the Photo-Secession. That led to another important step in the consolidation of photography's artistic status, the cementing of connections between photographers and the artistic community of painters and sculptors. Edward Steichen, already in close contact with Rodin, whom he had photographed in his studio, became the conduit through which first Rodin, then Matisse, Cezanne, Picasso, and other French artists sent their work to be shown in Stieglitz's gallery at 291 Fifth Avenue. Steichen was also responsible for Stieglitz exhibiting John Marin and thus coming into contact with other to-be-important young American painters like

FIGURE 41. *Alfred Stieglitz,* The City of Ambition. *Stieglitz developed a distinctive new approach to the technical and symbolic problems of photographing the city. Black-and-white photograph, 1910. (Courtesy of the Art Institute of Chicago.)*

Marsden Hartley and Arthur Dove. Stieglitz ceased showing photographs exclusively and filled the gallery with modern drawings, paintings, and sculpture. He introduced painters and photographers to one another, and taught them to take each other's work seriously, not in the imitative style of the earlier "painterly" photographers, but in a mutually complementary way. The connection, which became domestic in the liaison and marriage of Stieglitz and Georgia O'Keeffe, persisted throughout Stieglitz's long career.

Stieglitz never solved one major problem of an art world: how to organize art work so that people can make a living at it. His contemporaries and successors, if they were to work at photography full-time and be more than camera club amateurs, had to do that. If Stieglitz could not make a living selling prints as though they were paintings, no one could, and photographers had to do the work others were willing to pay for, craft work which could not straightforwardly explore an idea or emotion photographically. Steichen (1963), for instance, early learned to do commercial portraits; later he photographed fashionable women in fashionable clothes and stage and movie stars for *Vogue*, and still later worked for the government (Sekula, 1975). In all of these activities, the final product had to satisfy extraneous (i.e., alien to the developing tradition and history of the art) standards—make the subject of the portrait or the clothing look good, or satisfy a bureaucrat's or military man's public relations needs. Some people became very adept—Steichen certainly did—at working under such constraints. But those organizationally based constraints made it virtually impossible for photography to be more than a minor art form, imprisoned in craft standards tied to the necessity of doing someone else's business in order to make a living. Art photographers (Rosenblum, 1978), then and now, have maintained an uneasy balance between the work they do for others and that done for themselves (with the exception, relatively recent, of those who live by teaching [Adler, 1978]).

Many photographers found portraiture the least compromising and distracting paying work. Edward Weston (Maddow, 1973) relied on it throughout most of his life, though he hated the necessity of making a picture that would please the subject (rather than himself), in a sitting of perhaps an hour. Those were the craft standards he had to escape, standards enforced in the loose organization of fee-for-service professional work. Weston did some things to improve art world institutional organization so that artist-photographers might be able to make a living, but his accomplishments were less impressive than Stieglitz'. He founded the f64 group in San Francisco, dedicated as the name suggests to an ideal of sharp, clear photographs rather than soft-focus, "arty" ones. The organizational form and the aesthetic goal are both reminiscent of Stieglitz. He was the first American photographer to receive a Guggenheim Fellowship, a form of support which, while it has never sustained any photographer's career, has helped many of them to do important photographic projects. His influence, passed on by friends, sons, disciples, and imitators, has been enormous, especially, but not solely, on the West Coast.

Like Stieglitz, Weston helped connect the aspiring world of art photography to established painting. In his case, the connection was to the Mexican muralists. In 1923, he left his wife and family in California and moved to Mexico with Tina Modotti, another photographer. The Mexican artistic community took him in as a brother; he was close to Diego Rivera, for one, and his exhibitions resulted in sales as well as in critical praise.

Whether it was the example and influence of the muralists or just not having to satisfy the vanity of sitters who were paying for their pictures, Weston freed himself from the conventions of portrait photography and made a series of revolutionary unposed portraits (two of the best were of Orozco and Rivera). He ignored many other photographic conventions, revitalizing the still life, landscape, and genre picture as well. In every case, working for himself rather than for a sitter or publisher, Weston made pictures that interested established artists from subject matter that had become trite and stereotyped. Ignoring craft standards that were taken for granted in favor of standards more common in the world of high visual art, he developed a style that combined a stern realism with the symbolic effects of photographic tonalities. Throughout his life, he photographed his friends and lovers, dunes and rocks, common household scenes and effects, even vegetables, in ways that gained the respect of people and established institutions in the visual arts.

Documentary photographers had to fight the organizational constraints generated by the agencies for whom they made photographs, either political organizations, usually reformist and left-wing, or government agencies, sometimes reformist but more often interested in work that had some public relations value (in this differing very little from the advertising agencies other photographers were working for). The most interesting instance of overcoming the constraints of such organizational forms was the photographic unit Roy Stryker created for Rex Tugwell's Farm Security Administration during the 1930s (Hurley, 1972). The constraints were embodied in the standard format of the government-agency publicity campaign, with its press kits, canned news stories, and accompanying photographs showing what a good job the agency had done. Stryker, a protege of Rex Tugwell's and a quasi–social scientist, ran bureaucratic interference for his photographers, letting them explore subjects at length, without interference and without having to come up with predetermined images of the right point of view. At the same time, he gave them a substantial dose of social science thinking about what they were photographing, which insulated them against the tendency to deal in current stereotypes of art, politics, or public relations, and helped spawn the unit's characteristic documentary style.

Though the work of the Farm Security Administration was political or scientific or documentary in its original intent, Walker Evans and most of the other photographers also intended to make art. Evans knew artists in a variety of fields: painter Ben Shahn (who joined the unit as a photographer himself for a short time), poet Hart Crane, and writer James Agee (with whom he collaborated on *Let Us Now Praise Famous Men*), among others. His mind, eye, and critical working standards reflected his membership in that artistic community, so he was unwilling to make even minimal concessions to the discipline Stryker sought to impose; not surprisingly, he soon left the unit. But he stayed long enough to let it influence his own work deeply and to create a style that made painters and other established artists take the documentary photograph seriously (see figure 42).

An art world, finally, creates a history which shows how it has from its beginnings produced work of artistic merit and how a steady line of development has led inevitably from those beginnings to the present situation of undoubted achievement of high-art status. Remember that in the beginnings of any art world an enormous variety of work is produced by a host of local experimenters. Historians can choose selectively from what remains of that enormous residue to produce a history that validates the present situation. (Kuhn [1962] has described a similar situation in the history of science.) At some point in an art world's development, such historians appear and begin to construct a more or less official version of the medium's history, ignoring most of the work produced in the past and concentrating on a few workers and works which embody the aesthetic now regarded as appropriate for such a medium. American photography found its historian in Beaumont Newhall, curator of photography at the Museum of Modern Art in New York, whose history of the medium (Newhall, 1964) plucked out and canonized a few of the thousands of experimenters who participated in the process described earlier. (It is interesting to compare Newhall's selections with the much more catholic view of the history of photography presented by a chemist, Robert Taft [1938].)

Other arts making the transition from an innovation to be experimented with to a fully developed art world go through similar transformations. Having created the conditions for a large body of work to emerge, work which can be made and appreciated by people outside the local culture which spawned it, the participants in a new art world develop the organizations and institutions which identify it as art, rather than some of the other things it might be. They can then argue to the members of other art worlds that what they are

FIGURE 42. Walker Evans, Houses and Billboards, Atlanta, Georgia, 1936. *Walker Evans, working under the constraints of a government agency, created a style that made painters and other established artists take documentary photography seriously. Black-and-white photograph. (Reproduction courtesy of the Library of Congress.)*

doing is art, and the whole apparatus may then be incorporated into what that society publicly accepts as art.

LIMITS AND DECLINE

Art world growth eventually levels off, with a maximum of the resources which can be gathered and a maximum of the people interested in participating. Some art worlds reach this peak and remain there a long time. In the short run, they seem permanent, as the world of the novel or the film or the classical ballet seems to us now. But nothing, and that includes art worlds, lasts forever. Many change gradually, in ways we have already discussed. Many decline to the point where we might want to say that they have died, although few disappear completely (as we have seen, institutions preserve vast numbers of art works for which there are at any particular time no makers and no audiences).

Since art worlds grow through the diffusion of both organizations and conventions, anything which interferes with either kind of growth limits the growth of art worlds. Class, ethnic, regional, sexual, and national cultures, for example, limit the groups to which an art world can communicate its works. People who do not know the conventions on which an art work depends cannot cooperate in its production. Films may use characters and plot elements peculiar to one country, so that audiences from elsewhere will not, even with the aid of subtitles, appreciate subtleties and allusions, will perhaps not even understand the plot at all. Americans, for instance, find it hard to follow movies made in India, which refer to, and take for granted, a knowledge of a social organization and social and individual problems most Americans know nothing about. Similarly, Brazilian films make casual references to spirit possession that are meaningless to people from other countries, who thereby may miss crucial elements of a plot.

The differentiation of a society into subgroups—by ethnicity, age, sex, and class, at a minimum—makes it likely that each group will lack some of the conventional knowledge necessary to understand art works aimed at some other group. (This topic has been explored thoroughly in Gans, 1974; Bourdieu et al., 1965; Bourdieu and Darbell, 1966; and DiMaggio and Useem, 1978.) Ignorance among sizable social groups of the conventions which inform a work limits the work's spread to those groups (Bourdieu, 1968), and that limits the growth of the world which produces the work.

National and intrasocietal cultural differences do not limit the production of art works as they do their diffusion. Professional participants in art worlds often share the conventional knowledge of their craft across those lines, and use a professional lingua franca even if they share no other language. So musicians and singers can cooperate internationally to produce operas, and actors and technicians to produce films.

Art worlds decline when some groups that knew and used the conventions which inform their characteristic works lose that knowledge, or when new personnel cannot be recruited to maintain the world's activities. Stereography exemplifies such a decline. Although some American homes still had stereo cards and viewers as late as the 1950s, stereography was by then an anachronism for most people. The Sears catalogue for 1927, far from devoting pages to stereo products as had earlier catalogues, has a three-inch, single-column listing, on a page otherwise devoted to funny disguises, dribble glasses, metal crawling bugs, and "Dandy Little Steam Engines."

What happened? The public had not lost its taste for visual imagery. This was the era in which picture magazines, films, and eventually television became major forms of mass communication. New ways of satisfying that taste need not preclude older forms. If magazines, films, and television coexist, why should stereographs not have joined that entente? Nor can stereography have failed so dramatically because the purposes people used it for no longer interested them. We use visual imagery more than ever for educational purposes, as the growth of the educational film and television industries, and the wealth of photographs in school texts, attests. We still use visual materials to keep up with events in the larger world and for home entertainment (in the form of the projected slides which have partially replaced the family album).

If these commonsense reasons do not explain the decline of the stereograph, what does? My guess is that stereography failed to change its imagery and machinery rapidly enough to avoid the stigma, deadly in a style-conscious society, of being out of date. That change set in motion mutually reinforcing disintegrative processes, so that the institutions of the world of stereography began to come apart in the same interlocking way they grew. As sales decreased, manufacturers' incentive to invest in product development and to modernize their equipment diminished. They had less cause to commission new series of views from photographers, and increasing reason to simply milk their existing inventories. Photographers turned their attention and energy from this dying market to others that offered more opportunity. Customers lost interest in what was now quite clearly an outmoded activity.

Decline seldom proceeds to the point of total death. Stereographs remain in collections, music remains in scores and on recordings, even dance (the most ephemeral of the arts) remains in memories and new stagings. Equally important, many arts and genres in decline retain the loyalty of those who became involved in them at some time in their own development. Popular American music changes frequently—from Dixieland to jazz to big band swing to rock, for instance. Each of these types, and a good many subtypes, are still played and enjoyed today by people who grew up with them. Each wave of innovation leaves behind a shelf of sediment made up of the art makers and art appreciators who can't or won't switch their allegiance to the new wave that has taken over their field.

Art worlds, then, are born, grow, change, and die. The artists who work in them have different problems depending on the state of their world. The kind of work one can make and the fate it will have differ, too. Artistic work lasts when it has an organizational basis that preserves and protects it. Both commonsense and theoretical aesthetics make lasting a crucial criterion of artistic greatness, that is to say, of reputation. So the final chapter brings all the previous analysis to bear on the problem of reputation and uses those results to assess some common theories about art and society.

11·Reputation

I have made art worlds my central concern, treating them as the producers of art works, looking at their careers, workings, and results, rather than at those of individual artists. That runs counter to common sense, and most cultivated and learned opinion as well, which treat art work as the products of individual artists. We choose such perspectives not because one or the other is correct, the only proper way to look at the matter, but because looking at it one way lets us see something hidden in a different perspective. I have perhaps overemphasized the collective character of making and consuming art, to see what could be seen from that vantage point.

This last chapter pushes that perversity a step further, investigating the focus on the reputations of individual artists so characteristic of lay and professional thinking. Art worlds routinely create and use reputations, because they have an interest in individuals and what they have done and can do. Analyzing reputations will let me summarize the various analyses proposed earlier. Because every aspect of art world activities and organizations contributes to and affects the making of reputations and their results, discussing reputation as a social process easily lends itself to doing that job.

Analyzing reputations will also let me discuss some of the aesthetic questions that traditionally occupy students in the sociology of art. I noted in the Preface that, while I do not denigrate those interests, I intend to approach art in a more conventionally sociological way, looking at the social organization of people who work at art and of the audience which responds to it. I would not try to settle questions of relative artistic worth by sociological analysis. Nor would I try to assess the way social forces and influences impinge on and inform particular works of art, thus turning sociology into a kind of criticism. But the questions, answers, and approaches of the previous chapters necessarily have some relevance to those matters (as the earlier chapter on aesthetics, for instance, makes clear). So I will conclude by discussing that relevance, considering the problem of what lasts, which works persist (whatever that may mean) and how an understanding of lasting (which I will construe as a problem of reputation) affects our understanding of those aesthetic and critical concerns.

REPUTATION AS PROCESS

Art worlds, in a variety of interwoven activities, routinely make and unmake reputations—of works, artists, schools, genres, and media. They single out from the mass of more or less similar work done by more or less interchangeable people a few works and a few makers of works of special worth. They reward that special worth with esteem and, frequently but not necessarily, in more material ways too. They use reputations, once made, to organize other activities, treating things and people with distinguished reputations differently from others.

The Theory of Reputation

It makes sense to spend time and energy assessing and communicating reputations if you believe in a particular, intensely individualistic theory of art and how it is made, but not otherwise. The theory goes like this. (1) Specially gifted people (2) create works of exceptional beauty and depth which (3) express profound human emotions and cultural values. (4) The work's special qualities testify to its maker's special gifts, and the already known gifts of the maker testify to the special qualities of the work. (5) Since the works reveal the maker's essential qualities and worth, all the works that person makes, but no others, should be included in the corpus on which his reputation is based.

Note the historically and culturally contingent character of this theory. Many societies have never had such a theory (and as a result we know nothing about their artists):

> In the Middle Ages the individual artist remains invisible behind the corporate facades of church and guild. Greco-Roman and Chinese histories alone report in any detail the conditions of individual artists' lives. A few names and lines of text are all we have about Egyptian dynastic artists. The records of the other civilizations of antiquity in America, Africa, and India tell nothing of artists' lives. Yet the archeological record repeatedly shows the presence of connected series of rapidly changing manufactures in the cities, and slower ones in the provinces and in the countryside, all manifesting the presence of persons whom we can call artists. (Kubler, 1962, p. 92)

We presumably would have known about these artists, had we been there, because our theory of art makes it important to know who they are. But Western societies have not always made those distinctions either:

> The contested, but dominant, definition that our society gives to art and the artist is the fruit of a process of differentiation of human activities whose origin can be situated in the Renaissance. Beginning in Italy, at the end of the 15th Century, the activities of the painter, sculptor and architect, considered as radically different from the manual trades, achieved the dignity of "liberal" arts. The artist is no longer an artisan, but a creator, a sort of *alter deus* free from ordinary norms; the charismatic representation of the artist merges with an aristocratic image of the work of art, unique and irreplaceable. We are at the point of departure for the modern idea of the creator and the created object.
>
> The second stage coincides with the first industrial revo-

lution, that of the 18th Century. Beginning with that revolution, the artistic product tended to be defined in opposition to the industrial product. The machine is opposed to the hand of man, divided work to undivided, the production of a series of identical objects to the singularity of the unique object. The industrial reality which is translated, in humanistic moral philosophy, into the alienation of the assembly line results, in the economic order, in the negation of uniqueness, the essence of rarity. To show the specificity of their product in relation to the products of the artisan and of industry, artists tried to remove from their own practice the factor common to the other two, the awareness of the utilitarian plan: the philosophical theory of art as the finality without any purpose justified their survival. By attributing to themselves the monopoly of production of sublime purposelessness and of the essential difference (in opposition to the similarity of objects in an industrial series or the small difference which allows one to distinguish among objects from the same artisanal series) the artists of the 19th Century protected the rarity and, through it, the possibility of giving social and economic value to the symbolic goods they produced. (Moulin, 1978, pp. 241–42, my translation)

In short, the theory of art which makes it possible and worthwhile to create reputations is not timeless; it arises in societies which subscribe to more general theories emphasizing the individual over the collective, and under particular social conditions. Having arisen, it can then be exported to and adopted by societies which formerly did not bother about such things.

The first premise of the theory of reputation holds that artists have special gifts that are quite rare. Recall the definition Stoppard put into the mouth of Henry Carr in *Travesties*: "An artist is someone who is gifted in some way that enables him to do something more or less well which can only be done badly or not at all by someone who is not thus gifted" (Stoppard, 1975, p. 38). The definition emphasizes traits of the maker of fine works; it asserts that such works do not get made accidentally, that making great works is not something anyone could do on a good day, that the works get their value from being made by unusual people, of whom there are not many. If these unusual people do important work, then we need to know who they are so that we can help them do it, provide them with appropriate circumstances, and not interfere with them. Moulin (1978) and many others suggest that contemporary visual art, following the lead of Marcel Duchamp, has increasingly emphasized the artist over the work, insisting in effect that anything an artist does thereby becomes art.

Most adherents of the theory, however, do not think that everything an artist does is art. On the contrary, they think that artists create works—objects or events—which are especially beautiful or profound, works which stand out from the mass of superficially similar works. The theory recognizes that many people may, by following the rules which govern the making of art works, produce creditable musical performances, readable novels, and not entirely uninteresting paintings. By following the conventions, such workers will produce work others will recognize as competent. One might thus write a tragedy, using Aristotle's *Poetics* as a guide. Of course, that would not necessarily (or even likely) result in an important work. The theory holds, however, that people with special gifts can manipulate the available conventions, perhaps change them or invent new ones, and so produce works which are not just so-so or ho-hum but, rather, are extraordinary. Those works will stand out from the mass the way Dickens' novels stand out from the thousands of roughly similar works produced in nineteenth-century England, the way the recordings of Louis Armstrong stand out from thousands of similar performances by early jazz trumpet players. They have more, a lot more, of whatever characterizes beautiful or profound works than does most work.

Adherents of the theory do not agree on what these special works have. This question—the "what" that characterizes art works and especially great art works—divides aestheticians, audiences, and other art world participants. In one common conflict, some look to art works to be faithful to the world, to interpret and show it to us in a recognizable and yet new way, to explain and make us feel the strength of important philosophical concerns about the meaning of life and how people should live. Realistic fiction and painting, drama, and film which explore ethical, emotional, or social problems (documentary photography, for instance) satisfy that demand. Others look to art works to exhibit an internal order of superior interest, to deal with problems invented within a medium's tradition in a new, unexpected, or exciting way. Paintings devoted to the problems of how to depict light or volume on a two-dimensional canvas, photographs which deal with the paradoxes of visual representation, novels which rely on formal symmetries for their effect, and especially music which manipulates limited sound materials according to accepted rules in a way which leads us to admire the inevitability of the work's construction, all satisfy this second demand.

Many, if not most, aficionados of an art can find virtues of both kinds in work they admire. They enjoy Renaissance portraits both for the exploration of timeless human types and for experimentation with problems of light and geometry. They admire Dickens for his social analysis, his moral indignation, his ability to create unforgettable characters, and his skill in formal construction all at once. Some, more rigorous in their beliefs, attend only to one or the other set of virtues. The "what" of artistic excellence clearly varies from time to time and place to place. We might, in general, say that we expect the special works produced by specially gifted artists to express and to create in their audiences profound human emotions, and to do that (this may be less axiomatic) by their connection to fundamental (perhaps universal) human values and emotions.

Works and makers stand in reciprocal relation to one another. How do we know that artists have special gifts? By their works, which produce special emotional experiences and reveal their exceptional skills. But remember Trollope's experiment, reported in the first chapter, in which he undertook, at the height of his career, to publish stories under an assumed name, and discovered that the Trollope name created literary qualities apparently not otherwise discernible. We shouldn't be cynical about that. If we know that a person of superior ability made a work, we pay more careful attention to it, and thus can see what might escape the more casual inspection we give a work from which we expect nothing special. So we also know works by their makers, whose abilities give works a warrant they would not otherwise have. (It is more complicated than that. Works can take on a meaning because of the context created by their maker's other work; we appreciate the elaborate and complicated plotting of Dickens' late novels more by contrast to the picaresque plots of his earlier works.)

Since we infer artists' underlying but unobservable talent from the observable work they produce, and since the ability to make that inference is a crucial skill for any art world participant, we need to make it carefully. We want, especially, to base our inference on adequate evidence. The quest for adequate evidence takes several forms. We want to establish the complete and authentic canon of the artist's works, so that we can take into account everything that might help us make our judgment. We want to uncover cases of plagiarism, so that we do not credit an artist with someone else's work. Problems of attribution and authenticity also arise here.

Since artists know that other art world participants make reputational inferences from their work, they try to control the work that becomes available for making such inferences. They destroy work they don't want considered, or label it "unfinished"; if they are lucky, a court may (as French courts can) prevent the circulation of work they don't want publicly attributed to them. They distinguish categories of work, as contemporary photographers sometimes distinguish their "commercial" work (not to be considered in assessing them as artists) from their "personal" work (to be so used), according to the seriousness of their intentions in making it. They revise their work when they can, as Stravinsky and Henry James did.

The five premises, taken together, furnish the basis for making, maintaining, and unmaking reputations as characteristic art world activities.

Levels of Reputation

Artists are not the only ones to have reputations. Works have reputations, too. "The finest novel of the last ten years," "the greatest work of South American fiction," "one of the ten greatest paintings of the twentieth century"—members of art worlds say such things every day. They are not judging the people who made the works, but rather how well the work deals with the problems, possibilities, and constraints of its genre, of what George Kubler (1962) calls a "form-class." They compare the work to others like it, more or less without reference to who made it. An otherwise ungifted artist, contrary to the theory of artists' reputations, may get hot and make one great work. The work's reputation will overshadow its maker's. Likewise, a great work can be made but knowledge of its maker be lost or never recorded; Kubler mentions this as characteristic of many of the great artistic cultures.

Schools develop reputations, made up in part of the reputations of the individual artists who belong to them and the works those members create. Method acting and serial composition, for instance, have reputations—not necessarily universally agreed on—which are based on but not the same as the individual reputations of works and workers. The reputation of a school depends on some larger art world's assessment of the possibility of creating important work using the conventions characteristic of the school. Can you compose emotionally meaningful music if you accept the complicated constraints of the twelve-tone system? Can you compose music that embodies your own gifts and sensibility by leaving much of what is to be played to chance operations carried on by the performer on the occasion of each performance? Art world members who answer "no" to these questions automatically decide the reputations of all the artists who belong to those schools and all the works based on those theories.

Genres develop reputations, just as schools do, which reflect the consensus of the relevant art world about the degree to which important works can be done in them. White and White summarize the doctrine of the Royal Academy of Paris on the appropriate genres for serious painting:

1. Classical and Christian themes are the only proper subject matter.
2. Only the most "perfect" forms (as found in classical sculpture and the painting of Raphael) should be selected to portray such subjects.
3. Only a certain set of "nobly" expressive positions and gestures (again classical or high Renaissance in origin) are appropriate in the representation of the human figure.
4. The human figure is the highest form and expresses perfect "absolute" beauty.
5. Pictorial composition should preserve classical balance, harmony, and unity; there should be no jarring elements either of form or expression.
6. Drawing is the probity of art. (White and White, 1965, pp. 6–7)

Other genres—still life or scenes of the daily life of common people—could not, in this view, express the noble sentiments which alone could provoke proper artistic experiences in viewers.

Finally, media have reputations. Some media, such as easel painting in oils, have the highest possible reputation; they are art and no doubt about it. Other media, such as weaving or glassblowing, have lower reputations as minor or decorative arts. Still others (quiltmaking or whittling) have the reputation of folk arts or (soap operas or rock music) popular arts, and the media of some totally idiosyncratic productions (like the Watts Towers) don't even have a name, let alone a reputation. In each case, the reputation of the medium is a judgment as to the possibility of doing serious, important, or great art in it.

At whatever level, reputations develop through a process of consensus building in the relevant art world. Like all forms of consensus, the consensus on reputations, at every level, changes from time to time. Base media become noble media, the greatest work of the twentieth century is superseded by a new discovery (as are the greatest works of earlier centuries), genres fall out of favor, and artists thought second-rate rise in favor as stars fall.

Reputation and Art World

The theory of reputation says that reputations are based on works. But, in fact, the reputations of artists, works, and the rest result from the collective activity of art worlds. If we review the major activities of art worlds from this point of view, we can see how they all contribute to and depend on the making of reputations.

For reputations to arise and persist, critics and aestheticians must establish theories of art and criteria by which art, good art, and great art can be distinguished and identified. Without those criteria, no one could make the judgments of works, genres, or media on which the judgments of artists depend. Remember Danto's aphorism: "To see something as art requires something the eye cannot descry—an atmosphere of artistic theory, a knowledge of the history of art: an artworld" (Danto, 1964, p. 580). Likewise, historians and scholars must establish the canon of authenticated works which can be attributed to an artist, so that the rest of us can base our judgments on the appropriate evidence. The distribution system relies on these scholarly judgments to ratify its choices of what to distribute (and at what price):

> The two major facts which introduce, at the level of the supply [of classical paintings], guarantees of rarity and quality are the following. Each work put on sale is singular and irreplaceable: it is the unique product of the undivided labor of a unique creator. The authenticity and the originality, as well as the quality of works, are guaranteed by a corps of specialists, the historians of art. (Moulin, 1978, pp. 242–43, my translation)

Participants in the distribution system help shape the work by setting the conditions distributable works must meet—sculptures that are not too heavy for museum floors to bear, musical works not too long for audiences to sit through. Some go farther than that, taking an active role (as did the patrons of Italian Renaissance painters) in the design of the work. The state guarantees the right to control publication or distribution of work, which allows artists to control the corpus of what is counted as their oeuvre.

Since reputations, though made by the cooperative activity of art world members, do depend on the works made by artists, whatever contributes to the making of the works affects reputations, directly or indirectly. Fellow artists create a tradition, a world of conventional discourse, a gallery of exemplars to be imitated, conversed with, or rebelled against, a context of other works in which any particular work makes sense and gets meaning:

> Every important work of art can be regarded both as a historical event and as a hard-won solution to some problem. . . . any solution points to the existence of some problem to which there have been other solutions . . . other solutions to this problem will most likely be invented to follow the one now in view. As the solutions accumulate, the problem alters. (Kubler, 1962, p. 33)

Many other people, especially but not only those whose job is editing, help the artist make the innumerable choices that shape the work, and make some of them whether the artist wants their help or not. Reputations grow out of the way the art world assesses the relation between what an artist has done and what others doing similar work have done; the reputational process systematically ignores, by accepting the theory of reputation, the contributions of others to the works on which reputations are based.

Audiences, finally, recognizing the skillful use of conventional means and experiencing emotions and insights attributable to that skillful use, put the theory into practice and accept the inferences and conclusions about the maker suggested by what they know of the work.

All these participants in art worlds produce the circumstances in which artists define the problems they work on and find the solutions, embodied in works, which contribute, for good or bad, to their reputations. Kubler points out that the stage of an artistic problem's development, and the organization of the surrounding society, together define an artist's opportunities to engage in one or another kind of artistic endeavor. He describes, for instance:

> the slow-paced, patient painters, such as Claude Lorrain and Paul Cezanne, whose lives contain only one real problem.

> Both men were alike in their dedication to the portrayal of landscape.... The type flourishes only in those urbane periods when the ascendancy of special vocations allows persons of ruminative tendency the leisure to achieve their difficult varieties of excellence. (Kubler, 1962, p. 87)

On the other hand, other periods provide the setting for:

> versatile men. Their entrances may occur at either of two junctures, of social or technical renovation.... Such moments in the history of things occur when new techniques suddenly require all experience to assume their mold. Directors of cinema, radio, and television have thus transformed our world in this century.... The other moment for the appearance of the versatile men occurs when a whole society has been resettled along new lines of force after great upheavals, when for a century or two the endlessly complicated consequences, implications, and derivations of novel existential assumptions must be set in order and exploited. (Kubler, 1962, pp. 87–88)

By creating the circumstances that favor one or another kind of career and achievement, art world participants—here conceived on the largest scale as including all the members of a society—define the possibilities for making a reputation.

All the cooperation which produces art works, then, also produces the reputations of works, makers, schools, genres and media—reputations which are a shorthand for how good the individual work is as one of its kind, how gifted the artist is, whether or not a school is on a fruitful track, and whether genres and media are art at all.

Art worlds vary in size, as we have seen, from small, local, esoteric groups to large, inclusive, international ones. You cannot have the same kind of reputation in such different organizations, and some of them make it difficult to put the theory of reputation into practice. Consider the difficulties which arise from the peculiarities of some distribution systems. The theory assumes something like the condition of perfect information in the definition of perfect economic competition, that everyone whose opinion affects the formation of reputations has access to and knowledge of all the work relevant to his judgments. He has heard every piece of music, read every novel or poem, seen every play or film. Some large international art worlds—perhaps the worlds of grand opera or the feature film—approach this. Everyone who is interested hears or sees everything of interest (whether the original performance or a recording), knows every work of every worker, and can make truly informed judgments.

In many art worlds, however, the mechanism for weeding things out, so that informed people need concern themselves only with what is truly important to them, does not work very well. There is too much material, too much work, too many people to consider. The assumption of perfect information makes no sense. An informed observer of American literary magazines (Anania, 1978, pp. 8–9) estimates that at least fifteen hundred such magazines, containing original fiction, poetry, and criticism, were being published in the United States in 1978. Of those, "A few—just two or three—have circulations of about 10,000. . . . Most are printed in runs of less than 2,000 copies, and many have fewer than a hundred readers." No one can read all that. No one does. As a result, contemporary writers published by little magazines cannot achieve reputations that have wide currency and thus represent the consensus of a major art world, even though literature and poetry are undeniably major arts of international scope. That writers do not achieve major reputations does not mean that no one is doing work that would, by the standards of those worlds, deserve such reputations, only that the world's distribution system does not let participants know what they need to to make the comparisons that would allow credible judgments. That creates a painful dilemma for writers. The proliferation of magazines makes possible the publication of much more material than would otherwise ever be publicly available, but it prevents writers achieving the major reputations they would like, even though whatever minor reputations the present situation gives them is more than the nothing they would probably have otherwise.

Another difficulty arising from distribution systems concerns language. Music and visual art use languages that can, in some meaningful sense, be called international. But literature uses one of the world's languages, few of which are mutually intelligible. In practice, only a few Indo-European languages are known in enough countries that literature written in them has any chance of being considered in the global judgments which create international literary reputations. A novelist who writes in French or Spanish will be read more widely and have a better chance for an international reputation than one who writes in Portuguese, let alone one who writes in Hindi, Tamil, or Swahili. The latter languages are read by millions of people, but not by the people who make international literary reputations. The Nobel Prize committee in literature periodically awards the prize to someone who writes in a minor language and whose work is not widely known through translation into one of the European languages, but that seldom changes the situation very much. They may award the prize to an Icelandic novelist, but most members of the international audience do not read Icelandic and probably never will, so that the award is a gesture without consequence in the world of literature. If your linguistic community is small or unimportant, you cannot have a major reputation.

Reputations, resulting from the cooperative activities of participants in worlds of varying size, thus depend on, but do not automatically reflect, the qualities of art works as perceived and judged by those participants. That would only be true if we supposed that art worlds detected those qualities infallibly, never made a mistake, and never overlooked worthwhile contenders. The evidence that that is not true abounds; much of the discussion in earlier chapters addresses that point. The same evidence, just summarized so briefly, makes clear that crucial components of the theory of reputation are factually incorrect, especially those portions which ascribe the undivided responsibility and the praise or blame for the results to the artist acting alone, ignoring the contributions of all the others I have taken so much space to detail. We praise Picasso, not M. Tuttin who printed his "impossible" ideas, and Trollope rather than the old manservant who woke him at 5:30 with hot coffee. We would feel foolish if we did otherwise. As participants of one sort or another in all these art worlds, we necessarily share the beliefs on which collective action in them is based. But, analytically, we recognize that these are choices from a range of possibilities, choices whose sense is ratified by the adherence of art world participants to the premises on which they are based.

WHAT LASTS?

Most theories of aesthetics and the more traditional versions of the sociology of art insist on the possibility and the necessity of making judgments of quality about art works. They make reasoned arguments about how work of exceptional value can be distinguished from the ordinary and insist that that distinction must be the cornerstone of any rational or serious investigation of art as human activity. If art expresses basic cultural values or human emotions, some art will do that better than other art and will therefore be what ought to be studied to understand what is generically true of the phenomenon. Such an investigation might model itself on Aristotle's *Poetics*, taking the best specimens of a genre and inspecting them to see what they have in common. Traditional sociologists of art (e.g., Lowenthal, 1957; Lukacs, 1964; Goldmann, 1964, 1967) typically believe that to study the "close relationship between literary creation and social and historical reality. . . . the very peaks of literary creation may not only be studied quite as well as average works, but are even found to be particularly suitable" (Goldmann, 1967, p. 495).

But which works are better? To identify them by their congruence with the theory that is to explain them begs the question. Recognizing that, the common solution to the problem of identifying what is best is to appeal to common sense and collective experience, to what "everyone knows." What everyone knows—it is a fact of common observation—is that some works have lasted for years, centuries, even millennia. What lasting consists of is not very clear. It does not refer to simple physical survival, but rather to continued appreciation by large numbers of people. It is not unreasonable to see lasting as a phenomenon of reputation. That is, a work that lasts is a work that has a good reputation for a long time.

The appeal to what lasts as a way of identifying great art is an argument against applying relativism to the evaluation of art works. It admits the reputational process we have been concerned with, and sees that reputations that last are a product of consensus and that the consensus arises through an historical process. It admits all that because it insists on a version of the theory of reputation that makes all that, if true, irrelevant.

The theory that explains what lasts is a theory of universals. Aestheticians and analysts of art often wish to find cultural universals—modes of responding to art works that transcend particular cultures, and forms of art that evoke the same response, whatever and whenever they occur. If Shakespeare is admired in every country in which his plays are produced, the argument goes, it must be because the plays touch something so deep in human experience that everyone is vulnerable to them. In this view, works develop a lasting reputation because, with all the vagaries and contingencies of art world operation and reputation-building processes, some works always develop a reputation for having the highest quality. The reputational process occurs, but produces the same result everywhere. If that is true, then it must be due to some quality inherent in the work interacting with some fundamental and culturally untouched feature of human psychology and experience. Reputation, then, however produced, identifies works of real value if one is interested in aesthetics, works which explore historical and social reality in an exceptional way if one is a traditional sociologist of art.

We cannot say that this theory is incorrect and can be proved false. But neither can anyone prove it true, and much of the material presented earlier casts doubt on it, making analyses based on the premise suspect. The following arguments cast doubt but do not disprove. If you think the theory correct until proved false, it will remain valid for you; if you think it false if there are doubts about it, you will have reason to reject it. I am less concerned with the relevance of these arguments for aesthetics than for the sociological analyses which take works of art to embody and reflect fundamental values or emphases of a culture, so that their analysis can reveal the culture and can simultaneously show that society, in the largest sense, affects their fundamental emphases and character.

One doubt arises because art works last for other reasons besides being universally appreciated. Many works continue to enjoy high repute, not because anyone actively appreciates them, certainly not because large numbers of people actively appreciate them, but rather because they are historically important. Bakhtin points out that "of all the great writers of world literature, Rabelais is the least popular, the least understood and appreciated" (Bakhtin, 1968, p. 1), that no one reads him because no one enjoys him, and no one enjoys him because readers don't understand what he is about—the dethroning of pre-Renaissance authoritarianism through the use of the unofficial language of laughter and the marketplace to say what couldn't otherwise be said—and wouldn't enjoy something so alien to their own culture and experience if they did understand the point. Moulin similarly points out that many paintings by Old Masters enjoy a good reputation today not because people think they are particularly good—in fact, the cyclical revisions of critical thinking guarantee that such reputations will move up or down periodically—but because they are "historically important," an importance they do not lose when tastes change. History is still history (Moulin, 1967, pp. 431–32).

A larger problem has to do, not with what the reputation-making process selects, but rather with what it leaves out. As we have seen earlier, art worlds engage in a continuous process of selection, looking over possibilities and incorporating some of them, weeding out some people and things formerly, but no longer, thought well of. But these reputational changes happen largely to works which more or less approximate the standard practice of the art world. A much more crucial selection takes place when art worlds fail to notice work created by others besides integrated professionals. Mavericks are sufficiently near to art world practice, and sufficiently interested in calling the attention of the art world to what they do, that art worlds sometimes eventually incorporate their work, assimilating them after the fact of what they have done rather than during its making. But art worlds seldom incorporate naive or folk artists into their ranks. What those people do is often too different, both in conception and in form, from the art world's standard practice to be assimilable. It is stigmatized, as well, as being too crazy or eccentric to be taken seriously or as being too connected with the everyday life of common people to be treated as the special work of gifted people called for by the theory of reputation. The work of naive artists may exhibit special gifts, but it does not ordinarily speak to many people, being too private. The work of folk artists speaks to many, but is too commonplace to be anything special.

As a result, the process of selection through which art worlds operate and art reputations are made leaves out most of the works which might be, under other procedures of definition and selection, included in the corpus of what is recognized as art, good or competent art, and great art. The reevaluations of work which take place at other times or through the efforts of people from elsewhere show that the content of the "art" category is in fact contingent, not so much because Shakespeare's reputation varies, as because most of the Ferdinand Chevals and Simon Rodias, the Conlon Nancarrows and other unheard composers, the quiltmakers and peasant cart decorators are left out; for everyone we eventually hear of, hundreds never come to anyone's attention and never get counted in.

Theories which find evidence of a society's values and cultural emphases in its art, then, really find that evidence in the art which survives a complicated and historically variable process of selection and reputation making. Would such theories find the same result if they considered all the art made in a society? Perhaps. But that proposition needs to be explored rather than accepted on faith.

ART AND SOCIETY

There is another way to think about the relation between art and society. What I have said here about art worlds both arises from a more general theoretical orientation toward the study of society and contributes to the development of that orientation. What I have said about art worlds can be said about any kind of social world, when put more generally; ways of talking about art, generalized, are ways of talking about society and social process generally. Let me conclude by making the parallels and lessons explicit.

If we focus on a specific art work, we can usefully think of social organization as the network of people who cooperate to produce that work. We see that the same people often cooperate repeatedly, even routinely, in similar ways to produce similar works. They organize their cooperation by referring to the conventions current among people who participate in the production and consumption of such works. If the same people do not actually act together in every case, their replacements also know, and are proficient in the use of, the same conventions, so that the cooperation can go on without difficulty. Conventions make collective action simpler and less costly in time, energy, and other resources; yet they do not make unconventional work impossible, only more costly and more difficult. Change can occur, and often does, whenever someone devises a way to gather the greater resources required. Thus, conventional modes of cooperation and collective action need not persist, because people constantly devise new modes of action and discover the resources necessary to put them into practice.

To say all this goes beyond the assertion that art is social and beyond demonstrations of the congruence between forms of social organization and artistic styles or subjects. It shows that art is social in being created by networks of people acting together, and proposes a framework for the study of differing modes of collective action, mediated by accepted or newly developed conventions. It puts some traditional questions in the field in a context in which their similarity to other forms of collective action can be used for comparative theoretical work.

The discussion of art as collective action reflects a general approach to the analysis of social organization. We can focus on any event (a general term which encompasses as a special case the production of an art work) and look for the network of people, however large or extended, whose collective activity made it possible for the event to occur as it did. We can look for networks whose cooperative activity recurs or has become routine and can specify the conventions by which their constituent members coordinate their separate lines of action.

We can use such terms as *social organization* or *social structure* as a metaphorical way of referring to those recurring networks and their activities. In doing so, however, we should not forget that they are metaphors and inadvertently assert as a fact implied in the metaphor what can only be discovered through research. When sociologists speak of social structure or social systems, the metaphor implies (though its user neither proves nor argues the point) that the collective action involved occurs regularly or often (the qualifier, being implicit, is nonspecific) and, further, that the people involved act together to produce a large variety of events. But we should recognize generally, as the empirical materials require us to do in the study of the arts, that whether a mode of collective action is recurrent or routine enough to warrant such description needs to be decided by investigation, not definition. Some forms of collective action recur often, others occasionally, many seldom. Similarly, people who participate in the network that produces one event or kind of event may not act together to produce other events or art works. That question, too, must be decided by investigation.

Collective actions and the events they produce are the basic unit of sociological investigation. Social organization consists of the special case in which the same people act together to produce a variety of different events in a recurring way. Social organization (and its cognates) are not only concepts, then, but also empirical findings. Whether we speak of the collective acts of a few people (a family or a friendship) or of those of a much larger number (a profession or a class system), we always need to ask exactly who is acting together to produce what events. To pursue the general version of the theory developed for artistic activities, we can study social organizations of all kinds by looking for the networks responsible for producing specific events, the overlaps among such cooperative networks, the way partici-pants use conventions to coordinate their activities, how existing conventions simultaneously make coordinated action possible and limit the forms it can take, and how the development of new forms of acquiring resources makes change possible. (Other statements of this point of view can be found in the writings of, among others, Simmel [1898], Park [1950, 1952, 1955], Blumer [1966], and Hughes [1971], especially pp. 5–13 and 52–64].)

Similarly, the four modes of being oriented to an art world—as integrated professional, maverick, folk artist, or naive artist—suggest a general scheme for interpreting the way people can be oriented to any kind of social world, whatever its focus or its conventional round of collective activities. Insofar as the world has built up routine and conventional ways of carrying on those activities its members usually engage in, people can participate in it as fully competent members who know how to do easily and well whatever needs to be done. Most of what is done in that world will be done by people like that—the generalized analogue of integrated professionals. If the activity is one that every member of the society, or every member of some large subcategory, engages in, the folk artist may provide a closer analogue. Some people, knowing what is conventional, will nevertheless choose to behave differently, with predictable ensuing difficulties. Some few of the innovations such people propose may be taken up by the larger world from which they have differed, turning them (at least in retrospect) into honored innovators rather than cranks. Some will not know of the world's existence or care much about it, and will invent the whole thing for themselves—the generalized version of the naive artist.

In this way, we might say (with rather more warrant than it is usually said) that the world of art mirrors society at large.

Bibliography

Abbott, Berenice. *The World of Atget*. New York: Horizon Press, 1964.

Abrahams, Roger. *Deep Down in the Jungle*. Chicago: Aldine, 1970.

Adler, Judith. *Artists in Offices*. New Brunswick, N.J.: Transaction, Inc., 1978.

Anania, Michale. "Of Living Belfry and Rampart: On American Literary Magazines since 1950." *TriQuarterly* 43 (Fall 1978): 6–23.

Arnold, Bill, and Carlson, Kate. "The Bus Show." *The Massachusetts Review* 19 (Winter 1978): 710–16.

Ashley, Robert. "Interview with Philip Glass." *Music with Roots in the Ether*. Videotape, 1978.

Bakhtin, Mikail. *Rabelais and His World*. Cambridge: MIT Press, 1968.

Bauman, Lawrence S. "Legal Control of the Fabrication and Marketing of Fake Paintings." *Stanford Law Review* 24 (May 1972): 930–46.

Baxandall, Michael. *Painting and Experience in Fifteenth Century Italy*. Oxford: Oxford University Press, 1972.

Becker, Howard S. "Blessing San Francisco's Fishing Fleet." *Society* 11 (May–June 1974): 83–85.

———. *Outsiders: Studies in the Sociology of Deviance*. New York: The Free Press, 1963.

373

————and Walton, John. "Social Science and the Work of Hans Haacke." In *Framing and Being Framed*, by Hans Haacke, pp. 145–52. New York: New York University Press, 1976.

Bennett, H. Stith. *On Becoming a Rock Musician*. Amherst: University of Massachusetts Press, 1980.

Bergós, Joan. *Antoni Gaudí: L'home i l'obra*. Barcelona: Ariel, 1954.

Bihalji-Merin, Otto. *Masters of Naive Art*. New York: McGraw-Hill, 1971.

Blasdell, Gregg N. "The Grass-Roots Artist." *Art and America* 56 (September–October 1968): 25–41.

Bliven, Bruce, Jr. "Profile: George Fabian Scheer." *The New Yorker* (November 12, 1973): 51–56ff.

Blizek, William. "An Institutional Theory of Art." *British Journal of Aesthetics* 14 (Spring 1974): 142–50.

Blumer, Herbert. "Sociological Implications of the Thought of George Herbert Mead." *American Journal of Sociology* 71 (1966): 535–44.

Bollinger, Dwight L. "Rime, Assonance, and Morpheme Analysis." *Word* 6 (August 1950): 117–36.

Borges, Jorge Luis. "Pierre Menard, Author of Don Quixote." In *Ficciones*, pp. 45–55. New York: Grove Press, 1962.

Bourdieu, Pierre. "Outline of a Sociological Theory of Art Perception." *International Social Science Journal* 20 (1968): 589–612.

Bourdieu, Pierre, and Darbel, Alain. *L'Amour de l'art: Les Musées et leur public*. Paris: Les Editions de Minuit, 1966.

Bourdieu, Pierre, et al. *Un Art moyen: Essai sur les usages sociaux de la photographie*. Paris: Les Editions de Minuit, 1965.

Brief, Henry. *Radio and Records: A Presentation by the Record Industry Association of America at the 1964 Regional Meetings of the National Association of Broadcasters*. New York: Record Industry Association of America, 1964.

Bucher, Rue. "Pathology: A Study of Social Movements within a Profession." *Social Problems* 10 (Summer 1962): 40–51.

Bucher, Rue, and Strauss, Anselm. "Professions in Process." *American Journal of Sociology* 66 (January 1961): 325–34.

Bystryn, Marcia. "Art Galleries as Gatekeepers: The Case of the Abstract Expressionists." *Social Research* 45 (Summer 1978): 390–408.

California State University, Fullerton. *Overglaze Imagery: Cone 019-016*. Fullerton, Calif.: Visual Arts Center, California State University, 1977.

Catalog Committee, The. *An Anti-Catalog*. New York: The Catalog Committee of Artists Meeting for Cultural Change, 1977.

Cheval, Ferdinand. "The Fantastic Palace of Ferdinand Cheval." *Craft Horizons* 28, no. 1 (1968): 8–15.

Christopherson, Richard. "Making Art with Machines: Photography's Institutional Inadequacies." *Urban Life and Culture* 3 (1974a): 3–34.

_____. "From Folk Art to Fine Art: A Transformation in the Meaning of Photographic Work." *Urban Life and Culture* 3 (1974b): 123–57.

Chrysôstomo, Antônio. "Entrevista: Chico Buarque de Holanda." *Veja*, Rio de Janeiro (October 27, 1976): 3–6.

Cincinnati Art Museum. *The Ladies, God Bless 'Em: The Women's Art Movement in Cincinnati in the Nineteenth Century*. Cincinnati: Cincinnati Art Museum, 1976.

Clark, Larry. *Tulsa*. New York: Lustrum Press, 1971.

Clark, Priscilla P. "Deux Types de subventions: L'Assistance aux écrivains en France et aux Etats-Unis." *Bibliographie de la France* 24 (June 1976): 1232–42.

_____. "Styles of Subsidy: Support for Writers in France and the United States." *French Review* 50 (March 1977): 543–49.

Cohen, Ted. "The Possibility of Art: Remarks on a Proposal by Dickie." *Philosophical Review* 82 (January 1973): 69–82.

Coleman, James S., Elihu Katz, and Herbert Menzel. *Medical Innovation: A Diffusion Study*. Indianapolis: Bobbs-Merrill, 1966.

Collins, George R. *Antonio Gaudí*. New York: George Braziller, Inc., 1960.

Commins, Dorothy. *What Is an Editor? Saxe Commins at Work*. Chicago: University of Chicago Press, 1978.

Connell, Evan S., Jr. *The Connoisseur*. New York: Knopf, 1974.

Corn, Wanda M. *The Color of Mood: American Tonalism, 1880–1910*. San Francisco: de Young Museum, 1972.

Cooper, Grosvenor, and Meyer, Leonard B. *The Rhythmic Structure of Music*. Chicago: University of Chicago Press, 1960.

Cooper, Patricia, and Buferd, Norma Bradley. *The Quilters: Women and Domestic Art*. Garden City: Doubleday, 1977.

Cowell, Henry, and Cowell, Sidney. *Charles Ives and His Music*. New York: Oxford University Press, 1954.

Danto, Arthur C. "Artworks and Real Things." *Theoria* 34 (1973): 1–17.

_____. "The Artworld." *Journal of Philosophy* 61 (1964): 571–84.

_____. "The Transfiguration of the Commonplace." *Journal of Aesthetics and Art Criticism* 33 (1974): 139–48.

_____. "Munakata in New York: A Memory of the '50s." *The Print Collector's Newsletter* 10 (January–February, 1980): 184–89.

Darrah, William Culp. *The World of Stereographs*. Gettysburg, Pa.: William C. Darrah, 1977.

Dart, Thurston. *The Interpretation of Music*. 4th ed. London: Hutchinson, 1967.

Denisoff, R. Serge. *Solid Gold: The Popular Record Industry*. New Brunswick, N.J.: Transaction Books, 1975.

Dickie, George. *Aesthetics: An Introduction*. New York: Pegasus, 1971.

_____. *Art and the Aesthetic: An Institutional Analysis*. Ithaca: Cornell University Press, 1975.

_____. "A Response to Cohen: The Actuality of Art." In *Aesthetics: A Critical Anthology*, edited by George Dickie and Richard J. Sclafani, pp. 196–200. New York: St. Martin's Press, 1977.

DiMaggio, Paul, and Useem, Michael. "Cultural Property and Public Policy: Emerging Tensions in Government Support for the Arts." *Social Research* 45 (1978): 356–89.

Donow, Kenneth. "The Structure of Art: A Sociological Analysis." Ph.D. dissertation, University of California, San Diego, 1979.

Doty, Robert. *Photo-Secession: Steiglitz and the Fine-Art Movement in Photography*. New York: Dover, 1978 [1960].

Earle, Edward W., editor. *Points of View: The Stereograph in America—A Cultural History*. Rochester, N.Y.: Visual Studies Workshop Press, 1979.

Eliot, George. *Daniel Deronda*. Notes by Barbara Hardy. London: Penguin, 1967.

Eliot, Valerie, editor. *T. S. Eliot, The Waste Land: A Facsimile and Transcript of the Original Drafts Including the Annotations of Ezra Pound*. New York: Harcourt Brace Jovanovich, 1971.

Faulkner, Robert. *Big Hollywood, Little Hollywood: Composers at Work in the Business of Film*. New Brunswick, N.J.: Transaction Books, forthcoming.

_____. "Orchestra Interaction: Some Features of Communication and Authority in an Artistic Organization." *Sociological Quarterly* 14 (1973a): 147–57.

_____. "Career Concerns and Mobility Motivations of Orchestra Musicians." *Sociological Quarterly* 14 (1973b): 334–49.

_____. *Hollywood Studio Musicians*. Chicago: Aldine Publishing Co., 1971.

Forbes, Elliot, editor. *Thayer's Life of Beethoven*. Princeton: Princeton University Press, 1967.

Freidson, Eliot. *Profession of Medicine*. New York: Dodd, Mead, and Co., 1970.

_____. "The Division of Labor as Social Interaction." *Social Problems* 23 (February 1976): 304–13.

Fulcher, Jane. "The Orphéon Societies: Music for the Workers in Second-Empire France." *International Review of the Aesthetics and Sociology of Music* 10 (1979): 47–56.

Gans, Herbert. *Popular Culture and High Culture.* New York: Basic Books, 1974.

Gilot, Françoise, and Lake, Carlton. *Life with Picasso.* New York: McGraw-Hill, 1964.

Glassie, Henry. "Folk Art." In *Folklore and Folklife,* edited by Richard M. Dorson, pp. 253–80. Chicago: University of Chicago Press, 1972.

Goldfarb, Jeffrey C. "Social Bases of Independent Public Expression in Communist Societies." *American Journal of Sociology* 83 (January 1978): 920–39.

Goldmann, Lucien. *Pour une sociologie du roman.* Paris: Gallimard, 1964.

_____. "The Sociology of Literature: Status and Problems of Method." *International Social Science Journal* 19 (1967): 493–516.

Gombrich, E. H. *Art and Illusion: A Study in the Psychology of Pictorial Representation.* Princeton: Princeton University Press, 1960.

Griff, Mason. "The Commercial Artist: A Study in Changing and Consistent Identities." In *Identity and Anxiety,* edited by Maurice Stein, A. Vidich, and D. White. New York: The Free Press, 1960.

Griswold, Wendy. "Renaissance Revivals: The Continuing Interaction between Culture and Society." Ph.D. dissertation, Harvard University, 1980.

_____. "American Character and the American Novel: An Expansion of Reflection Theory." *American Journal of Sociology* 86 (January 1981): 740–65.

Haacke, Hans. *Framing and Being Framed: 7 Works 1970–75.* New York: New York University Press, 1976.

_____. "The Good Will Umbrella." *Qualitative Sociology* 1 (May 1978): 108–21.

Haber, Ira Joel. "The M. E. Thelen Piece." *TriQuarterly* 32 (1975): unpaginated.

Halverstadt, Hal. "Mary Buskirk: '. . . a sense of freedom.'" *Craft Horizons* 20 (March–April 1960): 9–11.

Hamilton, George E. *Oliver Wendell Holmes: His Pioneer Stereoscope and Later Industry.* New York: Newcomen Society in America, 1949.

Harmetz, Aljean. *The Making of the Wizard of Oz*. New York: Alfred A. Knopf, 1977.

Harris, Neil. *The Artist in American Society: The Formative Years 1790–1869*. New York: Simon and Schuster, 1966.

Haskell, Francis. *Patrons and Painters: A Study in the Relations between Italian Art and Society in the Age of the Baroque*. New York: Alfred A. Knopf, 1963.

Hennessey, Thomas. "From Jazz to Swing: Black Jazz Musicians and Their Music, 1917–1935." Ph.D. dissertation, Northwestern University, 1973.

Hibel Museum of Art. *Catalogue*. Palm Beach, Florida: Hibel Museum of Art, 1977.

Hirsch, E. D., Jr. "Carnal Knowledge." *New York Review of Books* 26, no. 10 (June 14, 1979): 18–20.

Hirsch, Paul M. "Processing Fads and Fashions: An Organization-Set Analysis of Cultural Industry Systems." *American Journal of Sociology* 77 (1972): 639–59.

Hitchcock, H. Wiley, and Perlis, Vivian, editors. *An Ives Celebration*. Urbana: University of Illinois Press, 1977.

Hoffman, Theodore. "The Bluestocking Theater and the Actor from Mars." *Columbia Forum* 11 (Fall 1973): 33–38.

Hoffman, Virginia. "When Will Weaving Be an Art Form?" *Craft Horizons* 30 (August 1970): 18–23.

Holstein, Jonathan. *The Pieced Quilt: An American Design Tradition*. Boston: New York Graphic Society, 1973.

Hooper, Finley. *Greek Realities: Life and Thought in Ancient Greece*. New York: Charles Scribner's Sons, 1967.

Hoos, Judith. "Herman Rusch: Prairie Moon Museum and Garden." In *Naives and Visionaries: An Exhibition by the Walker Art Center*, pp. 71–75. Minneapolis: E. P. Dutton, 1974.

Horowitz, Irving Louis. *Taking Lives: Genocide and State Power*. New Brunswick, N.J.: Transaction Books, 1980.

Hughes, Everett C. "Action Catholique and Nationalism: A Memorandum on Church and Society in French Canada." Unpublished, n.d.

———. *The Sociological Eye*. Chicago: Aldine, 1971.

Hume, David. "Of the Standard of Taste." *Philosophical Works*, vol. 5, part 3. Boston: Little Brown, 1854 [1752].

Hurley, F. Jack. *Portrait of a Decade*. Baton Rouge: Louisiana State University Press, 1972.

Ives, Charles E. *Memos*. Edited by John Kirkpatrick. New York: W. W. Norton and Co., 1972.

Ivins, William, Jr. *Prints and Visual Communication*. Cambridge: MIT Press, 1953.

Jackson, Bruce. *Get Your Ass in the Water and Swim Like Me: Narrative Poetry from Black Oral Tradition*. Cambridge: Harvard University Press, 1974.

————. *Wake Up Dead Man: Afro-American Worksongs from Texas Prisons*. Cambridge: Harvard University Press, 1972.

Jenkins, Reese V. *Images and Enterprise: Technology and the American Photographic Industry, 1839–1925*. Baltimore: Johns Hopkins University Press, 1975.

Johnson, Thomas. *Emily Dickinson*. Cambridge: Harvard University Press, 1955.

Kael, Pauline. "The Making of the Group." In *Kiss Kiss Bang Bang*, pp. 67–100. Boston: Little Brown and Co., 1968.

Kase, Thelma. "The Artist, the Printer and the Publisher." M.A. thesis, University of Missouri, Kansas City, 1973.

Katz, Elihu, and Lazarsfeld, Paul. *Personal Influence*. New York: The Free Press, 1955.

Kealy, Edward R. "From Craft to Art: The Case of Sound Mixers and Popular Music." *Sociology of Work and Occupations* 6 (February 1979): 3–29.

Kjørup, Søren. "Art Broadly and Wholly Conceived." In *Culture and Art: An Anthology*, edited by Lars Aagard-Mogensen, pp. 45–53. Atlantic Highlands, N.J.: Humanities Press, 1976.

Kubler, George. *The Shape of Time: Remarks on the History of Things*. New Haven: Yale University Press, 1962.

Kuhn, Thomas. *The Structure of Scientific Revolutions*. Chicago: University of Chicago Press, 1962.

Lerner, Robert E. "Literacy and Learning." In *One Thousand Years: Western Europe in the Middle Ages*, edited by Richard L. DeMolen, pp. 165–233. Boston: Houghton Mifflin, 1974.

Lesy, Michael. *Real Life: Louisville in the Twenties*. New York: Panthcon, 1976.

Levine, Edward M. "Chicago's Art World." *Urban Life and Culture* 1 (1972): 292–322.

Lewis, David K. *Convention: A Philosophical Study*. Cambridge: Harvard University Press, 1969.

Lichtenstein, Grace. "Cowboy Art Finds Home on the Range." *The New York Times* (February 10, 1977): 41, 45.

Lipman, Jean, and Armstrong, Tom, editors. *American Folk Painters of Three Centuries*. New York: Hudson Hills Press, Inc., 1980.

Lowenthal, Leo. *Literature and the Image of Man.* Boston: Beacon Press, 1957.

Luders, Theodore H. "A Plea for the Stereoscope." *American Annual of Photography* (1892): 227.

Lukacs, Georg. *Studies in European Realism.* New York: Grosset and Dunlap, 1964.

Lyon, Eleanor. "Behind the Scenes: The Organization of Theatrical Production." Ph.D. dissertation, Northwestern University, 1975.

_____. "Work and Play: Resource Constraints in a Small Theater." *Urban Life* 3 (1974): 71–97.

Maddow, Ben. *Edward Weston: Fifty Years.* Millerton, New York: Aperture, 1973.

Martindale, Andrew. *The Rise of the Artist in the Middle Ages and Early Renaissance.* London: Thames and Hudson, 1972.

McCall, Michal M. "Art without a Market: Creating Artistic Value in a Provincial Art World." *Symbolic Interaction* 1 (Fall 1977): 32–43.

_____. "The Sociology of Female Artists." *Studies in Symbolic Interaction* 1 (1978): 289–318.

McCoy, Esther. "Grandma Prisbrey's Bottle Village." In *Naives and Visionaries: An Exhibition Organized by the Walker Art Center,* pp. 77–85. Minneapolis: E. P. Dutton, 1974.

Mead, George Herbert. *Mind, Self and Society.* Chicago: University of Chicago Press, 1934.

Meyer, Leonard B. *Emotion and Meaning in Music.* Chicago: University of Chicago Press, 1956.

_____. *Explaining Music: Essays and Explorations.* Berkeley and Los Angeles: University of California Press, 1973.

Mills, C. Wright. "Situated Actions and Vocabularies of Motive." *American Sociological Review* 5 (1940): 904–13.

Mitchell, Joseph. *Joe Gould's Secret.* New York: Viking Press, 1965.

Mitias, M. H. "Art as a Social Institution." *The Personalist* 56 (1975): 330–35.

Moulin, Raymonde. "La Genèse de la rareté artistique." *Revue d'ethnologie Française* 8 (1978): 241–58.

_____. *Le Marché de la peinture en France.* Paris: Les Editions de Minuit, 1967.

Mukerji, Chandra. "Film Games." *Symbolic Interaction* 1 (December 1977): 20–31.

Nancarrow, Conlon. *Complete Studies for Player Piano.* Vol. 2. 1750 Arch Street Records S-1777. Berkeley: 1750 Arch Street Records,

1979.

Newhall, Beaumont. *The History of Photography*. New York: Museum of Modern Art, 1964.

Newman, Charles. "The Uses and Abuses of Death: A Little Rumble through the Remnants of Literary Culture." *TriQuarterly* 26 (1973): 3–41.

Newman, K. O. *Two Hundred and Fifty Times I Saw a Play, or Authors, Actors and Audiences*. Oxford: Pelagos Press, 1943.

Norman, Charles. *The Magic-Maker: E. E. Cummings*. New York: Macmillan, 1958.

Norman, Dorothy. *Alfred Stieglitz: An American Seer*. New York: Random House, 1973.

Park, Robert E. *Human Communities*. New York: Free Press, 1952.

———. *Race and Culture*. New York: Free Press, 1950.

———. *Society*. New York: Free Press, 1955.

Partch, Harry. *Genesis of a Music*. Madison: University of Wisconsin Press, 1949.

Perlis, Vivian. *Charles Ives Remembered: An Oral History*. New Haven: Yale University Press, 1974.

Peterson, Richard A. "The Unnatural History of Rock Festivals: An Instance of Media Facilitation." *Popular Music and Society* 2 (Winter 1973): 98–123.

Pevsner, Nicholas. *Academies of Art: Past and Present*. Cambridge: Cambridge University Press, 1940.

Phillips, John. *The Reformation of Images: Destruction of Art in England*, 1535–1660. Berkeley and Los Angeles: University of California Press, 1973.

Photographers' Formulary: Chemical and Laboratory Resources. Catalogue 3. Missoula, Mont.: Photographer's Formulary, Inc., n.d.

Reese, Gustave. *Music in the Renaissance*. Revised edition. New York: W. W. Norton, 1959.

Rehfeldt, Phillip. *New Directions for the Clarinet*. Berkeley and Los Angeles: University of California Press, 1977.

Reitlinger, Gerald. *The Economics of Taste: The Rise and Fall of Picture Prices, 1760–1960*. London: Barrie and Rockliff, 1961.

Roscoe, Lynda. "James Hampton's Throne." In *Naives and Visionaries: An Exhibition Organized by the Walker Art Center*, pp. 13–19. Minneapolis: E. P. Dutton, 1974.

Rosenblum, Barbara. *Photographers at Work*. New York: Holmes and Meiers, Publishers, Inc., 1978.

Rosenblum, Ralph, and Karen, Robert. *When the Shooting Stops
. . . the Cutting Begins: A Film Editor's Story.* New York:
Penguin Books, 1980.

Ross, Lillian. *Picture.* New York: Avon, 1969 [1952].

Rossiter, Frank R. *Charles Ives and His America.* New York: Liveright, 1975.

Rubin, Cynthia Elyce. "Shaker Stereo Views/Shaker Stereo
Views." *Clarion* (Winter 1978): 56–57.

Sanders, Clinton. "Psyching Out the Audience: Folk Performers
and Their Audiences." *Urban Life and Culture* 3 (October 1974):
264–82.

Sant'Anna, Affonso Romano de. "Chico Buarque: A musica contra
o silencio." In *Musica popular e moderna poesia brasileira*,
pp. 99–104. Petrópolis, Brazil: Vozes, 1978.

Schonberg, Harold C. "He Is the Dean and Da Vinci of the Copyists." *The New York Times* (June 4, 1978): D15.

Sclafani, Richard. "Art as a Social Institution: Dickie's New Definition." *Journal of Aesthetics and Art Criticism* 32 (1973a):
111–14.

———. "Art Works, Art Theory and the Artworld." *Theoria* 34
(1973b): 18–34.

Seiberling, Grace. "'Joyful to Receive the Impressions Thereof':
An Iconological Study of Victorian Albums." Unpublished, n.d.

Sekula, Allen. "The Instrumental Image: Steichen at War." *Art-
forum* (December 1975): 26–35.

Sherarts, Ted, and Sherarts, Sharon. "Louis C. Wippich: Clown of
Molehill." In *Naives and Visionaries: An Exhibition Organized by
the Walker Art Center*, pp. 87–93. Minneapolis: E. P. Dutton, 1974.

Silvers, Anita. "The Artworld Discarded." *Journal of Aesthetics and
Art Criticism* 34 (1976): 441–54.

Simmel, Georg. "The Persistence of Social Groups." *American
Journal of Sociology* 3 (1898): 662–69.

Sinha, Anita. "Control in Craft Work: The Case of Production Potters." *Qualitative Sociology* 2 (September 1979): 3–25.

Slivka, Rose. "Laugh-in in Clay." *Craft Horizons* 31 (October 1971):
39–47, 63.

Smith, Barbara Herrnstein. "Fixed Marks and Variable Constancies: A Parable of Literary Value." *Poetic Inquiry* 1 (Autumn
1979): 7–22.

———. *Poetic Closure: A Study of How Poems End.* Chicago: University of Chicago Press, 1968.

Smith, Cyril Stanley. "Art, Technology, and Science: Notes on Their

Historical Interaction." *Technology and Culture* 11 (October 1970): 493–549.

Smith, W. Eugene, and Smith, Aileen M. "Minamata, Japan: Life—Sacred and Profane." *Camera 35* 18 (April 1974): 26–51.

——. *Minamata.* New York: Holt, Rinehart and Winston, 1975.

"Southern Illinois: Letter." *Photographic Times* 6 (June 1871): 91.

Steichen, Edward. *A Life in Photography.* Garden City, N.Y.: Doubleday, 1963.

Stoppard, Tom. *Travesties.* London: Faber and Faber, 1975.

Sudnow, David. *Ways of the Hand.* Cambridge: Harvard University Press, 1978.

Sumner, William G. *Folkways.* Boston: Ginn and Co., 1906.

Sutherland, J. A. *Victorian Novelists and Publishers.* Chicago: University of Chicago Press, 1976.

Szarkowski, John. *Mirrors and Windows.* New York: Museum of Modern Art, 1978.

Taft, Robert. *Photography and the American Scene.* New York: Macmillan, 1938.

Talbot, George. *At Home: Domestic Life in the Postcentennial Era.* Madison: The State Historical Society of Wisconsin, 1976.

Thompson, Peter Hunt. "In Time." In *Untitled 9*, edited by Peter Hunt Thompson. Carmel, Calif.: Friends of Photography, 1975.

Tice, George. *Artie Van Blarcum: An Extended Portrait.* Danbury, Vt.: Addison House, 1977.

Trillin, Calvin. "I Know I Want to Do Something." *The New Yorker* (May 29, 1965): 72–120.

Trollope, Anthony. *An Autobiography.* Berkeley and Los Angeles: University of California Press, 1947 [1883].

Velho, Gilberto. "Accusations, Family Mobility and Deviant Behavior." *Social Problems* 23 (February 1976): 268–75.

——. "Projeto, emoção e orientação em sociedades complexas." *Boletim do Museu Nacional (Antropologia)* 31 (January 1979): 1–28.

Walker Art Center. *Naives and Visionaries: An Exhibition Organized by the Walker Art Center.* Minneapolis: E. P. Dutton, 1974.

Watt, Ian. *The Rise of the Novel: Studies in Defoe, Richardson and Fielding.* Berkeley and Los Angeles: University of California Press, 1957.

White, Eric Walter. *Stravinsky: The Composer and His Works.* Berkeley and Los Angeles: University of California Press, 1966.

White, Harrison, and White, Cynthia. *Canvasses and Careers.* New York: John Wiley, 1965.

Wilder, Alec. *American Popular Song: 1900–1950.* New York: Oxford University Press, 1972.

Wollheim, Richard. "Art and Life with the Very Rich." *New York Review of Books* 22 (May 1, 1975): 29–31.

Wörmer, Karl H. *Stockhausen: Life and Work.* Berkeley and Los Angeles: University of California Press, 1973.

Zack, David. "Ceramics of Robert Arneson." *Craft Horizons* 29 (January, 1970): 36–41, 60–61.

Zolberg, Vera. "The Art Institute of Chicago: The Sociology of a Cultural Organization." Ph.D. dissertation, University of Chicago, 1974.

———. "Displayed Art and Performed Music: Selective Innovation and the Structure of Artistic Media." *Sociological Quarterly* 21 (Spring 1980): 219–31.

Index

385

Designer: Wendy Calmenson
Compositor: Dharma Press
Printer: Thomson-Shore Inc.
Binder: John H. Dekker & Sons
Text: 11/13 Aster
Display: Bauhaus Light